DIFFERENT SPEEDS
AND DIFFERENT NEEDS

DIFFERENT SPEEDS
AND DIFFERENT NEEDS
HOW TO TEACH
SPORTS TO EVERY KID

Gary Barber B.H., P.G.C.E., M.A.
St. Michaels University School—Junior School
Victoria, British Columbia

·P A U L·H·
BROOKES
PUBLISHING CO®

Baltimore • London • Sydney

Paul H. Brookes Publishing Co.
Post Office Box 10624
Baltimore, Maryland 21285-0624
USA

www.brookespublishing.com

Book design by Erin Geoghegan.
Typeset by Aptara, Inc., Falls Church, Virginia.
Manufactured in the United States of America by
Sheridan Books, Inc., Chelsea, Michigan.

The individuals described in this book are composites based on the authors' experiences or real people whose situations are masked and used with permission.

The information provided in this book is in no way meant to substitute for a medical or mental health practitioner's advice or expert opinion. Readers should consult a health or mental health professional if they are interested in more information. This book is sold without warranties of any kind, express or implied, and the publisher and authors disclaim any liability, loss, or damage caused by the contents of this book.

Library of Congress Cataloging-in-Publication Data

Barber, Gary
  Different speeds and different needs : how to teach sports to every kid /
Gary Barber.
    p.   cm.
  ISBN-13: 978-1-59857-100-4
  ISBN-10: 1-59857-100-1
  1. Sports for children—Coaching.   2. Sports.   I. Title.
GV443.B339 2010
796.083—dc22   2010010966

British Library Cataloguing in Publication data are available from the British Library.

2014   2013   2012   2011   2010
10   9   8   7   6   5   4   3   2   1

*To Michael and Colin Barber: Great kids and
very fast runners!*

Contents

About the Author

Gary Barber, B.H., P.G.C.E., M.A., is a physical education teacher with over 30 years' experience teaching students of all ages, abilities, and varying needs. He was an international-level middle-distance runner and uses his knowledge as the head coach of Islanders Running Club, a running program especially designed for students who have experienced difficulties in other sports. Gary is also the head of SportWrite Education. This is a company that provides parents, teachers, and educators with resources to support all students in finding success and acceptance in sports and physical education.

A sought-after keynote speaker, Gary Barber offers presentations that combine his experiences as a father of two sons with autism with his knowledge of sports, physical education, and the very latest research from the field of special education.

Acknowledgments

I thank my wife, Michelle, and our wonderful sons, Michael and Colin. Their love and patient support throughout this project comforted "daddy" as he spent countless hours painfully trying to find letters on the keyboard. It is a shame that single-finger typing is not an Olympic sport: The gold medal would surely be mine!

I also thank my parents, Maureen and Brian Barber, and my sister, Helen, for their amazing support throughout my career in sports and education.

I am especially grateful to Rebecca Lazo, Senior Acquisitions Editor at Brookes Publishing. Her constant encouragement and belief in this book, combined with her outstanding professionalism, was instrumental in helping me to complete this project. Special thanks also go to Marie Abate and Steve Plocher at Brookes Publishing for their fine work in developing and supporting this manuscript.

I would like to extend my sincere appreciation for the hard work of Peggy Kellar, the project manager of this book. Many thanks, also, to Sheryl Rose for her attention to detail in copyediting.

I wish to thank my colleagues at St. Michaels University School, Victoria, British Columbia, for the discussions and feedback that helped to strengthen and guide this book as it evolved. I am grateful to Brian and Martha Hume for graciously suffering through every page of an appalling first draft.

Finally, this is a book to support children who learn, think, and behave in different ways. I have worked with thousands of children in my years of teaching and coaching; each child has contributed to the spirit of this book in some way. Thank you for your inspiration. I hope this book will help all children to find acceptance and joy in whatever paths they may choose in life.

Preface

This book is about people with differences. We all look different, behave in different ways, have different interests; yet despite our evolved sensibilities, we have never been very good at accepting people who are different from us. Throughout history we have condemned people with nonconforming views as heretics and perhaps even burned them at the stake. We have enslaved people who look different from us, and we have fought wars with people who have different customs than ours. We have declared many of our most brilliant thinkers to be either eccentrics or misfits. We have dismissed generations of children who did not learn at the speed or did not have interests that the education system deemed appropriate.

You would think in our modern society we should have made some progress on this issue. Today, we seem to be focused on categorizing and labeling different people with neat scientific descriptors. We have created a vast range of nomenclature to describe behaviors that we consider to be "disorders." We seldom look at the many positive features that accompany some of the challenges that people experience; in fact, we seem to focus more on what people cannot do.

This book is about young athletes with different needs.

These young athletes may have visible challenges (a wheelchair athlete or a person with Down syndrome), or less obvious difficulties (perhaps it is a sensory impairment or a learning disability). They may be children who just need a bit of support to help them become confident. This book aims to educate teachers, coaches, and parents about the needs of these "different" children who are seeking to find acceptance in sports, and in a broader context acceptance in life. These children are not really different, for what I hope to convey is the idea that there is a part of all of us in this book. We all, at some point in our sporting lives, have had a struggle or a setback, have been marginalized, have been bullied, or felt emotionally insecure. If you truly value sports and all that they have to offer, I urge you to reflect on your own experiences and consider the following: "Is this how I want my child, or the children that I coach, to be treated? As a coach, how can I make my sport enjoyable and accessible for all athletes who want to participate?" I ask you to start by accepting the differences of these children; consider all of them to be capable of making meaningful contributions while honoring their personal potential.

> If a man does not keep pace with his companions, perhaps it is because he hears a different drummer.
> —Henry David Thoreau

We are all different. Let's accept and celebrate that simple fact!

Creating a Sports Environment in Which All Participants Can Thrive

Seventeen years ago I walked into the staff room of a school in which I had just been hired to teach physical education. I was full of ideas and confidence, and I felt ready to deliver what I thought would be a high-quality program to my eager students. I believed that I could inspire them to become courageous young athletes, and I especially relished the opportunity to work with kids who had a reputation.

Before starting my first class I picked up a book already gathering dust on the coffee table. Sent by the Ministry of Education, it was an A–Z manual of physical or mental challenges that could influence a student's learning. I opened the first page and read the title: "A for Autism." I had heard the term but had no idea what it really was, or how it manifested itself in students. I continued flicking through the pages and jumped from "Attention Deficit" to "Cerebral Palsy" to "Tourette Syndrome." It made for unsettling reading as I quickly realized that years of university training had not prepared me to effectively teach kids with those kinds of challenges. It became obvious to me that the teaching techniques and activities that I had been trained to use were designed for the fit and athletically capable. Students with learning difficulties or physical/mental challenges were expected to "tag along. Just don't expect that you're going to get much out of them" (the exact words of a university physical education professor). I put the book down and headed off to teach my first class. I tried to reassure myself that these were rare conditions and were not likely to be found in a typical student population. I couldn't have been more wrong.

There are times when our lives take a direction that we would never have imagined. A few years ago my wife and I were pushed down such a path when we were informed that both of our sons had an autism spectrum disorder (ASD). I thought back to that day—"A for Autism"—I knew nothing then about this issue; now, I certainly know a lot more. Many parents try to cope with a trauma or challenge by learning as much as they can about the situation they face. The hope is that the more you learn, the more effective you will be in helping your child through the difficulties that he or she faces. My wife and I, both teachers, read voraciously and we started to build our knowledge of autism and associated disorders. It was inevitable that this knowledge would be integrated into our teaching styles.

I have seen firsthand the challenges that children with special needs have when sports are presented in a manner that is generic and seemingly only applicable to the typical population. Well-meaning coaches—many of them teenagers working in recreation programs—struggle to include these students. I have observed that too many children were failing, not because they were not capable or lacked interest in the sport, but because they were being taught in a manner that exacerbated their challenges. Students with attention deficits were being forced to sit still and listen to lengthy coaching instructions; not surprisingly, they became disruptive and were treated as a disciplinary problem. Children with coordination difficulties were being made to perform skills that were so complex that they were almost certain to fail. Students with learning challenges were asked to follow sports strategies that they could not understand. Surely we should be designing our sports programs for everyone to find a measure of success, not just the capable students.

Everybody has some experience with sports. From mandatory gym classes in school to community recreation sports programs, we all have stories about how sports were presented to us. Sports may have inspired us and brought great joy; maybe we were indifferent and felt bored; or perhaps it was something that was painful and prompted us to drop out. This book includes many personal anecdotes drawn from the experiences of students, teachers, parents, and coaches. Their stories are both encouraging and, at times, disturbing.

There is extensive research and reporting on the physical benefits of exercise and a student's overall development; there are many social benefits as well. Whether children have a physical disability, a learning challenge, or just find physical activities difficult, they should benefit from being included with their peers in physical education classes, extracurricular athletic activities, and club sports and from just having fun!

As a teacher and coach, I have seen the joy that sports can bring children when someone takes the time to build an environment where they are valued and respected. I have seen young athletes beam with delight when they have mastered a challenging skill or made an authentic contribution to the team. Success is possible for all children, and it is the purpose of this book to provide coaches, teachers, and parents with the knowledge to achieve this goal.

Terminology

This book uses the words *kids, children, students,* and *young people* interchangeably. Although I have written this book for young people, the issues and teaching strategies are not age sensitive; that is, they can effectively apply to teenagers and young adults as well. Some suggestions might be more appropriate for a particular age group, and adaptations can be made to appeal to an older or younger group of athletes. Note that in any situation, it is important to deliver age-appropriate instruction to individuals, no matter their disability or challenge.

The Purpose of This Book

This book will help

- The child with learning difficulties
- The young athlete who can't seem to follow or understand the coach's instructions

- The child with a disability who has difficulty being involved in sports
- The young athletes who have not developed their physical skills at the same rate as their peers and are starting to have a crisis in confidence
- The children who are either shy or not particularly competitive but want to play sports as long as they don't get hurt
- The child who has difficulty in forming and keeping friends
- The students who seem conscious of their physical challenges (obesity, anorexia, excessive or limited height)

This book is for the teacher or coach who

- Wants to find ways of helping all athletes achieve success
- Recognizes the need to vary the way sports programs are delivered (i.e., taught)
- Wants to help children who might easily drop out of sports
- Understands that sports programs must be built on the developmental needs of the children, not the needs of the coach
- Recognizes that how the program is presented will shape the attitudes of the athletes and their parents

This book is for the parents who

- Want to see their child fully involved in sports
- Want to see their child happy, accepted by peers, and given the same opportunities as everybody else
- Recognize the importance of role modeling positive behavior
- Want to learn how they can become advocates for their child while avoiding adversarial approaches

CHAPTER 1

Sports for All, or for Just the Talented Children?

S ports are supposed to be fun, and they probably are if you can run fast, throw far, and catch or kick a ball. But if you lack those basic skills, playing sports can be a frustrating experience, and unless presented in a manner that accommodates those difficulties, sports may become something to be avoided.

Our societies greatly value sports, and we have spent centuries (if not millennia) creating and refining the sporting experience. From the ancient to the modern Olympic Games, on the sports field, and in the gymnasium, we have sought ways to showcase our sports abilities. Some athletes find immense success and fortune; others participate purely for the joy that sports brings them. Every weekend across the planet, legions of young athletes can be found energetically sprinting across their sports fields, responding to the enthusiastic exhortations of parents and coaches alike.

Schools, community organizations, and recreation centers have traditionally been the lens for focusing our sports programs. In the community, parents are viewed as the initiators of the sporting experience as they enroll their children in community programs. After a while, parents seem to take on the role of facilitators. They volunteer for coaching or administering their children's opportunities. Generally, the opportunities that are provided start with the philosophy that everybody plays.

Parents of athletically capable children seem to gravitate to coaching roles, and soon selection policies are introduced to sift through the athletic talent and create representative teams. Children whose skills are slower to develop are left standing on the sidelines cheering on their friends, whereas the gifted students receive the rewards for their genetic blessings.

In my experiences as a sports coach for many years, when I have observed the kinds of young athletes participating in school or community sports, I have noticed the absence of athletes with ASDs, attention deficit disorders, or learning difficulties. Students who were obese, the shy and the timid, those with developmental delays, or those with poor coordination did not seem to fully participate in community or school sports teams. So where were these young people? Were they simply just not interested in sports? Or did they find that their personal challenges restricted them from participating or finding enjoyment in sports? Did they feel welcome in sports programs or did they feel discouraged? Rimmer (2005) discussed the notable absence of people with disabilities in regular physical activity. Using data from the *Healthy People 2010* report (U.S. Department of Health and Human Services [DHHS], 2000), Rimmer noted that only 13% of people with a disability exercised vigorously for 20 minutes, three times per week, compared with 25% of people without a disability.

Whatever their reasons for not consistently participating in sports, the consequences of physical inactivity for young people are staggering. Sedentary behavior is increasing, according to the *Youth Risk Behavior Survey* (National Center for Chronic Disease Prevention and Health Promotion [NCCDPHP], 2007), and diseases such as insulin resistance, hypertension, and type 2 diabetes are being observed in young overweight people (Rosenbloom, 2002). While we are investing money in programs that encourage healthy living, there are still children with physical challenges, teenagers with learning disabilities, or adults with a weight (and self-image) problem who are still struggling to find a place in sports. In researching this book, I interviewed far too many adults and young students who described their sporting opportunities as being unrewarding at best, demeaning and discriminatory at worst.

If we truly value sports and all that they have to offer, surely our sports institutions (e.g., clubs, school teams, community organizations) are morally obliged to provide opportunities for the marginalized members of society as much as our capable participants. Before I develop the theme of this book, I would like to share two anecdotes from my own sports experiences.

Sport for All?

The message on the poster clinging to the gym wall read *Sport For All*. It was a catch phrase and program that the British government had decided was worthy of millions of pounds of investment. It seemed a noble concept, with everyone having the same chance to play as everybody else. There would be equal opportunity to practice and compete, there would be excellent coaching, and students would be able to enjoy the benefits of all that sports could offer. Of course all of that was lost on me on that cold and miserable day in November 1973. Although I didn't know it then (after all, I was only 10 years old), the event that transpired would underpin my thoughts about physical education and sports, especially for young people.

I was a skinny student and by far the youngest and smallest student in my grade. You could probably say that I was slow to develop. Studying wasn't important to me, and all I wanted to do was play. I idolized professional soccer players, cried when England failed to win the World Cup of soccer (something I would have to get used to throughout my adult life!), and pretended to be a top athlete running in the Olympics. I climbed trees, split logs for my father, and cut grass for my neighbors. I loved sports and, like many children of that age, firmly believed that I was very good. I expected my physical education (PE) teacher would affirm this grandiose view once the lesson started.

My classmates and I ran out onto the school sports field. We were all told to wear our gym clothes; mine included a skimpy T-shirt based on the assumption that the class would be held in a warm gym. I was wrong! We were pushed outside to face a sharp November wind that cut through my shirt; I shivered almost uncontrollably while waiting for instructions from the teacher. We asked for permission to wear our coats, and this request was denied. He mumbled something about us being "a bunch of wimps." I didn't know what a wimp was. I hoped that it was something good!

Our teacher suddenly walked away from us and headed into the school building. We were not sure what was happening. He didn't say a word. Was the PE class over before it had even started? We all trembled with the cold, a few of us whimpered and cried, and a few others started some mischief. After 10 minutes our teacher reappeared, suitably attired in a warm winter jacket and woolen hat, lovingly nursing a mug of piping hot tea. Tucked under his armpit was a brand-new soccer ball. We excitedly gathered around him; after all, we didn't see brand-new equipment at our school that often. This was a special day: Who was going to be the first to score a goal with this ball? "Could we borrow it at recess?" we asked him. "No!" he sharply replied. I still thought this was going to be a great lesson, with new equipment, a great game of soccer, playing with my friends. Yes, this was going to be fun!

Then the girls were sent off to the playground to play netball (a game with skills similar to basketball). A few of them protested, "Why can't we play soccer?" Our teacher told them that soccer was a boys' game, that girls weren't tough enough (his exact words), and they couldn't play. The sign read *Sport For All*—this included girls, just as long as they didn't want to play soccer!

We were quickly split into two groups; the first group he titled "The Stars." These were the big kids: athletically capable and eager to show our teacher what they could do. They moved onto the soccer field, replete with goals, nets, and, yes, the brand-new ball. I watched my friends move off to the soccer field and then looked at the children who remained. We were a ragtag crew of the overweight and excessively skinny, the hyperactive, and the just plain disobedient. Our teacher could barely mask his smug grin when he gave us our name: "You are 'The Dregs.'"

We were dismissed to the far corner of the field, actually a patch of rough ground, without a ball, a coach, or any instructions. Basically, he just wanted us to get out of the way. I scampered off to the equipment room and found another brand-new soccer ball sitting on the shelf, gleaming as if it were one of the Queen of England's Crown Jewels. It was pumped up and ready to go. I plucked the ball off the shelf and excitedly ran toward my fellow "Dreg-Mates." In the corner of my eye, I saw my teacher literally sprinting across the field toward my group (I can't remember if he spilled his tea—I can only hope so). "Who told you to take that ball?" he bellowed. "That is not for you; it's too good for you; get another one." We all looked bemused. Why couldn't we play with a brand-new ball like "The Stars"?

At the end of the lesson I was taken into the gym and received "six of the best"—the euphemism for six strikes with the cane—for being "a very disobedient little boy." I was 10 years old and weighed less than 60 pounds.

So what happened to my classmates? Not one of "The Stars" excelled in sports at a level higher than school sports. Many of "The Stars," tired of being yelled at by this aggressive coach, turned their attention to other sports. Most dropped out of sports altogether. My overweight friends remained overweight; perhaps that is hardly surprising, given the sports culture my teacher promoted. Many of my friends learned to loathe sports. At a recent reunion with these school friends, conversation recalled those blustery November days in PE. The feeling around the coffee table was unanimous: We survived PE rather than thrived on it!

It is clear that teachers and coaches play a powerful role in shaping the sporting interests of young athletes. Rather than being a positive and nurturing influence, the sporting environment created by my teacher was toxic and damaging. I can vividly remember children who were verbally, and occasionally physically, abused. Girls' and boys' sports options were stereotyped and restricted. Students with physical issues were either ignored or ridiculed, often by fellow students, and sometimes this occurred with the full support of the teacher. He created an environment that glorified success and ability. He had no time for children with learning difficulties. His one and only template for learning either worked for you or it didn't. He viewed concepts of participation and personal potential with scorn.

Is it really surprising that so many children leave school with negative views of sports and healthy living?

A Different Approach

My next PE teacher (Grades 6–12) was the antithesis of my last teacher. This young man wanted the best for each student, and he quietly went about finding ways to inspire us. He knew that a few of my friends needed (and wanted) a direct and technical manner of coaching. He also knew that many students preferred a more supportive and understanding approach. At recess, this coach could be found in the gym offering extra guidance to children with physical challenges. He tempered the arrogant and guided the talented; basically, he understood people and he knew how to help us. After school, he was busy taking us all over the country to sports competitions. On the weekends, he competed for Great Britain in track and field—his role modeling inspired many.

This teacher became extremely popular. He managed to relate to the students on an influential level, and yet he retained an appropriate professional distance and respect. Participation rates in school sports soared. Students who never would have even considered sports were now valued members of the sports program. An increase in school spirit, participation, and overall performance was evident as our teams (soccer, cross-country, and track) started to win major trophies.

The two styles of coaching in these anecdotes are clearly diametrically opposed. The first one reinforces age-old stereotypes and is dismissive of students lacking obvious athletic talent. The other approach promoted participation and the development of personal potential and found ways for students of all abilities to enjoy sports. Emerging from these two personal stories is the central theme that anchors this book.

How Can We Make Sports Attractive for Students with All Ranges of Abilities?

Consider these numbers.

- Thirteen percent of American children are obese (NCCDPHP, 2007), with 30% (6- to 11-year-olds) rising to 50% (16- to 19-year-olds) being overweight (*National Health and Nutrition Examination Survey, 1999–2002*; National Center for Health Statistics, 2002).

- Forty-six percent of American children participate in no physical education at all (NCCDPHP, 2007).

- Fifty-six percent of people with a disability do not participate in physical activities, compared with 36% without a disability (DHHS, 2000).

- Almost 8% of American students have a recognized learning disability (Altarac & Saroha, 2007; *Morbidity and Mortality Weekly Report*, 2008).

- Between 5% (National Health Statistics, 2008) and 10% of students have attention deficit difficulties (Szatmari, Offord, & Boyle, 1989).

- One in one hundred ten students has an ASD diagnosis (*Morbidity and Mortality Weekly Report*, 2009).

- Thirteen percent of students have anxiety disorders (DHHS, 1999).

- Two percent of prepubertal students and 8% of students in puberty experience depression (American Family Physician, 2000).

When we assemble all of these numbers into a typical student or athlete population, we have to acknowledge the likelihood that some of these children are going to have these issues. Does your school or sports club have a plan to address the needs of these children and help them to find success in sports?

When I look at some sports programs, I cannot help but think that many are designed to benefit only the fit and the healthy. It is easier to ignore the needs of children who need extra help and just concentrate on talented young athletes, but I find that to be morally repugnant. Ensuring the well-being of all young people (physically, emotionally, and socially) should be at the forefront of a coach's motives for working with young athletes.

Making Sense of Sports Science Research

Sports—like politics—is one of the few things about which just about everyone has an opinion. Most people have either played on a team or participated in a race, and these experiences form the foundation of what they consider "good sports." "Good sports" may mean the championship title for the coach who wants to build a winning team; for the parent who is volunteering, it may be making sure that every student in an underprivileged community can have a chance to play. For some students, "good sports" may be having the opportunity to play with their friends. The pursuit of "good sports" is even exemplified by a country that is prepared to spend huge sums of money hosting prestigious international events. Whatever interpretation we use to give sports meaning, it is something that we clearly value.

To better understand our involvement in sports, research scientists have received extensive government funding to examine everything from how the body adapts to practice (exercise physiology) to how the body moves (biomechanics), to how we behave in sports (sports psychology). Now, when we consider questions such as why we participate or what makes us drop out of sports, we can provide theories that have moved beyond ill-informed opinion. There are many sports research journals, and some offer complex theories that are so esoteric, few coaches will ever be able to use that information. What teachers, coaches, and parents ultimately want to know is, "How can I use sports science information to help my athletes?"

This book aims to strike a balance between research and pragmatism. I have drawn on some of the research to support or contradict many popular opinions as to what makes "good sports." Good coaches reflect on their style and consider if their opinions and knowledge blend with the current research that suggests what is best for students.

I encourage all readers to examine their beliefs and practices—especially those that relate to how their sport is structured and taught to students with different challenges. People who carry ultracompetitive motives for competition, and who couldn't care less if a student with difficulties is excluded, will likely be dismissive of this book—paradoxically, these are probably the people who could use this book the most!

The Three Legs of Sports

Three areas have emerged from extensive research that identifies the barriers facing people with challenges: architectural, program, and attitudinal issues (Schleien, 1993).

Architecture is a term that has been used to define the accessibility of sports facilities and buildings for people with challenges. No matter how good a sports program is, or how wonderful and compassionate the coach may be, this is all moot if the athlete cannot get through the front door and into the gym.

Program issues refer to how the sport is designed. It considers whether the sport has qualified staff who understand the needs of people with differences. It asks whether the school or organization has the equipment needed to successfully modify an activity to allow a young athlete to find success. Limitations in such areas have been identified as barriers to the full inclusion of these young athletes in sports programs (Devine & Broach, 1998). Whether it is a stigma or a stereotype, exclusion or marginalization, negative *attitudes* toward people with challenges is considered one of the most frequently occurring barriers to full inclusion in sports (Bedini & Henderson, 1994; Shank, Coyle, Boyd, & Kinney, 1996).

This book focuses on two of these areas: 1) ways to structure a sports program that promotes full inclusion and 2) how attitudes toward students with challenges are formed and how they can be used to promote acceptance.

Robert Ferguson (2002), founder of the Harvard-based Tripod Project, suggested the three "legs" of a sound education to be content, pedagogy, and relationships. Without one of these "legs," the student's program becomes unbalanced and can falter. Having an excellent knowledge of a sport's content (skills and tactics) is not necessarily enough to help a student develop if you don't know how to teach that content effectively or fail to establish an inspiring and supportive relationship with the student. It does not matter what you teach this student if the environment is threatening, discouraging, and (inadvertently—or worse, purposely) designed to amplify the student's difficulties; this student is likely to drop out. My purpose is to help teachers and coaches create a positive and rewarding sports environment, one in which the athlete feels secure and accepted by other members of the group.

Getting Started with Sports

As a starting point, we need to understand why students even bother with sports. What is it about sports that makes students want to participate— sometimes even if it does not bring them joy? Why do some people eventually drop out of sports? Why are students with differences especially vulnerable to withdrawing from sports? What issues can we address so that everyone may enjoy the benefits of sports for life?

Why Do Young People Participate in Sports?

Numerous surveys have investigated why young people participate in sports. Ewing and Seefeldt (1992) asked more than 26,000 students (ages 10–18) why they participate in sports and their reasons for dropping out of a sport. Having fun was cited as the primary reason for participating and a lack of fun underscored their reasons for withdrawing. Weiss (1993) suggested that motives for participating in sports also seemed to cluster in three main areas:

- The development and demonstration of physical competence
- The desire to gain social acceptance
- The desire to have fun

The way the sporting environment is presented and students' perception of their competence influences their enjoyment of physical activity. Research has shown that teachers and coaches (especially of elementary school–age children) exert a strong influence in the development of a student's attitude toward physical activity (Pieron, Telama, Almond, & Carreiro da Costa, 1997; Sallis et al., 1992).

Being accepted by your teammates (peers) has been identified as an important predictor of later social competence and emotional adjustment (Stone & LaGreca, 1994). Research has also shown the value of promoting a fully inclusive sports environment; the younger the students, the more accepting of differences they seem to be (Odom & Diamond, 1998).

Another survey (Lee, Whitehead, & Balchin, 2000) of almost 6,000 students—girls and boys in equal numbers, ages 7–12—reported that the reasons people participate in sports are

- To have fun
- To improve skills
- To do something that they are good at
- To have the excitement of competition
- To get exercise
- To play with a team
- To enjoy the challenge of competition
- To win

How Many Young People Participate in Sports?

The U.S. government follows youth sports participation through a system called the Youth Risk Behavior Surveillance System (YRBSS). YRBSS tracked the behavior of students in Grades 9–12 and found that two out of three students did not participate in any vigorous physical activity (NCCDPHP, 2007). Only 53% of students attended physical education classes once per week. Perhaps this should not be surprising: A sample of private and public schools revealed that only 8% of elementary schools, 6.4% of middle schools, and 5.8% of high schools provided daily physical education for their students (Burgeson et al., 2000). Data charting the sedentary recreational habits of the nation's youth reveal a troubling trend toward sedentary lifestyles: One in three students spend more than 3 hours per day either watching television or looking at a computer screen (Kaiser Family Foundation, 1999; NCCDPHP, 2007).

The Canadian government conducted the *General Social Survey* in 2005 and noted a trend toward inactivity in young people. Rates of participation for teenagers (15–18 years) fell from 77% in 1992 to 59% in 2005. Children ages 5–14 participated in organized sports even less, with rates of 55% for boys and 44% for girls. A clear link between income and participation was identified; with a family income of less than $40,000, 42% of children participated in sports. This number increased to 63% if the family income was $80,000. The survey recognized the important role that parents play in inspiring (and possibly motivating) students to participate in sports. Almost 60% of participants had a parent who was involved in sports or modeled an active, healthy lifestyle. With no parent involved in sports, rates of participation fell to 35%.

It is clear from these numbers that many children and teenagers are inactive. Why do they not participate in sports? In one extensive study, 85% of parents reported that they had serious concerns about the way youth sports programs were presented (Frankl, 1998), but this only hints at part of a much bigger issue: Are students of all ranges of ability being provided the opportunities to participate in sports?

What Are the Benefits of Organized Sports?

The benefits of healthy participation in sports are well documented in the research:

- Sports help to develop an appreciation of health and fitness.
- Sports provide participants with a sense of belonging (Dykens, Rosner, & Butterbaugh, 1998).
- Sports create opportunities for participants to learn new skills.
- Sports can provide personal challenges and a sense of achievement when the challenges are successfully overcome (Seefeldt, Ewing, & Walk, 1992).
- Exercise can enhance self-esteem and promote personal confidence (Calfas & Taylor, 1994).
- Exercise can reduce stress and depression, according to the Surgeon General's report (DHHS, 1999).

- Daily activity has been shown to enhance general health and reduce the risks of disease connected to sedentary behavior: juvenile diabetes, cardiovascular disease, and the debilitating effects of obesity (Canadian Fitness and Lifestyle Research Institute, 2002).
- Physical activity is an effective means of inhibiting the progression of disease (Murphy & Carbone, 2008).

Participation in sports seems to benefit academic performance:

- Research has shown that involvement in after-school programs can enhance student achievement, improve work habits, and lower absenteeism (Hamilton & Klein, 1998).
- Keays (1993) noted the importance of sports in a study showing that most elementary school–age students would rather play sports than do anything else. The study also revealed that high school–age boys would prefer to fail in their studies than be viewed as incompetent on the sports field.
- Participants in a 2-year physical education program were able to sustain concentration for longer periods and had higher levels of achievement than a control group (Sallis et al., 1999).
- A strong connection between aerobic fitness and academic performance in core subjects studied by students in Grades 3–5 was identified in research by Castelli, Hillman, Buck, and Erwin (2007).
- Jordan and Nettles (1999), in a study of adolescents, found that students participating in sports and who have positive and effective adult role models will make greater personal investments in their learning.
- The Active Living Research Project by the Robert Wood Johnson Foundation (2007) reported that healthy students learn more effectively and achieve more academically.
- Chomitz et al. (2009) reported a link between fitness and academic achievement. Their study, which accounted for gender, social economic status, and ethnicity, revealed that children (Grades 4–8) who demonstrated good levels of physical fitness performed better in standardized math and English exams than classmates who either did not participate in PE or had poor levels of fitness.
- Hanson and Krause (1998) reported that science achievement in girls was enhanced when they participated in sports. The reasoning for this is intriguing; they suggest that the confidence that girls can build from their participation can help them become less intimidated by the domains that have traditionally been thought of as male dominated (e.g., engineering, science, math).

Participation in sports offers considerable benefits for people with disabilities:

- Playing sports decreases physical dependence (Noreau & Shepard, 1995).
- Sports can improve social inclusion.

- Sports promote understanding and acceptance of people with differences. Participation in the Special Olympics was noted for enhancing perceived physical competence and peer acceptance among participants compared with nonparticipants (Weiss, Diamond, Demark, & Loval, 2003).

- Sports can improve fitness and thereby reduce the severity of many challenges (Damiano & Abel, 1998).

Why Do Young People Drop Out of Sports?

Young people drop out of sports in significant numbers. Petlichkoff (1996) reported that almost 70% of students between 7 and 18 years of age will withdraw from organized sports. The most commonly cited reasons for dropping out of sports include a lack of fun and a lack of personal success. Too much emphasis placed on winning and excessive pressure from parents, coaches, and peers are also recognized as sources of discontent. Martens (1996) proposed two ideas that underpin a student's reasons for participating in sports: "the fun principle" and "the self-worth principle." The ideas underlying these principles are fairly obvious: We want children to have fun and feel valued from their sporting experiences. Martens stated that "as we take the fun out of physical activities, we take the kids out of them" (1996, p. 306). These principles are also undermined when children are "over-organized, constantly instructed, evaluated, over-drilled, replacing unstructured play with calisthenics, and using physical activity as a source of punishment" (Brady, 2004, p. 40).

It is clear that students' perceptions of their athletic abilities also determine the degree of their ongoing commitment to a sport. Students with low self-opinions need a nurturing and encouraging coaching environment; they require a lot of support from their parents, and they need to feel valued and accepted by peers. Coaches who fail to promote such an environment will likely amplify the low feelings of self-worth among such children, who eventually will drop out of sports.

Sport Is a Public Affair
In contrast to the achievement in the classroom where passing or failing a math test can be an unobserved private experience, a hit or a strike is witnessed by teammates, opponents, coaches, parents, and spectators (Scanlan, 1986, p. 113).

Athletically talented children also drop out of sports. Demanding high levels of performance, a distinct lack of enjoyment in practice and competition, and excessive parental involvement were cited as contributing factors to young athlete burnout (Coakley, 1992). Disliking the coach was also identified as a significant reason for young people to drop out (Gould, Feltz, Horn, & Weiss, 1982).

Pierce (1981) reported the results of a survey of 543 young people (ages 10–17) who were involved in various sports. Sixty-two percent said that "not playing well" and "making mistakes" worried them. Those results were probably not surprising, for we know that young athletes are eager to please their coaches and impress their friends. What was more startling was the statistic that reported 51% of respondents claimed sources of stress prevented them from playing their best. What were the sources of this stress? Eleven percent were worried by parental comments, 25% by the coach's comments, and 25% by the comments of their peers.

Martens (1996) stated that an athlete's feelings of self-worth are diminished by a coach who expresses frustration at the athlete's current level of skill and difficulty at performing at a desired level. Failing to recognize the athlete's effort and improvements further undermines the child's perception of competence.

All Children Want to Play, But Not All Children Want to Play Sports

It is true that some young people simply do not like sports. Their interests may lie in other areas, and they may not feel any need to be competitive or energetic in sports. Children who prefer sedentary choices are often pressured by their parents to be more athletic. They flit from one sport to another in a desperate attempt to find something at which they can succeed. Coercion is seldom a successful tactic when trying to have a reluctant student participate in a sport. Parents may wish to explore options that go beyond some of the more traditional sports choices; sometimes it is a matter of finding the right fit. Progressive schools and sports clubs offer a number of different programming choices. Following are some programming choices that can be offered to student athletes.

Wellness Strand

Students with no athletic or competitive inclinations are encouraged to pursue choices connected to health and personal wellness. These choices might include yoga, Pilates, aerobics, or games that have a recreational focus (e.g., ten-pin bowling).

Active Living Strand

The athlete may participate in the competitive sports offered but avoid the intensity of high performance; that is, he or she can play the game just for enjoyment. Intramural competition and exhibition games are ways to meet the competitive needs of these athletes.

High-Performance Strand

Participants in this strand practice with a highly competitive focus. They receive excellent coaching and are encouraged to pursue both individual and team goals.

What Are the Costs of Not Participating in Sports or Physical Activity?

Rates of participation in organized sports plummet in the teenage years, admittedly due to a broad range of issues such as starting relationships, finding employment, and being self-conscious about body changes due to puberty. As these students no longer participate in organized sports or after-school sports programs, increasing numbers are returning home to unsupervised environments. The U.S. census of 2000 revealed that 9% of children ages 5–11 years and 41% ages 12–14 years are left without adult supervision on a regular basis. Organized sports can provide not only purposeful activity with all of its inherent benefits, but also a secure environment while parents are at work. Yet many children are choosing "screen time" such as television, computer games, and electronic communications (texting) over physical activity. The average American student is now watching between 3 and 4 hours of television per day (American Academy of Pediatrics, 2001; NCCDPHP, 2007). Andersen, Crespo, Bartlett, Cheskin, and Pratt (1998) noted that children with television viewing habits of 3–4 hours per day had greater body mass indices (BMIs) and skinfold measures (both key indicators of weight issues) than children watching 2 hours per day or less. Another study suggested a strong link between the sedentary behavior associated with prolonged screen time and elevated blood pressure in children (Martinez-Gomez, Tucker, Heelan, Welk, & Eisenmann, 2009).

A lack of physical activity (including sports) carries the increased risk of ill-health issues. Research from the U.S. Office of Disease Prevention and Health Promotion (*Healthy People 2010*, DHHS, 2000) also showed that since 1980, the number of young people who are overweight has doubled. More than 10% of children between the ages of 2 and 5 are overweight; this increases to 16% for children 6–19 years of age.

The costs of inactivity are staggering. Physically inactive people are twice as likely to develop heart disease as regularly active people, and more than 108 million American adults are considered either obese or overweight (President's Council on Physical Fitness and Sports, 2009). If sports are not presented in a manner that is socially and physically appealing to people whose preference is inactivity, these issues and their immense costs to society—including health care costs, lack of productivity, and so forth—will increase.

Final Thoughts

This book could churn out page after page of health statistics in support of the view that participating in sports is important for the individual and for society. We need to move beyond numbers, however, and reach a practical understanding as to why our sports systems struggle to encourage and embrace people with differences to participate in healthy leisure pursuits.

CHAPTER **2**

Inclusion and Sports

Inclusion is a philosophy that seeks to provide ways for young people from all backgrounds and all ranges of ability to find genuine acceptance from others. Respecting diversity is at the core of inclusion. Norwich (2005) defined inclusion as "a focus for tackling all forms of discrimination, unfair disadvantage, and exclusion." Inclusion is an important concept, but it has inherent difficulties being successfully incorporated into sports. Sports are, by virtue of their structure, usually exclusive. In many sports, teams can only field a certain number of players, and those athletes with skills that don't meet the desired standard are denied the opportunity to play. Athletes with excellent capabilities tend to be rewarded with more opportunities to play, receive more attention from the coach, and get more recognition for their successes. Students with challenges in a sports environment that lacks support and understanding of their needs will not receive the same benefits as their more capable friends. Inclusion is a philosophy that values all children equally. This chapter looks at guiding principles that will help coaches and organizations build an appropriate environment in which all athletes can participate.

A Call to Action!

In July 2005, the U.S. Surgeon General, Richard H. Carmona, issued *The Surgeon General's Call to Action to Improve the Health and Wellness of Persons with Disabilities* (DHHS, 2005). In this announcement, Carmona stated,

> Every life has value, and every person has promise. The reality is that for too long we have provided lesser care to people with disabilities. Today, we must redouble our efforts so that people with disabilities achieve full access to disease prevention and health promotion services. (p. 1)

This call to action has four main goals:

- Increase *understanding* nationwide that people with disabilities can lead long, healthy, and productive lives.
- Increase *knowledge* among health care professionals and provide them with tools to screen, diagnose, and treat the whole person with a disability with dignity.
- Increase *awareness* among people with disabilities of the steps they can take to develop and maintain a healthy lifestyle.
- Increase *accessible* health care and support services to promote independence for people with disabilities.

The words italicized in these goals are themes that are the foundation of this book. *Understand* the needs of children with challenges. Acquire and use *knowledge* to support each healthy child's development. Increase community *awareness* of the challenges these young athletes face in sports, and then design programs that not only increase their *access* to sports but actively promote their full acceptance into typical sports environments.

Athletes First

This book promotes the view that children are more than a label or a neat phrase that defines the symptoms or characteristics of the challenge; these young people are athletes first. They are children who want to play, be liked, have friends, and leave every game and practice feeling valued. If we stop treating them as a condition and view them like any other children, we will help create the tone that an inclusive context seeks. Some might argue that these comments just reflect sentiments of political correctness, but the athlete-first (also known as the person-first) approach is more than a contrived argument of semantics. For example, if a child has leukemia, you would not describe that person by the disease. You would likely say that child has leukemia. The disease doesn't define the person or his or her strengths or interests.

Equality in Sports

Mackay (1986) identified three elements that constitute equality:

- Equal opportunities
- Equal outcomes
- Nondiscrimination

Although issues of equality are vigorously applied in the workplace and other aspects of our society, these principles are not uniformly respected in many sports environments. Children of lesser ability are not always given equal opportunities or authentic sports experiences. Is this discrimination, or are these some of the practical issues that emerge when children with challenges try to participate in certain sports situations? Inclusion does not demand that a child with severe challenges be a member of the Olympic team. Inclusion means providing our young athletes the opportunities to practice and compete in an environment that respects their personal potential. In many circumstances, a child with challenges can fully participate in sports if the coach or organization makes accommodations or modifications in the way the program is tailored to this child.

Does Discrimination in Sports Still Occur?

Recent high-profile stories are a sobering reminder that negative attitudes toward children with challenges or differences are still held. Here is a sample of news stories from the past few years:

- A young child with Down syndrome wanted to try out for a soccer team. By all accounts she performed well during practice to merit inclusion in the team. The coach decided to exclude the child from competition, believing her disability limited the team's chance for success (Austin, 2007).

- A baseball organization paid for the Little League boys' team to attend a championship game, but the organization did not pay for the girls' team. The girls were eventually awarded $1,000 each at the B.C. Human Rights Tribunal (Hume, 2008).

- A sports organization banned a young Muslim girl from playing soccer because she wanted to wear a hijab (headscarf) (Wyatt, 2007).

- A young girl who had no opportunities to play rugby in her community wanted to play on the boys' team. The team was accepting, the sports organization was not (Hume, 2008).

> "Nothing about us without us."
> —a maxim of disability support groups

Sports, Inclusion, and the Law

Our societies take the issue of inclusion very seriously. Legislation in many modern countries enshrines the fundamental rights of individuals to fully participate in society without facing institutionalized prejudice. The American with Disabilities Act of 1990 (PL 101-336) made it illegal to discriminate against an individual with a disability. The law also required state and local government facilities to be made fully accessible for use by people with various challenges.

Least Restrictive Environment

There are occasions when the child just does not have the physical or cognitive capabilities to participate in a meaningful way. At what point is it okay to suggest that a young athlete find sporting experiences elsewhere? Education legislators have grappled with this issue for years. They have created the term *least restrictive environment (LRE)* to define the context for this issue. According to Section 504 of the Rehabilitation Act of 1973 (PL 93-112), LRE requires that

> To the maximum extent appropriate, children with disabilities, including children in public or private institutions or other care facilities, are educated with children who are non-disabled; and special classes, separate schooling, or other removal of children with disabilities from the regular educational environment occurs only if the nature or severity of the disability is such that education in regular classes with the use of supplementary aids and services cannot be achieved satisfactorily.

I have observed far too many sports organizations and school sports teams exclude children with challenges because it is either easier or more convenient to leave them out. An inclusive philosophy stands opposed to such practices—such a philosophy also has the legal support of powerful organizations.

Other pieces of legislation have required sports organizations to pursue more inclusive sports practices. In 2001, the European Union revised the *European Charter for Sport* (R [92] 13 rev., pp. 3–5) to both implicitly recognize the value of sports and create a framework for safe participation in sports for every individual:

The *European Charter for Sport* states that sports should

- Ensure that all young people have the opportunity to receive physical education instruction and the opportunity to acquire basic sports skills
- Ensure that everyone has the opportunity to take part in sports and physical recreation in a safe and healthy environment
- Ensure that everyone with the interest and ability has the opportunity to improve his or her standard of performance in sports and to reach levels of personal achievement and/or publicly recognized levels of excellence
- Protect and develop the moral and ethical bases of sports and the human dignity and safety of those involved in sports by safeguarding sports and participants from exploitation for political, commercial, and financial gain, and from practices that are abusive or debasing, including the abuse of drugs and sexual harassment and abuse, particularly of children, young people, and women

Sport Canada released a policy on *Sport for Persons with a Disability* (2006). The purpose of the document was to eliminate barriers that prevent people from fully participating in sports. The policy challenges "[a]ll stakeholders in sport to create and support an integrated athlete/participant centered sport model that ensures the seamless progress of athletes/participants to the full extent of their abilities and interests" (p. 31).

How Are Young People Excluded from Participating in Sports?

Exclusion from sports is something that can be be deliberately orchestrated by the leader (e.g., having a coach move a player off the field) or ruthlessly communicated by the peer group (e.g., peers telling one player not to play with them). Exclusion can take two forms: complete or functional exclusion. In *complete exclusion* the young athlete with challenges is not allowed to participate with their peers; this athlete is essentially segregated. *Functional exclusion* is something these young athletes are more likely to experience; they may be allowed to join a team but often will be denied any meaningful experiences. A study by Falvey, Givner, and Kimm (1995) recorded children's responses when they were included or excluded in sports. When excluded, they stated that they were angry, frustrated, lonely, inferior, worthless, untrusted, and so forth. When included, they used words like *secure, confident, accepted, liked, normal,* and *important.*

> As a society, we must decide that diversity is valuable. Diversity is not just a reality to be tolerated, accepted and accommodated, it is a reality to be embraced and valued! When some people are excluded from the social fabric of our communities, that fabric contains a hole. When the fabric contains a hole, the entire fabric is weakened.
> (Boiduck, 2004, p. 7)

What Are the Barriers to a Fully Inclusive Sports Environment?

It would be great if all coaches and organizations were to fully embrace an inclusive sports philosophy, but there are barriers to its full implementation. Many coaches are volunteers and, although well intentioned, may not know how to work with athletes with a broad range of challenges. Although this book will explore the different teaching techniques that coaches can use to promote inclusion, this is not enough. A paradigm shift in the attitudes and beliefs held by some coaches is also needed. Here are a few examples of barriers that could inhibit an inclusive philosophy.

Cliché-Driven Coaching

Coaches who draw on sports clichés as a source of wisdom or justification for their coaching techniques generally do a disservice to children with difficulties in sports. Some common clichés, such as "It's all in the mind," "Second place is first loser," "That's the way we have always done it," and its companion, "That's the way that I was taught, and it worked for me, didn't it?" are tiresome, worn-out views that limit the coaches' understanding of children with different needs.

One cliché, "If it ain't broken, why try to fix it?" is well suited for a description of a piece of machinery, but it does a great disservice to children. Some children will thrive in sports no matter what style of coaching or instruction they receive, but how successful is a program if a significant number of participants end up discouraged and drop out?

Emerging from these clichés are demeaning assumptions about children who have difficulty in sports. The ridicule and exclusion that many of these young people experience falls into the category of bullying. A clichéd interpretation of bullying and harassment includes phrases such as "It's just boys being boys," and "They just need to blow off steam!" Too often these difficulties are translated by children—and sometimes inadvertently promulgated by coaches—into a view that these behaviors are sanctioned by the coach and in the sports organization. A coach who argues, "He must have done something to invite the bullying" or states that "Kids must learn to work it out themselves" diminishes the seriousness of these behaviors. Cliché-based coaching philosophies could be a "red flag" about the coaches' attitudes and their expectations of young athletes; parents may wish to proceed with caution.

> The culture of exclusion posits that isolating and marginalizing the stranger is appropriate, acceptable and sometimes even laudatory. (Sapon-Shevin, 2003, p. 25)

Unrealistic Adult Expectations for Young Athletes

Coaches of young athletes must have a sound technical knowledge of the athletes' physical capabilities and an understanding of the people they are working with. However, I have observed that it is a common practice to impose adult expectations of effort and achievement on young developing athletes. It should be obvious that young children and teenagers have developing physiological and psychological systems and that they need to be gradually introduced to more complex and demanding methods of practice as befits their bodies' ability to adapt. Put simply: Adult methods and quantities of training are not developmentally appropriate for young athletes.

Coaches also need to understand why the young athlete is participating in the sport. When there is a disconnect between the athlete's motives for practicing or competing and the coach's expectations, conflict and dissatisfaction for both parties can emerge. The athlete may be accused of lacking determination or commitment. The student may feel the coach is trying to make him or her behave (compete) in a manner the student finds uncomfortable. How many times have you heard a coach demand that the athlete "suck it up, kid," when more often than not, this distressed and tearful athlete just needed some compassion and support?

Stereotypical Misunderstandings

In researching this book, I have heard the following statements:

- "These kids [with challenges] are just not interested in sports."
- "It costs too much to develop special programs for these kids."
- "Our coaches don't have the knowledge to deal with them."
- "We don't have the facilities to help out."
- "We're not a babysitting service!"
- "Sports were never meant to be inclusive. It's simply survival of the fittest."

But for the "babysitting" remark (which was so outrageous I wanted to include it to show that ignorance still festers in sports), most of the aforementioned remarks are typical. Their concerns are unfounded, however. Coaches can be trained, facilities can be modified (usually without significant cost), and, most important, children will attend if a sport is offered in a manner that supports their needs.

Inclusion Can Be a Polarizing Topic

It is fair to acknowledge that inclusion can be a polarizing topic. There are passionate advocates for children with challenges who will wave legislation at sports organizations and shout discrimination if they don't get their way. These parents want to see their children fully involved (which is just), but some demand that the child has rights and needs that supersede all others (which clearly is not just!). Some take a more subtle approach, quietly engaging community sports leaders and trying to strike up partnerships of collaboration. Whatever sports this child with a challenge participates in, the activities must be able to preserve and enhance his or her sense of dignity and let the child build on personal success. It is important that advocates for inclusion do not use their arguments to place a child with serious challenges in a situation where he or she cannot possibly find success.

Absolute positions—whether they are for or against inclusion—often take the child out of the analysis. We should not look at children as fixed entities; they are constantly changing and challenging our assumptions about their capabilities. A child who struggles one year may transform himself into a highly competent young athlete the next. These changes can be at the physical, emotional, and social level, and we need to look for and expect the best in our children. The following account from a fifth-grade teacher highlights this view:

> If I told you that Jim was going to be our athlete citizen of the year, you would have laughed at me and said that is ridiculous. Jim had experienced a tough fourth-grade year; he wasn't very nice to the other kids. He took setbacks on the sports field in bad humor, and he hated losing to the point that he sulked incessantly. In fifth grade he returned to school and became the most helpful, kind, and considerate young man. He was given lots of responsibilities, and he

became a trusted leader of the other students. What brought about this dramatic change? I believe it was always in him. Maturity, praise, and encouragement helped to draw these skills out of him.

What Can Parents Do to Help Promote Their Child's Inclusion in Sports?

There are many great coaches looking after our young athletes. They are educated, guided by ethical conduct, and seek to provide a sound developmental program for their athletes. But there are also coaches who are bullies. They are argumentative, inflexible, and create an adversarial atmosphere that does little to foster respect. You may be able to identify the bullies easily, for their reputation often precedes them. But as the advocate for your child you are entitled to respectfully ask the sports organization or school if they have a policy of inclusion and what authentic opportunities exist for the child with challenges. You may wish to determine if there is a coach who is particularly skilled at working with children with challenges. This is an important question, as research has repeatedly shown that a child who feels a sense of attachment to a significant figure (e.g., a coach, parent, or teacher) is more likely to be motivated to learn (Glasser, 1986).

A parent's attitude toward sports has been shown to be a powerful determinant of the child's view of sports (Biddle & Goudas, 1996). Parents who actively support their child's interests and who participate in sports themselves are influential in shaping the decisions of a child uncertain about participating. Research has also shown that parents who are highly sociable, have well-developed emotional expressiveness, and are involved in vigorous play with their child will have a positive influence on their child's peer status (Putallaz, 1987).

Sadly, a disturbing trend is that many school boards either have made daily physical education an elective or have written it completely out of the curriculum. This will only be changed with parent advocacy and lobbying. Schools need to hear how important sports are for all students, not just for the elite teams. Parents should ask that the school provide as many teams or opportunities as necessary to meet the interests of children of all ranges of abilities.

Inclusion in Sports and the Reggio Emilia Approach

The Reggio Emilia approach to inclusive education offers an innovative method to help students with challenges find acceptance. Although this method (developed in Italy) was designed for early education, it has elements that sports coaches may wish to adopt to help them improve their inclusive program. The main goal of this approach is to help each child build a strong sense of belonging to the community and to strengthen the child's identity as an individual (Gandini, 1993).

One of the hallmarks of this philosophy is that all children are viewed as capable—even if they face a variety of challenges. Parents are considered partners in the educational or coaching process and are encouraged to play an active and supporting role in the program (Spaggiari, 1993).

Cooperative learning, peer support, individualized goals for the young athlete, activity choice making, and visual schedules are practical methods the Reggio Emilia approach uses to develop the potential of each child. How might this apply to coaching?

Cooperative Learning

In this approach to learning, the coach will develop clusters of students and direct them to look after each other. It is important to include at least one influential or popular child in each group and avoid clustering the popular and talented children together! The coach may then select a skill development or tactical problem for all the members of the group to think about and then develop some solutions. For example, a coach of Grade 5 basketball students wants to develop their ball handling skills (dribbling). He presents a concept: "Today we are going to play Basketball Wheel of Good Fortune." The coach shows a "wheel" that he has made out of cardboard—it is a circle with five pie-shaped segments. He divides his students into five groups of three. Each group is given the same instruction: "I want you to create a game that develops your dribbling skills. To give you some ideas, they could be dribbling relays, dribbling games of tag, and so forth. Create your own rules for this game and write the details into the Wheel of Good Fortune. When you are done, we will play the game." This type of activity can be designed or modified in a manner that promotes positive interaction among teammates and promotes the inclusion of those with less well-developed skills. A young athlete with poor basketball skills might have an excellent ability in creating fun and exciting games and will be admired by teammates.

Making Choices and Expressing Knowledge

Choice making within a sport's activities allows the athletes to work at their own pace and skill level. It is also an effective means of diminishing the athletes' exposure to criticism or mockery when they make a mistake in practice. For example, a soccer coach divides the group into smaller clusters and develops a series of practice stations that will help to develop the skills the coach feels the athletes must work on. The stations can have graded levels of skill challenges. There will be an activity for those who are struggling with the fundamentals of the skills and a station for athletes who need enrichment. If this soccer coach is looking to develop shooting skills, the stations might include shooting a bouncing ball, shooting a still ball, shooting a ball that is rolling away, and so forth.

Another belief of the Reggio Emilia approach is that children are capable of expressing their knowledge in many different ways, something that has been described as the "hundred languages of children" (Malaguzzi, 1993). Traditionally, achievement in sports has been acknowledged by the athlete's performance outcome. The Reggio Emilia approach would also use the child's knowledge of the activity, expressions of emotion, and use of symbolic representation (e.g., pictures drawn, journals kept) to build a more complete picture of achievement, one that recognizes the behavioral, cognitive, and affect components of the self.

The development of autonomy, the recognition of diversity, and the strengthening of self-concepts are important features of this approach and should serve as the essential foundations for a coach or teacher who wants to develop an inclusive sports program.

Benefits of an Inclusive Sports Environment

There are many benefits to providing an inclusive sports environment to students. Here are a few examples of benefits:

- Students and young athletes without disabilities tend to develop more positive attitudes toward and an appreciation of the challenges faced by children with special needs when placed in an inclusive sports environment (Vogler, Koranda, & Romance, 2000).

- Successful inclusion programs were noted for improving attitudes of acceptance, understanding of differences, and the self-concept of athletes (Block, 1999).

- When athletes without disabilities volunteer to help teach their friends in a peer-tutoring program, research suggests that this can help develop the fitness of children with challenges (Halle, Gabler-Halle, & Bembren, 1989).

- An inclusive sports environment helps students develop loyalty, intimacy, and self-esteem (Martin & Smith, 2002).

> Having an opportunity to experience a range of valued (sports) roles is empowering because it reduces isolation, increases social interaction, and enhances the person's feelings of self-worth.
> (Lord, 1993, p.16)

- In a research study, students ages 9–11 years with mild intellectual disabilities were incorporated into a general education class, and all students (including students without disabilities) were given cooperative activities. After a 5-week period, the students without disabilities reported significantly higher levels of social acceptance of the children with disabilities. A control group did not have the opportunity to engage in cooperation-building activities, and their levels of acceptance of children with disabilities did not change (Jacques, Wilton, & Townsend, 1998).

Building a Sense of Community and Belonging: Coaching Tools and Techniques that Promote Inclusion

Many coaching tools and techniques that promote inclusion are simple but effective. These tools include the following:

- *Team chants and songs:* These chants and songs are badges of identity and can create a sense of group membership.
- *Acknowledging the achievements of each child:* It is important to acknowledge the achievements of each child based on each child's effort rather than on an outcome.
- *Team photos:* Photos build a sense of cohesion among team members. Team photos and group social events are important vehicles for building athletes' positive sense of connection and self-worth. Conversely, excluding a child from a team photo is also a powerful message that would surely convince the child that he or she does not belong on the team.

Other techniques that "inform" teammates that a student is a fully recognized member of the team (whether the teammates like it or not) include the following:

- *Using the "halo effect":* Identify influential people in the group and have them mentor the child through various activities.
- *Providing each child with a position of responsibility and opportunities for leadership:* Most team sports have rituals that precede the start of the game: leading the team out onto the field, tossing the coin to decide which team starts, leading a team cheer, and so forth. Choosing a vulnerable young athlete for these leadership opportunities may help to increase his or her sense of value to the team.
- *Creating a cherished ritual:* Once per practice, allow a student to wear a certain special jersey or other highly valued artifact.

Final Thoughts

A fully inclusive sports environment will consist of a program in which athletes of all ranges of abilities are welcomed. The program will be structured with modifications and accommodations for different learning styles and physical needs. There will be excellent institutional leadership with policies that protect the rights of individuals and outline the responsibilities of members to promote acceptance. The coaches and parents will role-model kindness and compassion. They will take a key role in educating young athletes in the virtues that extol acceptance of children with differences.

There will be evidence of collaborative partnerships between the organization and parents as they share information that will help the athletes. There will be visible signs of success in this program: Attendance will be high, there will be a joyful atmosphere, the program will have an excellent reputation in the community, and athletes will be praised and recognized, reflecting a positive sports environment.

CHAPTER **3**

The Importance of Play and Sports in Children's Development

There are few statements about humans that can transcend cultures, genders, and ages, but this one is an example: A human being never loses his or her capacity or need to play. Play, a critical part of our development, prepares our brain to be flexible to meet the challenges placed before us. According to the U.N. High Commission for Human Rights (1989), play is so important that it is recognized as a fundamental right of every child.

Play is a driving force for our exploration of the world. Play helps us to learn how our bodies operate and helps determine and possibly extend the limits of our physical capacity. Play brings us limitless opportunities to forge social relationships and experience a broad range of emotions. For many people, play is a natural experience and its rewards are instant and gratifying. For some people, the lack of success in play may, in fact, be a marker of difficulties that could impede their overall development.

> Play is to the child what thinking, planning, and blueprinting are to an adult (Erikson, 1950, as cited in Ewen, 2003, p. 177).

Play is simple and can be unstructured. At other times, play can be full of complex rules that mutate as the game unfolds. It sounds confusing, and for some children (e.g., those with an ASD) it is confusing; such children fail to interpret the nuances of a game that evolves as it is played. But play is beneficial even for children who have difficulty understanding the subtleties of some types of play; the actions and gestures of play can be considered an expressive language for nonverbal children.

Many researchers have attempted to describe the importance of play in our social lives; there are, however, so many theories about play that even the lightest coverage could consume this book. Here are a few examples just to provide some context:

- *Rough-and-tumble play*: This is a very important mode of play for a child who is kinetic (i.e., constantly on the move) and enjoys physical contact in games.
- *Mastery play:* This is a form of play that is designed to solve a problem.
- *Sensorimotor play:* This form of play satisfies a need for sensory stimulation.
- *Cooperative play:* This kind of play teaches us how to get along with others.
- *Onlooker play:* In this kind of play a child watches others play, then engages in activities on his or her own.
- *Solitary play:* This kind of play consists of a child playing by him- or herself with little regard for others playing in the vicinity. Parents observing their child engaging in solitary play should not necessarily conclude that their child has social interaction difficulties. We all like to be on our own occasionally and children are certainly no different. However, ongoing solitary play may inhibit the development of age-appropriate social skills, and this should be monitored by caregivers.
- *Fantasy play:* Some children are especially adept at creating wonderful imaginary worlds to explore. They often use role playing to immerse themselves in a characterization from a book or film.
- *Cathartic play:* This is play that the child uses to release pent-up energy or perhaps act out frustrations and disappointments.

> You can discover more about a person in an hour of play than you can in a year of conversation.
> —Plato

Play is particularly beneficial for children who have been discouraged from engaging in physical activity. Burdette and Whittaker (2005) suggested that unstructured play is an important tool to promote the kind of physical activity that may be attractive to children challenged by obesity. They also noted the positive influence of play on mood states.

Troubling Trends Affecting Play Opportunities

The way that children play in our society is changing, and there are some troubling trends emerging that may actually hamper a child's play opportunities. These troubling trends include the "adultification" of play, coaches who inhibit creativity in sport, the "sterilization" of play experiences, competition for time in the school's curriculum, technology and fitness fads, and parental concerns related to safety that can cause children not to participate in unstructured play. These topics are discussed in the following sections.

The "Adultification" of Play

Should all children's play be "child centered"? A child's play can mimic aspects of an adult's behavior, for example, pretending to drive a car, pretending to be a top athlete winning a running race, and so forth. Even though the play context is an adult one, it is still child centered and can be a joyful, rewarding experience. My concern is with a process that I term *adultification of play*. This term refers to a situation in which adults are designing the place, the time, and the type of play for children, instead of letting the children lead the play.

Many parents have been able to provide enriched opportunities for their children. Their kids are enrolled in programs where their safety is ensured, where there is a strong educational quotient, and where their child mixes with other children of a similar background. The predominant belief system when it comes to sports and play is that the child will receive enrichment, and this will enhance the child's path to life success. When the adultification process is used, sports and play may become something that is packaged, available at a fixed, scheduled time (e.g., every Saturday morning from 9 to 10 A.M.), and likely to be followed up with a rewarding trip to a fast-food facility. Somewhere lost in this safe and supervised structure is spontaneous creative play. Why is spontaneous creative play important? Play that is rigid and is presented as a prescribed series of activities with a specific outcome limits the imagination of its participants. Children (and young athletes) who are encouraged to improvise around a theme can create wonderful solutions to problems, whether they are tactical challenges on the sports field or ways of resolving conflicts. Spontaneous creative play allows children to celebrate their uniqueness.

Play is important to adults, too, but we prefer to call it sports. Some of us are prepared to spend huge sums of money either watching it or participating in it, but it is really not that much different from the activities that a child undertakes in the sandbox. We decide upon a leader (or the team captain). We have rules in place to ensure that the game is played fairly. Sometimes people break the rules, and we need an arbiter to help us settle the dispute (the parent in the case of a child, the referee in the case of the adult).

This contrasts with how a child plays. For example, a child will imagine a whole variety of ways to play a game of tag, whereas adults, when playing sports, employ coaches and analysts to pursue the scientific study of strategy and scheme. Our sports have developed their own languages, codes of conduct, and expectations of performance. Whereas children dream of ruling their own make-believe world, many adults imagine hoisting the world championship trophy above their head.

Coaches Who Restrict Creativity

Creative play is an important part of a child's development. Using the imagination to solve problems or invent ways to have fun helps children in many of the ways already discussed in this chapter. As sports are often used by parents as a medium for play, an important question is whether creativity is encouraged and recognized by the coach.

In many countries, sports are so engrained into the culture that children often practice hour after hour in pursuit of glory in this passion. These practices often take the form of unsupervised and unstructured free play. Consequently, these children develop highly refined skills and innovative (creative) ways of solving challenges within the game.

In too many sports environments, adults have become excessively involved in the young athletes' development, and this has generated a risk of "overcoaching." Overcoaching occurs when coaches who cannot exercise self-restraint (or simply don't know better) stand on the sidelines yelling at the players about what to do and how to do it. Overcoaching can have detrimental effects on athletes. These athletes may feel controlled and feel fearful that the coach will rebuke them if they don't follow instructions or if they make a mistake. Such players can seem devoid of imagination when a novel situation presents itself within the game. A culture of fear, coercion, or control seldom brings the best out of any athlete.

> Creativity is a type of learning process where the teacher and the pupil are located in the same individual.
>
> —Arthur Koestler

Players who have been encouraged to express their creativity within the framework of the game and are emotionally secure enough to take risks tend to stand out. If we want to ensure that all of our athletes are challenged, we should provide them the opportunity to be creative. Coaches are advised not to criticize play that doesn't fit the template but, rather, to recognize the idea with praise, even if the execution was not successful.

The Sensory Sterilization of Play

Play is important in developing not only children's social and physical skills, but also their sensory systems. Activities that stimulate the senses and require the child to process these sensations and interpret them are increasingly being neglected in sports programs. Cutbacks in classroom physical education and the sensory sterilization of community playgrounds are depriving children of experiences that they need to stimulate their senses. Playground equipment, such as merry-go-rounds and swings, are being banned across our playgrounds as we aim to further cut the small number of accidents that are caused by these pieces of equipment. Also, although gymnastics have been a very important part of the PE curriculum, schools, fearing litigation, increasingly are choosing not to include these athletic skills in their programs. The sensory needs of young athletes are not being adequately developed. Areas such as vestibular stimulation (the balance system), spatial awareness, and proprioceptive integration (having the ability to sense where your body is relative to the space around you) are not being sufficiently challenged in some sports programs. Children crave these kinds of experiences (witness the lengthy lines for roller-coasters and intense fairground rides). Sterilizing play experiences can hinder children from developing these important sensory skills. How will this be changed? Realistically, the most practical means will be to incorporate more gymnastics back into our school physical education classes.

Competition for Time in the School Curriculum: Learning at the Expense of Play

Schools have long wrestled with the demands of finding adequate time in the curriculum for the vast range of subject and learning opportunities available. The No Child Left Behind Act of 2001 (PL 107-110) was designed to increase the standards of children's literacy and numeracy. One of the unintended consequences of this act was that academic time was found at the expense of recess and physical education. The Center on Education Policy (2008, February) reported that 20% of all elementary schools decreased the amount of recess time and 9% decreased the amount of physical education in order to meet math and literacy curriculum expectations. Although it has been over-stated in the media that this act has decimated recess (the average recess time in elementary schools dropped from 37 minutes per day to 24–30 minutes), of schools with minorities representing 50% or more of the student population, 14% of these schools scheduled no recess at all for Grade 1 students (U.S. Department of Education Fast Response Survey System, 2005). The absence of recess opportunities were found in 14% of schools for students from families with low socioeconomic status and living in urban environments (U.S. Department of Education Fast Response Survey System, 2005).

Ladd, Kochenderfer, and Coleman (1997) suggested that children given adequate amounts of recess time improved their ability to focus attention on academic tasks. Jarrett (2002) also noted the strong connection between student learning and activity time (recess). The lack of play opportunities has been a disservice to young children, who need to play to help facilitate their learning.

When physical education and recess time at school are cut from school programs, the educational equivalent of outsourcing is occurring. Schools that are unable to fund and provide sports programs for their students are offloading this responsibility to parents and outside sports organizations. Outsourcing sports and activity programs favors those children who are economically secure and denies opportunities to children from low-income backgrounds. Outsourcing also effectively denies opportunity to children with challenges, as many private outside organizations are ill prepared to accept children with challenges or special needs.

Technology and Fitness Fads

Few would dispute the importance of having sports programs that emphasize energetic activity as opposed to the passive involvement offered in video games. An unlikely paradigm shift may be taking place in the way that physical activity is being presented in combination with video games. Increasingly, new video games that pair fitness with technology, such as the Wii and Wii Fit systems, are being offered. This technology requires physical activity to successfully operate the game. Interaction with these virtual athletic environments offers intriguing possibilities for children who may respond well to controlled visual stimuli in an environment in which they feel in control and safe, such as at home. However, no clear evidence supporting the efficacy of these new games on fitness and exercise adherence has been identified (Daley, 2009).

Parental Concerns Regarding Safety

The need to protect and raise our young is a biological imperative that directs the behavior of responsible adults, so it is understandable that parents are concerned when they allow their children to play in unstructured situations. I don't know if rates of crime against young children have increased over the past few decades, but our instant technological access to news stories of appalling crimes is making parents more cautious than ever. The days of allowing young children to roam the neighborhood, creating their own games and seeking adventures, have been replaced by structured and supervised playtime. Parents of young children are registering them in sports programs, believing that they are play activities. Can sports provide a child with the benefits of play? Yes, as long as the coach incorporates playful activities as opposed to having the children focus exclusively on high performance and winning.

> Play needs to be cherished and encouraged, for in their free play children reveal their future minds.
> —Friedrich Froebel (1887)

Play and Brain Development

Play has been shown to influence the development of the brain's cerebellum (a structure that coordinates movements; Pellis & Pellis, 2007). A child with poor coordination skills is encouraged to engage in a broad range of play activities to help stimulate the cerebellum and help it to develop. These children may be marginalized from effective play interactions because of their lack of skill, but withdrawing from play interactions only serves to compound their difficulties.

Play has also been identified as taking a key role in the pruning process of dendritic connections in brain cells (neurons). A newborn has an excess of brain cell connections, so the brain, for the sake of efficiency, decides to cut down the number of these connections and concentrate on developing a few "superhighways" to carry the brain's messages. A child's desire to play reflects the need to help facilitate pruning these excess connections. Some research suggests that children with an ASD have poor pruning abilities

(Pellis, 1992). Compounding their brain's ineffi-
ciency (especially in the areas of communication
and social skills development), children with an
ASD are noted for their lack of play interactions
with others. There is some suggestion that attention deficit disorder (ADD) may be the result of
the overactivity of play urges within the nervous
system (Panskepp, 1998).

> Play reaches the
> habits most needed
> for intellectual
> growth.
> —Bruno Bettelheim

Coaches and Sports

What constitutes a sport, how it is structured and taught, and what it is
supposed to mean to a team or individual defies a concise definition. Many
coaches' understanding and philosophical approaches to sports are drawn
from their own experiences. Sports from an adult perspective is likely to be
about competition and striving for personal excellence; from a child's perspective, it may be more about fun and friendship. Sports meanings emerge
out of the attitudes, values, and interests of those participating.

The purpose of sports is steadily changing. In the ancient Olympic
Games, sports were an opportunity to display athleticism and—in some
events—the beauty of movement. In the Middle Ages, sports in England
were used as a means of social control (until riots broke out and Henry
VIII had to ban soccer!). Today, sports for adults are both entertainment and
health promotion. It has also become a mechanism for a child's enrichment
or, in the minds of some parents, a means of allowing children to play in a
supervised structure.

Sports are not always a successful medium for promoting the development of all children. An examination of sports environments where students
drop out, feel alienated, or feel rejected invariably reveals that there is an
absence of fun in the practices and excessive pressure in competitions. You
tend to hear statements from students such as "My teammates take the game
too seriously," or "I was constantly being yelled at." Resilient kids may learn
to cope, but for children who already have fragile confidence or marginal
interest, this is enough to discourage them.

In researching this book, discussions with several coaches revealed a
wide range of views of what coaches believe actually constitutes fun. One
coach said, "The kids just did as they were told. Having fun is just an attitude
and the right kind of kid will bring that attitude to practice. Kids with bad
attitudes shouldn't come!" He didn't sound like a lot of fun to me! Another
coach thought that too much of an emphasis on fun and play interfered with
learning; he didn't like seeing his athletes "goofing off."

There was, fortunately, a more enlightened coach who believed that play
needed to be at the core of her practices. When she incorporated these elements,
she found that the children learned that much better. Sports activities that are
fun tend to be presented with variety. The practices never get too repetitive.

Several studies have considered what fun actually means to young athletes. Hastie (1998) interviewed female field hockey players; they reported that fun for them consisted of interactions with friends, being part of a team, playing games, and developing skills. Mandigo and Couture (1996) stated that challenge, skill, participation, and locus of control (being able to exercise decision making in your choice of activity) were important elements of fun. Cothran and Ennis (1998) noted that children viewed fun as a process that increased their engagement in the activity; coaches tended to view fun as an outcome.

Striking a Balance Between Play and Sports: Recommended Ratios of Sports and Play

The way that we play is never static, and the needs of a teenager are obviously going to be different from those of a young child. What ratio of playfulness to sports is needed by a developing person? Although a later section of this chapter addresses the broader issue of when a child is ready for sports, the following recommendations will help coaches balance skill development and play:

Ages 5–8 years: 80%–90% play, 10%–20% skill development

Ages 8–12 years: 60%–70% play, 30%–40% skill development

Ages 12–15 years: 40%–50% play, 50%–60% skill development

Ages 15 years and older: 20% play, 70%–80% skill development

These recommendations dovetail with the long-term athletic development model (also mentioned later in this chapter) that stresses the importance of "*Fun*damentals" in young children's introduction to sport (Balyi & Hamilton, 2004).

Play does not mean that the activity has to be disconnected from the purpose of the sport. Many games can develop the child's skills but in a manner that is playful. Sometimes it is not so much what the activity is but how it is presented by the coach. For example, children who struggle to complete a formal distance running workout will joyfully play games of tag and likely achieve the same physical benefits.

Parents' Role in Facilitating Play

Role modeling healthy play behavior is an important part of parents' relationship with their child. It is clear that the exercise habits or sedentary choices of parents are inevitably embraced by their children (Anderson, Hughes, & Fuemmeler, 2009). Playing with a child is important, not only because it helps the child to develop physically, emotionally, and socially, but also because games of "rough and tumble" with Mom or Dad can be some of the most treasured memories in a child's development.

When Is a Child Ready for Sports?

This is an important question, but it is one with no easy nor formulaic answer. Parents—especially those with a child who has a disability or other challenges—want to support their child's inclusion but may be uncertain that this is the right thing to do. Their assessment of their child's readiness for sports needs to consider the child's physical development, social and emotional competence, and interest or motivation in the sport.

Physical Development

The various measures of a child's physical readiness for sports—height, weight, gross and fine motor skill assessment, and so forth—provide parents with observations and data that can guide their thinking, but human physical development is not a uniform linear progression where everyone develops at the same rate. Some children have precocious development and are physically able to participate in organized sports (and competition) from a very early age. Other children may have well-developed emotional resilience and social skills but have delayed physical development. Shephard (1982) noted there could be as much as a 4-year range in physical maturity when a child reaches 12 years old; this might translate into a 30- to 40-pounds weight difference between children who mature either very early or late. Such variance obviously carries significant implications for students where size in sports conveys an advantage or limitation.

There has been much research that has considered the risks of intense training and specialization with young athletes. From my own experience, I can recall 20 athletes being selected when 12 years old for the county cross-country running team. By the time we reached age 18, there were only two of us still participating in the sport. Most of my teammates were on a "scrap heap" with broken bodies and broken spirits. They practiced a lot harder than me in their early teenage years but they were not able to sustain the intensity and expectations that they experienced. The International Federation of Sports Medicine cautioned that the early and intensive specialization of exercise programs in children "lacks physiological or educational justification" (1991, pp. 23–24); the American Academy of Pediatrics (2000) has affirmed this view.

High rates of injury, emotional instability, social adjustment difficulties, and low self-esteem have been identified as risks to young athletes who train very hard (Pooley, 1981; Seefeldt et al., 1992; Williams, 1998). Although parents and coach may enjoy the performances of high-achieving young athletes, research has repeatedly shown that the connection among success, early maturation, and long-term achievement is at best tenuous (Magill, 2001; Matsudo, 1996; Rowland, 1998; Sage, 1984). Rowland stated that the "anatomical, physiological and psychological immaturity of children may place them at greater risk during athletic training and competition" (1990, p. 253). Wiersma (2000) reported that almost 98% of athletes who specialize in a sport at an early age do not reach the highest levels as adults. Barynina and Vaitsekhovskii (1992) reported that swimmers who specialized at a later age advanced at a greater rate than swimmers who specialized early.

Identifying Your Physically Developed, Talented Athletes

When it comes to the identification of sporting talent, all is not what it seems. Some young children enjoy success because they are simply more physically developed and biologically advanced than their opponents—that is, they have started to grow earlier than another athlete. Research has shown that these children are likely to receive more encouragement and opportunities than children who mature at a slower rate (Malina, 1984).

The Relationship Between Talent and Success Is Not Always Clear

The successful athlete is not necessarily the one who is the most naturally talented. Some children can be athletically talented and yet not successful, whereas other children may have precocious physical development and be successful but not athletically talented.

Success at a young age—although enjoyable for the athlete (and the proud parents)—is not particularly meaningful in the grand scheme of development. Puberty is often the great equalizer; as bodies can drastically change shape, the diminutive child at the back may suddenly power forward and express hidden talents. The "star" athlete no longer enjoys the biological advantages of precocious development and now has to work hard for success. Success in sports is certainly to be enjoyed, but it is not uncommon to find some teenagers run much slower times than when they were younger.

The following story describes the need for coaches and parents to build a framework of success that recognizes the changing needs of the child—even the most capable young athlete.

Too Much, Too Soon?

At the age of 11, one of our students was already an outstanding middle distance runner. With her long limbs and rake-thin body, she swept her rivals away with an imperious ease. Her talent was obvious and she was placed on a hard training regime by an overzealous coach. She easily won championships; sometimes she was minutes ahead of her nearest rival. When she turned 12, the excessively hard training and success continued. Journalists were knocking on the family door begging for interviews and photo shoots. She appeared on the front cover of running magazines, signed a shoe contract—all this before she had even left elementary school. Some ill-informed commentators thought she was a certainty for an Olympic gold medal. Television cameras were assigned to gather archival footage of this superstar in the making; she dared not have a bad race.

While the plaudits continued to pile on her young and slender shoulders, more astute observers noted that she was not the happy girl of earlier years. Not only had she adopted a sullen disposition, but the lively spring in her step had started to fade. With the inevitable arrival of puberty, she quickly adopted the mature frame of an adult and race victories were no longer assured. Dissenting opinions started to question this little girl's mental tenacity or physical skill. Some people said, "She is just not trying hard enough," but what she really needed was encouragement and support. At the age of 14 years old, our future Olympic gold medalist, unable to repeat the performances of two years earlier, left the sport. She never ran again.

This story is but a glimpse into the world of the child sporting prodigy. This is a world in which its star pupils live in the talented extreme of the bell curve—that beloved vehicle of the sports statistician. They are the tallest, the strongest, the fastest, and yet they still have the mind of a developing child. The risks and burdens of overtraining, excessive expectations, and overwhelming success at such a young age are many; it proved to be the undoing of this young girl.

Emotional and Social Competence

Assessing the physical skills of a young athlete is relatively straightforward; a coach can ask the student to perform an activity and then draw conclusions from their observations. The coach can then decide whether the athlete is ready to participate at a certain level. Assessing emotional and social competence is a more subjective and complex process with inherent difficulties as to how to appropriately use the information. A young athlete may be fully ready for the physical challenges that a sport presents but may lack the social sophistication or emotional flexibility to cope with demands of the activities.

For example, at the age of 7, my eldest son wanted to participate in a summer community soccer program. Physically, he was very athletic; he could outrun most children of his age and had well-developed coordination. His emotional and intellectual development significantly lagged his physical development. Consequently, he had a very difficult time understanding that when someone took the soccer ball away from you, that was part of the game. He became very distressed when tackled and it was clear that he was not ready to participate. Two years later, he is now fully engaged and is a joyful participant.

Assessment of emotional and social development carries a number of caveats:

- Conduct your assessment through the eyes of the child. Don't assess the child with emotional benchmarks that are suitable for adults. For example, don't expect the child to be emotionally disconnected when things don't go according to plan.

- Use this assessment information to identify areas of support and need rather than using it to restrict or deny participation to a young athlete.

- Maturity is a variable and nebulous concept that has no close ties to age. Precocious or delayed maturity does not necessarily indicate that a young athlete is ready for enhancement or should be held back.

- Students with differences may have difficulties in social settings, and this may be something that is characteristic of their challenge. For example, some students with an ASD can become shy, anxious, and withdrawn in social settings. Their lack of social skill in the sports setting should not be used to preclude their involvement; with appropriate support they will actually benefit from social interactions.

- Some students may have competent emotional and social skills and yet become uncertain and withdrawn in a sports setting. Children who exhibit such characteristics are likely to quit sports (very quickly) if they perceive the environment to be unsettling. If coaches and parents can identify this need in advance, a plan of support (mentoring or using an aide) can help these athletes.

- Sensitivity on how information is gathered and used (maybe even shared with parents) is critical. Coaching ethics should underpin the coach's purpose in this process.

Coaches will, realistically, not have the time nor inclination to use a questionnaire to increase their understanding of their athletes in these two areas. Here is a checklist of questions that can be used to assess the emotional and social competence of young athletes:

Checklist to Assess the Emotional and Social Competence of a Young Athlete

- ❏ Empathy—Does this young athlete show empathy with peers, adults, and coaches?
- ❏ Ability to work in teams—Can this athlete comfortably accept the ideas or efforts of other students?
- ❏ Leadership—Does this young person demonstrate leadership qualities or interests? If so, in what ways can the coach use them to develop the athlete's confidence and self-esteem?
- ❏ Conflict management—How does this student manage conflict? Does he or she require support from influential figures (e.g., parents, referees, coaches), or is the athlete capable of resolving conflicts on his or her own?
- ❏ How influential is this person in the social setting? Does he or she seem to prefer being alone or desire strong social connections?
- ❏ Emotional flexibility—What skills does this young athlete have in self-regulating his or her emotions? Does the student have control of his or her emotions in a focused and consistent manner?
- ❏ Can this athlete recognize the emotions of other students and use this information in appropriate ways?

Motivation and a Young Athlete's Participation in Sports

There are students—with all ranges of ability—who participate in sports with great enthusiasm and only need to be directed by the coach; it would seem that they have the strong desire to challenge themselves and are likely to enjoy competition. Other students may be reluctant participants and are coerced, persuaded, or manipulated by their parents to "at least give it a try." The reasons for wanting to participate in sports are more complex than a simple "You either like it or you don't!" Understanding the sources of motivation is essential if a coach or parent is to be effective in supporting children with interests in sports.

Motivation can be better understood, and at a more personal level, when we study a young athlete's motives for participation. *Motives* are the personalized origins of our behavior, and it is these that guide us toward our goal. Motives may include:

- Our personal *needs*—what it is that we hope to get from participating in the activity. Some children just participate in sports for the possibility of establishing friendships (affiliation needs); others are comfortable in their own company and will pursue individual activities. Some children play sports because they want to win (achievement needs), and they are deeply unhappy if the outcome is not favorable. Other children may participate simply because it is something that they like to do and, win or lose, the sport is still fun.

- Our *attitudes* shape our view of the sporting opportunity.

- *Incentives* can be what we may receive from participating in the sport. These rewards can be internal (known as intrinsic motivation) and could include things such as happiness, fulfillment, or a sense of accomplishment. External rewards (known as extrinsic motivation) may include things such as prizes, ribbons, or money awards. Incentives can exert a powerful influence on our involvement in sports.

- Our *interests* in the sport—or the activities presented in it—shape our involvement. Failure to consistently satisfy our interests in a sport will likely contribute to boredom and/or withdrawal from the sport.

It is acknowledged that there is a vast range of (often contradictory) philosophical and psychological theories about motivation; thus, a comprehensive review would only be a distraction. My purpose in the next section is to consider ways of identifying the sources of motivation that determine a child's readiness for sports.

Achievement Motivation Theory

The achievement motivation theory offered by McClelland, Atkinson, Clark, and Lowell (1953) and Murray (1938) suggested reasons why some people are more motivated to achieve things than others. This theory has three components: the expectation of succeeding at the task, the perceived value of the goal, and the individual's need for achievement. These components merge in the mind of the athlete and will determine his or her motivation to pursue goals.

The Expectation of Succeeding at the Task   Capable young athletes are likely to enter practices or competitions with the expectation that they will perform well. Delivering a performance that wins recognition reinforces their perception of competence. Young children who have low self-esteem (especially when they have constructed this view from their negative experiences in sports) will probably not believe that they are capable of successfully completing the complex tasks that a coach assigns. Watching the ease with which more talented children achieve these goals may reinforce their negative perception of their athletic ability. Building a program for each young athlete to find success takes us into the realm of goal setting.

Many coaches will understand the power of using goal setting to help their athletes strive for personal improvement in their sport. The principles of effective goal setting have been extensively researched and written about in business, self-help, and sports psychology literature; readers wishing more extensive coverage will be better served with books from those areas. I will focus on the SMART principles of goal setting. For goals to be effective, they need to be

Specific—"I want you to run a lap in a certain time."

Measurable—"By the end of this season I want you to have practiced 15 times."

Attainable—"I really believe that this is a goal that you can achieve; it may require hard work, but it is definitely something that is possible."

Relevant—"The skills that I want you to practice will work on the area that you seemed to be having some difficulty with."

Time specific—"Let's evaluate your progress in 1 month's time."

Effective coaches understand that the appropriate use of goal setting for children with challenges in sports is a powerful tool to help promote acceptance. Using these SMART goals will, in turn, increase these young athletes' expectation of finding success. Coaches who fail to modify the team's goals for these students essentially set them up for failure and can increase the children's self-perceived sense of worthlessness.

The Perceived Value of the Goal   Some goals in sports represent the pinnacle of athletic achievement—an Olympic Games gold medal, winning the World Cup of soccer, winning the Super Bowl, and so forth. The perceived value of pursuing these goals is quite obvious to the athletes and coaches. At less lofty levels of athletic aspiration, the importance of a goal is all in the interpretation of the athlete. Some children just don't find the competition that important, whereas for other athletes, this seems like the most important thing in their lives. Younger children often rely on others to articulate the perceived value of sporting goals. Coaches and parents are important communicators of the significance of the goal and can either provide balance and perspective or skew its interpretation in a harmful way.

Research has shown that when a parent places significance on the outcome of a race or game, the more important it becomes to the athlete. When parents express more interest in the athlete's mastery of skills, the more intrinsically motivated the athlete becomes (Swain & Harwood, 1996).

Students who are slower to develop their athletic skills or who have other challenges should probably avoid coaches with highly competitive motives. Some of these coaches have the tendency to amplify the importance of the child's sporting event so that its context and performance expectations are elevated to that of a professional athlete. Placing a high demand for performance on these young shoulders and expecting a win at all costs undermines the child's healthy development. The following story comes from an experience I had as a young boy. It illustrates how parents, coaches, and young athletes can perceive a single game differently.

The Final Score

We had to win the final game of the season in order to win the championship. The coach had sent out scouts to analyze the performance of our opponents and look for tactical weaknesses. He had studied the referee and felt that he knew his style of game management. No detail in game preparation had been overlooked; our uniforms were washed and pressed; the soccer pitch had been scoured for divots; we were told to be in the changing room 1 hour before the game for a technical meeting. We were 10 years old, and I had no idea what a technical meeting was; I just wanted to play the game. After 1 hour of wagging fingers, aggressive "go get them" talk, and soccer tactical talk that lost me after 10 minutes, we were released to actually play. The game was close, and my coach paced up and down the sideline screaming instructions, criticizing every decision the referee made against us. Some of my teammates' parents were getting agitated, and several scuffles broke out. It was a very intense atmosphere.

With 2 minutes left, we were tying this game, but we needed the win for the championship. I was playing defense and missed a tackle that let in my opponent for a clear shot on goal. Fortunately, he missed, but I can vividly recall the rage of my coach, teammates, and several other parents because of my error. I felt terrible and wanted to cry.

The game ended in the most awful way. The referee blew the whistle, and a split second later we scored the winning goal. The goal was disallowed, and parents and my coach ran onto the pitch. All I can recall is a lot of shouting and screaming and people being pushed about. The police had to be called to settle things down. Despite the coach's behavior, most of my teammates actually looked back on that season with pride; we had finished second overall and played some good games.

What Is an Individual's Need for Achievement (N-Ach)?

This is a feature of achievement motivation that describes an athlete's desire for accomplishing tasks. Those who have a high need for achievement (N-Ach) either choose moderately challenging tasks (where success is almost certain) or extremely difficult tasks, hoping to find out just how far they can push themselves. Athletes who participate in sports because they enjoy the challenge and want to see just how far they can push themselves are said to be task oriented.

Some young athletes with poorly developed athletic skills may have a low N-Ach. With this type of motivation, they may choose either very easy tasks that they can achieve or tasks so difficult that they will surely fail. An explanation for those choices was offered in Crocker and Wolfe's self-worth theory (2001). Crocker and Wolfe suggested that young athletes can actually protect their self-esteem by withdrawing effort. Similarly, failure to achieve an advanced skill may be perceived by more skilled athletes as a reflection of the task's complexity, not the athlete's poor skills. In a paradoxical manner, this helps to preserve the young athlete's self-esteem. As athletic ability is considered to be so important, a poor performance that is perceived as a lack of effort, rather than limited ability, can preserve the athlete's image status.

The need for achievement is not a fixed entity and can change with support from influential people. McClelland suggested that increasing the young athlete's N-Ach can be developed by encouraging independence, using sincere praise and rewards for achievement, and helping athletes recognize the importance of a challenge.

N-Ach in Athletes with Challenges: Sources of Motivation

One of the most persistent stereotypes about children with challenges is that their needs somehow erase any competitive drives or interests they may have. Some coaches have used this view to exclude these young athletes from authentic competition. Observers of the Paralympics Games will clearly see high levels of N-Ach as these athletes vigorously push themselves to achieve their goals. Sources of motivation for young athletes with challenges include needs for acceptance, fear of failure, fear of rejection, and ego orientation. These topics are discussed in the next sections.

Need for Acceptance (N-Accept)

As the focus of this book is promoting acceptance for all children in sport, I would like to suggest that another source of motivation is a need for acceptance (something I call N-Accept). I would venture that most participants in sports would like to feel valued and accepted by their peers and the sports organization. This need fluctuates according to the type of interactions the athlete experiences. With consistent rejection and hostility, the need for acceptance in that environment deteriorates until, finally, the child withdraws.

In parenting, you often hear the phrase, "That child is being very needy." It is important for coaches to recognize that their athletes want so much more than technical suggestions on how to kick a ball. The "needy athlete" wants to enjoy the company of others, be recognized, and feel that he or she can make an authentic contribution to the team.

Fear of Failure

The fear of failure is also recognized as a source of motivation in some athletes. Athletes who perceive the value of the goal to be extremely important may develop a fear of all the consequences if the goal is not achieved. Fear of failure can be a powerful motivator in the short term, but when children are motivated in such a way, it quickly undermines their sense of enjoyment in the activity.

Fear of Rejection

Fear of rejection is a corollary to this construct. Children who fear that they may not be accepted by their peers may be motivated to behave in ways specifically designed to attract attention and recognition. If these attempts lack social sophistication, they can actually amplify the child's sense of isolation. Some children are motivated by what has been termed *performance avoidance*. This is when the athlete makes a concerted effort to avoid being viewed as incompetent by others.

Ego Orientation

For some people, the main reason that they are involved in sports is because of their ego orientation. This is a view that is exemplified by the win at all costs mentality that is often perceived as being endemic in sports. The values associated with excellent sportsmanship—honesty, fair play, respect—are not likely to be found in an athlete or coach who has a profound ego orientation. Trash talking, intimidation, and finding ways to circumvent the rules are characteristics of an individual who values a winning outcome more than participating in the sport itself.

Parents with a strong ego orientation may take the roles of volunteer coach or spectator in the child's sports life. A loss of perspective, a sense of outrage when refereeing decisions go against the individual or team, and a lack of self-control are characteristics of parents overwhelmed by an ego orientation. It should be acknowledged that everybody has some degree of ego orientation. When we participate and do well, we feel good about ourselves. That is healthy and builds our confidence.

> One can never consent to creep when one feels an impulse to soar.
> —Helen Keller

Intrinsic and Extrinsic Sources of Motivation

Intrinsic motivation focuses on the idea that we need to feel competent and exercise a degree of personal control over the situations in which we participate.

With intrinsic motivation, young athletes derive satisfaction and pleasure from the mastery of challenges placed before them.

Like other sources of motivation, a young athlete's desire to participate can vary in intensity and duration. Young athletes, especially those with challenges, cannot be expected to maintain high levels of ongoing intrinsic motivation; they will likely need some support from coaches and parents. Understanding the athlete's motives for participation and then ensuring that the activities are built around this purpose will contribute to the athlete's personal enjoyment.

Example: A young athlete who really wants to achieve a certain time for 800 m running will likely thrive on a program that has specific fitness goals that will help him or her to achieve that time. If the athlete starts to experience a whole series of setbacks (perhaps injury or illness), personal enjoyment might be more difficult to achieve. The athlete would likely benefit from the support of an influential figure (a peer, parent, teacher, or coach) to help regain the intrinsic drive for the goal.

The importance of encouragement was supported by research (Vallerand & Reid, 1984) demonstrating that young athletes' intrinsic motivation and perceived competence increased when they received positive comments about their effort and performance.

Extrinsic motivation focuses on the use of rewards and incentives to activate and direct behavior. Many people equate rewards with sporting bribery—"If you do this, you will get that." Given the media attention and huge sums of money thrown at sports superstars, it is easy to understand the attraction that these rewards hold for young athletes. When the athlete achieves the goal by drawing on this type of motivation, it seems to justify this approach. If the athlete does not achieve what he or she expects, the extrinsic source of motivation may detract from ongoing participation in this sport.

Research by Deci (1975) suggested that the use of rewards (an extrinsic motivator) in a situation in which the athlete was otherwise intrinsically motivated carries the possibility of changing the athlete's reasons for participation. The idea is that a child who runs on the cross country team—simply because he or she likes to run—and receives ribbons may then only run if a ribbon (a reward) is offered. Deci and Ryan (1985) then proposed the cognitive evaluation theory, which suggested that ribbons (in our example) can take either an informational or a controlling function. When the ribbon took an informational position (reminding the athlete of the achievement), it enhanced the intrinsic motivation and the child's feelings of competence. When the ribbon took on a controlling function, it weakened the athlete's intrinsic motivation.

Research has suggested that girls seem to be more intrinsically motivated to participate in sports whereas boys are more extrinsically motivated (Synder & Spreitzer, 1979). Boys seemed to focus on the sports outcome; although outcome was important for girls, the benefits of friendship development were considered to be particularly important. One study suggested that competitive sports (as a source of extrinsic motivation) undermined the confidence, self-esteem, and self-perception of personal appearance of girls who experienced difficulties in sports (Marsh & Peart, 1998). Students who seem to lack a strong competitive drive may be better suited where there is a greater emphasis on social and personal development; for example, activities with a wellness focus such as Pilates, aerobics, dance, and so forth.

Competition: Friend or Foe?

Invariably, when considering a child's readiness for sports we can get drawn into the issue of competition. From the athlete in the race to the company competing for market share, from the Little League baseball arena to the worker interviewing for the job, competition infuses almost every element of society. Despite this, competition seems to carry the connotation that it is an unattractive quality. The phrase "You're too competitive" is a familiar refrain.

Competition in itself is benign, but how it is presented by the coach or team determines the identity it takes on. Unfettered levels of competition can be unattractive, and unless it is restrained by calm coaches, it can produce the behaviors that many people find distasteful: arguing with referees, violent conduct, poor sportsmanship, and so forth. A sports culture that has extreme levels of competition and pressure to succeed is not well suited to a child experiencing learning or physical challenges.

The following account from a running coach of high standing details the adverse effects of extreme parental pressure on a young boy.

Mom Knows Best

I will never forget what happened to Sam. His mom marched him over to the track and said to me, "I want you to make him into the best runner in the world." She was deadly serious. I looked at the boy, 13 years old, who was very keen to join our running club. We would practice three times a week, but I could tell that Sam was running a lot more, and he was always tired. It transpired that his mom was making him run twice a day, every day. Every run she made him do was hard, and it seemed to me that he was never allowed to rest. I told his mother that he would end up being injured, miserable, and eventually resentful. I told her that she should let me do the coaching. The mom agreed but continued to drive her son ever harder.

One day Sam complained of a deep pain in his thigh, and a bone scan revealed a serious stress fracture of the femur. The physician prescribed complete rest for at least 12 weeks. This advice was ignored by his mother, who felt that Sam was able to compete in the area championships on the weekend; apparently "the doctor didn't know what he was talking about." You could have heard the scream miles away as that femur fractured. Sam spent a few weeks in the hospital, and it was 8 months before he jogged his first step. Perhaps it is not surprising that within the year Sam had dropped out of sports, attempted to run away from home, and went through a turbulent phase in his adolescence.

The Competitive Achievement Model

There are some people who undoubtedly support the idea that the younger the child starts practicing and participating in sports, the better. The thinking is that the early introduction of sports skills and opportunities will confer a distinct competitive advantage over children who come to the sport later. Sadly, children with developmental needs more suited to play find themselves immersed in competitive programs for which they are not yet ready. This view has been described in the competitive achievement model (Hellison & Templin, 1991). The competitive achievement model is a paradigm in which coaches and parents place considerable emphasis on winning rather than learning. These coaches will likely deny equal access to all participants (i.e., only the athletically capable children get to play). Coaches may superimpose adult values and expectations on children, even though the child is neither physically nor emotionally ready for such direction.

There are countless tales of parents aggressively steering their child on paths that they believe will bring high standards of success. In several high-profile cases, parents (some of whom have had high-level athletic success themselves) have been banned from sports facilities or removed from competition arenas because they have been hostile and abusive. Smoll (2001) described this phenomenon as the reverse-dependency trap—the parents rely on the success of their child to generate the self-worth they need. These coaches and parents are often inspired by the stories of high-profile, extraordinarily successful overachieving athletes who started out as child prodigies: Tiger Woods picking up a golf club at age 4, Wayne Gretzky breaking ice hockey records from the moment he could skate. These parents look to organized sports for programs that will boost their child's opportunities for success. Even if the program doesn't promote their preferred sporting philosophy, they are prepared to export it from the sidelines—invariably drawing themselves into conflicts with referees, coaches, and other parents. Some proponents of this philosophy—admittedly at its most extreme—account for the tales of assault and intimidation that find their way into the media: all in the name of sports!

Legal Action Against an Eleven-Year-Old

I can recall my former soccer coach informing me that I had let the team down because I couldn't attend the last game. I was told that I would be taken to court—I'm not sure on what grounds! I was 11 years old and ran tearfully home to tell my parents that the police were going to take me away. My dad had some very strong words with that coach.

Supporters of the Competitive Achievement Model believe that losing is part of life, so, in the vernacular, "Suck it up, kid!" This and other like-minded clichés have reinforced the idea that sports are only for the capable, and in true Darwinian fashion, if you are not good enough, you either need to try harder or move on to something else. It is true that there is value in defeat; life's lessons are often learned more through setback than success. However, when we are dealing with young developing minds and bodies, defeat and disappointment must not be framed by the coach or parent as a damning verdict on the child's abilities. Positive reinforcement of each child's contributions is needed (regardless of outcome) to promote inclusion and acceptance (Graham, 1992).

Some physical educators (Pangrazi, 2001; Siedentop, 1998) have argued that the competitive achievement model has no place in sports for children younger than the age of 12 years. Pangrazi and Dauer (1992) suggested that competitive sports for elementary-age children run the risk of being exclusive and undermine the development of children who have yet to express any athletic potential that they may have. The Coaching Association of Canada (1996) has recommended that children should be able to participate in appropriately designed competitive sports environments after the age of about 11 years.

Cooperation and Sports: Moving Beyond "Duck, Duck, Goose!"

Cooperative activities that promote caring, sharing, and respect have been offered as alternatives to a competitive sports model (Orlick, 1982). Yet I believe the concepts behind cooperative sports have not been widely embraced and probably have been misunderstood. Using cooperative themes in your coaching is not the application of New Age mysticism! Cooperative play and learning is something that focuses on developing group processes. In strategies such as *think-share-perform* (Dyson & Grineski, 2001), all participants in a group are given a challenge (a physical challenge in a sports setting) that is analyzed, various strategies are explored, then actions are decided upon through negotiation before being performed. This approach has been shown to help develop the cohesion of a sports team. It has also been shown to enhance the motivation to participate in sports and subsequent learning (Polloway, Patton, & Serna, 2001). Research has shown that cooperative activities develop the fitness of athletes who find sports challenging (Grineski, 1996) and strengthen the support offered to these kids by their more able peers (Dyson, 2001).

Not everyone finds the principles behind cooperative sports appealing. In the book titled *In Defense of Elitism*, Henry (1995) argued that the modification of sports activities (for children with challenges) dilutes the spirit of competition that should be a natural extension of sports.

Beware of Sporting Extremism: Trusting the Coach

Remarkably, the *child as the victim* mentality does have a way of reinventing itself. A few school districts have decided to ban playground games of tag, dodgeball, gymnastics, and many other activities. The reasoning is that the child may get injured (thus the fear of litigation), and the self-esteem of children who are repeatedly "caught" in the game will be damaged. It reminds me of a complaint that I once received from a parent: "Why is it that Gary Barber makes children run in PE? My daughter can't run very well, so therefore he is damaging my daughter's self-esteem!" Even though I had children of all ranges of abilities supporting our cross-country running team (with a participation rate of 80% of the school population), this parent demanded that running be banned from the school program. At the other extreme are those parents and coaches who have become embroiled in confrontations. Whether it is disagreement over tactics, selection decisions, or perceived injustice, feelings run high and a few people react irrationally. We have seen players, parents, and teachers assaulted and abused. "It is only sports" is a familiar refrain, and yet for those who become passionately involved, this saying seems to take on a different identity. Trying to strike a sports context that is balanced, one that allows for free-flowing excitement and unrestrained positive emotions is desirable but challenging to achieve. In many areas of life, we defer to the opinions of experts and accept that their knowledge and experience should guide us. I don't tell the heart surgeon what tools to use or how to go about repairing my heart. I just let him get on with his job. In sports, it seems that everybody has an opinion. Many of us have had experiences playing or watching sports, and we feel we are suitably qualified to venture an opinion about a team's play.

> Sport liberates potential—not just physically, but psychologically, too.
>
> —Tony Blair, former British prime minister

People who do not trust or respect the coach can be passionate exponents of their contrary view. Dealing with these people can be challenging, and this is where the school or sports organization should have a code of ethics to guide conduct. Competitive extremism ultimately does a disservice to the parents who are volunteering their time to coach young kids; it also does a disservice to the athletes, who feel pressured and intimidated.

So which philosophical stance is most appropriate for a coach wishing to promote inclusiveness? Coaches and parents will arrive at that determination by examining the motives and assessing the readiness of each child. Competition is a natural and healthy part of sports, and when balanced with cooperative techniques of teaching, the underpinning philosophy is one in which all children can thrive.

How Coaches Can Design Age-Appropriate Sports Programs

The long-term athlete development model was created by Balyi and Hamilton (2004) to help guide coaches in designing age-appropriate sports programs. This model recommends a series of sequential steps that build sports skills and recognize the varying needs of athletes at different stages of their development. The first two phases of this model are critical, for this is where the foundation for acceptance or attitudes that reinforce exclusion are formed. The model breaks the athlete's development into the stages discussed next.

The *Fun*damental phase introduces the skills, rules, and language of the sport (terminology) to boys ages 6–9 years and girls ages 6–8 years. Agility exercises, plus activities that promote balance and coordination, are important skills to be developed in this phase. I incorporate knowledge of the sport through storytelling; the goal is to inspire each child to want to continue in sports. A recommendation in this phase is that the young athletes attempt many different sports and do not specialize. As noted before, in my experience early specialization is counterproductive and can impair an athlete's long-term development.

In keeping with the philosophy of the *Fun*damental phase, Cote (2005) and Salmela (2005) stressed the need for children to engage in what they termed *sand-lot games*. These activities emphasize fun and can be both child initiated and child directed. The children organize themselves, create their own rules, and solve their own problems without adult intervention.

When Kids Organize the Practice

When I was a kid, we played soccer for hours. Not just 1 or 2, but literally 4 or 5 hours at a time. We had no soccer teams; there wasn't any money about for leagues or anything like that. We would just get a bunch of us together on the village green, a few lads would take off their coats, and a game would spontaneously start. We had no referees (Dad was always at work), no coaches. We organized ourselves and we developed some great skills. Hour after hour of playing will do that to you.

In the second phase of the long-term athlete development model, the athletes increase their knowledge of performance as they "Learn to train." This phase targets the development of boys ages 9–12 years and girls ages 8–11 years. Flexibility and endurance, speed and strength (using the athlete's own body weight) combine to continue overall physical development. Although sports competitions may be an important source of motivation for young athletes, this model recommends that the ratio of training to competition be 70:30.

It is interesting to cross-reference these recommendations with the programs of some sports organizations that have their young athletes engage in highly specialized training and vigorous competition well in excess of the recommended ratio. If competitive sports opportunities are offered at these young ages, and parents believe their child will thrive, they should be applied with care and consideration for the needs of all children. Such programs must be built around fun, inclusion, acceptance, equal participation, and a nonthreatening environment.

The next phase of this model is "Training to train," aimed at boys ages 12–16 years and girls ages 11–15 years. Skill development is still the primary component of this phase, with aerobic development being a key component. The phase "Training to compete" (ages 16 years and older) prepares the athletes for competition by incorporating event-specific skill specialization into the program. "Training to win" is focused on adults. As the athletes physically mature, they are more capable of adapting to training regimens that prepare them for competition, and the ratio of competition to practice changes to 60:40. At the end of a competitive career, the athletes move into retirement and, it is hoped, use their skills and experience in coaching.

It should be acknowledged that this model needs to be adapted for people with challenges. The age ranges suggested in this model may not apply to someone with a congenital challenge or someone who has recently acquired a disability (e.g., paralysis from an accident). Some individuals may not progress past the *Fundamentals* phase due to the complexity of their challenge, which is fine as long as they are not purposely excluded from healthy competition.

Success for All Participants in Sports

Creating opportunities for talented students to find success in sports is relatively easy; they will likely thrive on any task that is assigned them. But how does a child with challenges or physical or developmental disabilities find success in sports? First, you have to provide these children with the opportunity to play. This may seem like a statement of the obvious, but when you see studies (Pate & Hohn, 1994; Pate et al., 1995) showing that 59% of high schools allowed students with physical disabilities to be exempt from physical education courses, it becomes apparent that many of these children are not being provided sports opportunities.

Teachers and coaches should never make the flawed assumption that these children are any less interested in their progress, their desire to be successful, or their need to be recognized than their peers without disabilities. This is an important issue and worthy of much reflection; too often kids hear messages that they are "not good." They may already hold the view that they are a "liability" on any team and have formed a negative opinion about their athletic potential and self-image.

> It's already difficult for some kids to fit in, but it is especially challenging when the school is very competitive and can't seem to find a place for you . . . it makes you feel like a loser.
>
> —Recollection from an elementary school teacher

Effective coaches design healthy competitive experiences for all of their athletes and are guided by a code of ethics that includes how the team—and officials—conduct themselves in the game. This plan considers how they will respond when things don't go well and so forth. Teaching and coaching techniques that can implement such a plan are discussed in the second section of this book.

Authenticity in the Sporting Experience

Success in sports for children is only found when they are given authentic opportunities to participate. What is an *authentic experience?* I can certainly tell you what it isn't. Putting a player in for the last minute of the game is not authentic. Soccer players who only allow a teammate to throw the ball in and then never pass to him or her are not facilitating an authentic experience. Pouring lavish and exuberant praise on a child who has finished absolutely dead last in a race is not believable and not authentic for the child.

Don't assume that children with challenges want a sugar-coated version of sports. Yes, the teacher or coach may need to adapt the program in such a way that allows the child to develop and achieve personal success, but this framework must include support that is meaningful and avoids belittling language and tokenism.

In an authentic coaching and learning environment, the athlete can develop his or her skills at an appropriate pace, with a degree of challenge that is respectful of his or her abilities, and using processes that draw on physical, cognitive, and behavioral skills. The coach should alternate roles from being the disseminator of information, to mentor, to provider of resources to help the athlete reach the goal. In a traditional model of coaching the coach dispenses wisdom. Ask yourself: Do you challenge the child's other domains of learning? In the cognitive domain (i.e., thought processes), do you coach to make the child think about game situations (i.e., present a problem and then find a solution)? Do you teach all athletes how to analyze their own performances and the performances of their rivals? Do you use techniques that try to draw information out of students so that they may build on their knowledge of the sport?

In the affective domain of learning (i.e., feelings and emotions), do you create situations in which a whole range of positive emotions can be freely expressed? When this is allowed, there are often outbursts of uninhibited and joyful emotions.

An authentic sporting experience means

- Being valued for your contributions
- Having a meaningful amount of playing time
- Receiving quality coaching (not superficial)
- Setting goals that require hard work to achieve them
- Benefiting from positive social interactions

These examples are not authentic sporting experiences:

- Playing a sport for 40 minutes and only touching the ball once
- Being "subbed" into the game for the last few minutes of the game. (When the outcome has already been clearly decided, such participation is like a consolation prize!)
- Being placed in the outfield, never being allowed to catch or throw the ball, and being blamed when a run is scored

- Never being passed to in the game
- Not receiving the same recognition as other kids (favorites)
- Having to face an exclusive social culture—one that is built around cliques and favoritism
- Consistently providing the child with immediate gratification to build the belief that success is a right and does not need to be worked for, which denies the child the thrill of success grabbed from the possibility of defeat

Success, or lack of it, is built on the kind of environment that the athlete participates in. If the predominant message is that defeat, setback, and disappointment are harmful to the child's overall development, then not surprisingly the child will quickly learn that sports have nothing positive to offer. Conversely, coaches presenting disappointment as a learning opportunity and teaching that competition is a chance to measure personal effort and improvement will evoke a different response from their athletes.

A study by Dodd (1990) noted that 75% of children (ages 10–17 years) who were interviewed said they didn't particularly care if no score were kept during any sports games that they played.

One Kick Is Not Enough

Nobody wanted me on their team. I was basically a bit useless. For a while I really wanted to play and would come home crying and complaining that I never even touched the soccer ball. Eventually, I gave up caring.

Final Thoughts

Sports, when presented in a manner that is age appropriate and fosters positive relationships among its participants, confers many distinct benefits. However, children who are not ready for sports or find themselves in an environment that is not inclusive or accepting of differences may withdraw from the activity and be denied its benefits. If we wish to build an inclusive sports environment, one in which all children feel valued and can develop their potential, coaches and teachers will need to have an understanding of the importance of play and how to successfully incorporate play into sports.

An understanding of children's learning and needs profiles will help to determine when it is appropriate for them to start a sport. Their readiness will be contingent on their level of age-appropriate maturity, their sophistication with social interactions, their ability to listen and comprehend instructions, and their mastery of basic physical skills. I have seen some children thrive at 10 years old in community sports programs (focused on fun), whereas others have not been emotionally or physically ready. It is clear that coaching styles need to match the maturational status of the athletes. Coaches must avoid concluding that a student who has yet to express sports capabilities lacks ability. This does a great disservice to students who are late maturers (Horn & Lox, 1993).

There is no hard and fast rule that states when the introduction of a student to a sport is appropriate. Consultation with coaches and other parents and observation of your student (child) in action will shape your views. However, I recommend that you don't rush to have a child participate in sports. If the child is not ready, coercing him or her will backfire and not achieve much of anything. Some children are enrolled in sports programs but lack the emotional readiness for successful inclusion. Such children should spend more time playing until they mature. Conversely, a child who seems to be very competitive—a sure sign is the number of arguments about sporting injustices in playground games—may well be demonstrating his or her need for structured sports and athletic challenges.

CHAPTER 4

Attitudes, Participation, and the Development of Friendships in Sports

S tudents understand only too well the relevance of attitudes in their sporting lives. They quickly learn that having a "good attitude" is rewarded—usually by praise from coaches and parents. They have learned that coaches will encourage them to bring a "positive attitude" to a challenge and how easy it is to develop a "negative attitude" toward sports. Sometimes, we confuse our young athletes by telling them to "lose the attitude!" The study of attitudes is a science in itself with such a vast amount of information available that it could overwhelm a reader and take us off topic. My purpose here is to help coaches, teachers, parents, and young athletes and their peers understand how attitudes about sports are formed and how they can either promote acceptance or reinforce exclusion.

What Are Attitudes, and How Are They Formed?

An attitude has been described as "a relatively lasting cluster of feelings, beliefs and behaviors directed toward specific persons, ideas, objects or groups" (Rajecki, 1982, as cited in Baron & Byrne, 1984, p. 126). When we have created an attitude, we have evaluated a situation and decided what it means to us. Based on our interpretation of that situation, this belief will then carry a connotation in our mind; it will either be viewed favorably, as in a positive attitude, or with concern, as in a negative attitude. The attitude may be a simple one based on personal experience, such as "I don't like doing push-ups; they make my arms sore." Or the attitude may be a more complex belief that has developed from discouraging experiences when feelings and beliefs were amplified by other people: "I hate sports; everybody laughs at me when I make a mistake."

There are many features of attitudes:

- They can be brief or long lasting.
- They may be deeply entrenched or easily changed.
- They can be highly personal or shared by a group.

We often develop our attitudes by observing others and being influenced by their attitudes, a process that is termed *social learning.* Positive role modeling is an important way to promote healthy and respectful attitudes and can have a long-lasting effect on the attitudes of young students.

We often participate in situations (sports) that are consistent with our attitudes. If our experience is a good one, it will strengthen the attitude and increase the likelihood that we will participate in similar situations in the future. If sports are fun and the environment promotes acceptance, the young athlete will likely continue to participate. The converse is also possible.

Adopting or imitating the views of a powerful figure (e.g., the most popular student in the class) can increase the possibility of acceptance. Conversely, taking a different stance may increase the chance that the individual attracts criticism. The implication is that a child struggling in sports may seek acceptance from peers by adopting attitudes that he or she does not necessarily believe. Group pressure to ridicule a child facing challenges can be self-perpetuating unless there is intervention from an influential figure (e.g., the coach, a popular peer).

What Makes an Attitude Toward Sports Positive or Negative?

Numerous studies emphasize the importance of having a positive attitude toward sports (Fland, Blair, & Blumenthal, 1992; McGinnis, Kanner, & DeGraw, 1991), but exactly what makes an attitude positive? The sporting experience can be defined in many ways. A positive experience for some children will be fully linked to outcome—if they win (or at least perform very well), then the assessment is viewed as favorable. Other young athletes with a different set of expectations may have a positive view if they simply get to play with their friends, or perhaps if they are praised for their effort. In a sad paradox, there are some participants who may find they had a positive experience in a practice (or game) when they were either left alone or not jeered by their teammates.

Attitudes are closely tied into the motives of participation; if these needs are not met (on a repeated basis), then the attitude (or reason for participation) may change. The negative attitudes that should concern parents and coaches are those that are firmly held and make the child believe that sports are something to avoid. Sports environments that expose the challenges that a child faces, then holds the child up to ridicule, can create negative experiences in the mind of the athlete. If a child is resilient, he or she may be able to cope for a while, but eventually it becomes too much, and the negative attitude creates avoidance behavior.

The Influence of Attitudes on Coaching and Teaching

The attitude of coaches or teachers toward the program that they are leading or the students that they are working with has been identified as a critical variable in the quality of their coaching effectiveness (Aicinena, 1991; Smith, 1993). Not surprisingly, a coach or teacher holding negative attitudes about the sport or the particular students playing in it undermines the students' quality of experience (Faucette & Patterson, 1989; Xiang, Lowy, & McBride, 2002). Although the formation of attitudes about students and performance can be developed from any number of sources, Doolittle, Dodds, and Placek (1993) noted that a coach's personal experiences in sports (either in school or the community) can often be resistant to self-examination. However, other studies have shown that a coach's attitudes can be changed by experiences while coaching, especially if the individual becomes reflective (Clarke & Hubball, 2001; Curtner-Smith, 1996).

How Can You Change or Influence Attitudes that Inhibit Participation or Make a Student Feel Excluded?

It is all very well identifying the origin of the attitude and its strength, but con- cerned parents and coaches may feel that they need to help the child change the restrictive attitude. How is this done? Persuading people to change their views is a lucrative field in the study of human behavior. The advertising industry relies on its ability to persuade you to choose a particular prod- uct; political parties rely on persuasion to change your view and encourage you to vote for them. Parents and teachers draw on the same skills to help encourage a child to take a healthy risk in learning. But can you change the attitude of a child who absolutely refuses to take part in sports?

What are the characteristics of persuasion? What makes some people very good at persuading others to change their attitude, whereas other com- municators fail to achieve their goal and only make their targets become even more entrenched in their view? The following example demonstrates an approach to convince a reluctant child to participate in sports.

Barry is an 11-year-old who likes to play on the computer but is reluctant to join in sports. The only time he tried a team sport—baseball—he lasted four practices before being asked to leave by the coach. He was disruptive, disin- terested, and argumentative. Barry cannot concentrate for too long, and many of his teachers suspect that he has ADD. This is probably inaccurate, because when Barry finds something interesting, he can concentrate for extended periods and can produce some good work. His attitude toward sports has hardened (maybe as a result of his baseball experience), and he has not been encouraged to be active by his teachers. His parents have always assumed that he just prefers solitary activities—playing computer games—and that Barry is just one of those children who doesn't like sports. On a recent trip to the family doctor, Barry's parents were informed that Barry is putting on weight. His parents have decided to enroll him in the local soccer team. Barry is refusing to go. "Why should I? I hate sports!" What can Barry's parents do to change his attitude?

The Features of Persuasion

There are three areas that determine the power of persuasion:

- Who is doing the persuading? Will this person be influential or ineffective?
- What will they say, and how will they say it?
- How will the message recipients respond?

In Barry's case, the individuals who are most likely to influence or change his attitude are his parents, teachers, or new coach. A close friend may also have some sway over Barry. As his attitude toward sports is set, he has bad memories, and he sees no purpose in participating, a careful plan will be needed to bring the desired attitudinal change. It should be noted that people with a strong need for social approval (they want other people to like them) are easier to persuade than those who don't really care what others think of them. Research also suggests that individuals with low self-esteem are easier to persuade than those with high self-esteem (Brockner, 1983).

Who Is Doing the Persuading?

Effective communicators use their knowledge in clear and efficient ways to change beliefs. But knowledge alone is not enough. Charismatic communicators use their speech—in tone, style, and speed—to sway the minds of the listeners. Liking the communicator also determines how effective the attempt at persuasion will be. The individual who works with Barry will need to be able to understand his needs and look for ways that will encourage Barry to take a risk. If this person is someone whom Barry trusts and is friendly with, the attempt has a greater chance for success.

What Will They Say, and How Will They Say It?

It is highly likely that Barry is going to resist initial attempts to persuade him. Sometimes parents connect emotions, behavior, and consequences in one broad sweeping message: "How will you ever have friends if you don't join this team?" This is hardly going to strike an agreeable chord in Barry! The message may carry more persuasive power when a commitment to participate is linked to a reward. Barry is not intrinsically motivated—given the choice, he will avoid sports. There has to be something else that will change his defiant attitude; words alone will not achieve that aim. As soon as you mention reward or incentive systems, the connection to bribery is made, which evokes emotional responses from critics. Obviously the desire is to have Barry participate because he wants to, because it is fun, and not just because he is going to get a reward. The effectiveness of a reward system is all in the design. Behavioral psychologists are highly skilled at shaping behavior by using reinforcers for positive changes; this might include stickers, ink stamps, paper certificates, and points that can be accumulated and then cashed in for a reward (preferably something that is not food based).

A series of incremental steps, with built-in recognition for any positive changes that Barry makes, may be designed in the following manner:

- Barry's parents just happen to drive past the sports field where the other children are practicing. They stop the car and watch for a few minutes. Barry's parents make no comments.

- The following week, the process is repeated. Barry's parents comment about the fun that Barry's friends seem to be having. No attempt to have Barry participate is made.

- Discussion around the family dinner table is led by the parents. They detail how the sports club is going on a trip—not sports related (the movies, and so forth)—and how much fun this club seems to have.

- Barry's parents invite a child who plays on the sports team over for a playdate.

- On the day of the next practice Barry is told that they are going to watch the team play. Barry can then ask a few people on the team to join him for a treat.

- Increasingly the parents are preparing and gently directing Barry toward taking the risk to participate. The parents need to counsel the coach on Barry's needs. The coach can use a few influential and popular kids to greet Barry and look after him in the practice.

- The parents should observe from the sidelines and lend a quiet but reaffirming voice of support. Hopefully, Barry will see out the practice. Give him lots of praise—not saccharine; that particular currency has little value—to recognize his effort and genuine accomplishment by taking a risk. Reward Barry with something that he likes to do and that has to be earned—more computer time? Barry may now see a connection among sports, friendship, and his other hobbies.

- If the sporting environment is well balanced, blending competition, fun, friendship, and social opportunities, the chance of Barry changing his attitude toward participation increases.

- The coach and Barry's parents will need to support him for quite a while as his confidence is fragile at best and his resilience to setback is limited.

How Will the Message Recipients Respond?

The power of persuasion fades when it either undermines or is disconnected to the athlete's motives for participating in a sport. A young athlete who just wants to be part of a team and does not have a very strong desire to achieve high levels of performance may well be resistant to a message that tries to persuade him or her to behave in a different way. Conversely, persuasion is very effective when an athlete has motives for participating that match the intentions behind the message. For example, an athlete with a strong need for achievement and who may be recovering from injury would embrace a persuasive message about his or her athletic capabilities.

The Role of Conformity in Excluding or Accepting Young Athletes in Sports

There are occasions when young athletes change their attitude or behavior so that they may conform to social norms. Conformity is a powerful process that creates pressures on an individual to follow a set of social rules or behaviors (something that is also called social norms). These norms can be positive rituals that welcome all athletes into a sport; for example, the coach may expect all athletes to join in a team cheer. Perhaps the team has a special way of making a newcomer feel welcome. Participation in the traditions of the club increases the possibility of acceptance.

Sometimes the social norms are unwritten, and this can present a challenge for young athletes lacking confidence or a child with special needs. Students with an ASD are not skilled at picking up subtle social cues; this can present difficulties for them to find acceptance in groups where such codes exist.

Sometimes the social norms pressure individuals to behave in ways that perhaps are discordant with their personal belief systems. Hazing is a well-known initiation practice in which new members of an organization have to comply with requests before they are accepted. Some of these rituals are fun and do not subject the individual to abuse (physical, verbal, and so forth). The predominant view is that hazing is team building and enhances the cohesion of the organization. Few sports outwardly sanction hazing behavior, but many still allow initiation ceremonies. These need to be monitored, for this is fertile area for exclusion, discrimination, and bullying to take root. Sometimes the initiation practice is demeaning to the individual, and this is clearly unacceptable.

If acceptance into the sports club involves either coercion or the perception of threat, this constitutes a hazing practice. Hazing is particularly damaging when it appears to have the sanction of the coach. It is great to make children feel welcome and make their entry into the club a memorable experience, but it is completely unacceptable to force them (either through coercion or through subtle pressure) into hazing activities. It is strongly recommended that a sports organization's risk management policy refer to hazing and give coaches a clear guideline as to what is acceptable.

The effects of conformity on athlete behavior are influenced by a number of principles, including group size, similarity, and expertise (credibility).

Group Size

Group size is an interesting feature of conformity. It is a principle that has been extensively studied in business in attempts to understand what group processes are at play in research and development. Three people in a group exert a significant effect on conformity, but the relationship is not linear; that is, the more people in the group, the greater the conformity (Wilder, 1977). What is important is the profile of the three or so individuals in the group that have influence. People who are perceived by others to be "low status" will exert only a limited influence on the group norms of behavior. Students with challenges—especially in the areas of social interactions—will likely have to conform to things they do not necessarily believe just to gain acceptance. High-status individuals can exert a significant influence on a group; this influence can be used to promote acceptance or to exclude.

Similarity

When athletes feel that they "belong" in the group and are surrounded by like-minded people, there is a greater degree of conformity. Social identity theory (Tajfel & Turner, 1979) suggests that membership in a group boosts the athletes' feelings of personal identity as well as provides a connection to the group identity. This is of importance to young athletes, especially those with recognized challenges, who have experienced difficulty being accepted in other social circles (school, clubs, and so forth). Social comparison theory (Goethals & Nelson, 1977) suggests that people will interact more positively when they meet someone who seems to be like them and in a different way to people they perceive as being dissimilar.

Respect and Expertise

An athlete's respect for the coach and teammates is built on trust, credibility, and the level of expertise. Coaches who are strong communicators, who have a good level of technical knowledge (expertise), and who can be trusted to act in a manner that supports and leads all athletes will be influential figures. Coaches who are respected are likely to have athletes who conform more than athletes who do not respect the coach.

Why Do Some People Not Conform?

From *The Catcher in the Rye* (Salinger, 1945) to *Rebel without a Cause* (Lindner, 1944), literature has long celebrated the uniqueness of someone who wants to be remembered as an individual. Young people with special needs are intriguing individuals. Although their behaviors, their needs, and their way of living are sometimes not easily understood, they have strengths and talents just like any other children. Many of these children do not easily conform to the social norms associated with sports, often because they don't understand them. Some sports have unwritten rules. For example, in ice hockey it is expected that you protect the goalkeeper; in soccer, it is expected that players kick the ball out of play when an opponent is injured, and so forth. Children with learning challenges may fail to pick up the subtleties of these "codes," and this failure tends to marginalize them even more.

Conformity and the Halo Effect

Getting along with your peers is an important motive for children who participate in sports. Everyone wants to be liked, and if possible, to be very popular. Invariably, popularity in sports is closely connected to ability: Children with well-developed sports skills are highly regarded by their peers.

Conforming to the group norms has always been a powerful motivator. The army understands this only too well and builds in all kinds of traditions and rituals that reward and demand conformity (thus, following orders). Children involved in sports will recognize that performing to a high level attracts recognition and popularity. Unfortunately, it is more difficult to be popular if your skills are underdeveloped. Children tend to exclude kids who are lacking in skill and perceived as being "different," and these children tend to either remain alone or participate on the fringes of the group.

The desire to be accepted sometimes translates into inappropriate behavior from the excluded child. This child may mimic the actions of the popular child or the peer group in order to gain recognition. The child may take greater risks to win approval; these risks, sadly, may include bullying another child.

When children (and adults) want to achieve popularity, sometimes they believe that "hanging out" with the most popular and powerful individual will win them the respect that they desire. This phenomenon is known in psychology as the *halo effect*. This may be advantageous if the popular child is welcoming and excludes nobody; it does, however, give the influential child a sense of power and control over other children, and when misused, this forms the core of bullying behavior.

Guozhen, Jinghai, Yimin, and Shaoqiu (1992) investigated the effects of conformity on moral judgment. They found that a situation directed by an authoritarian adult conveys the greatest influence on the judgments of children (ages 8–12 years). A coach who demands that his players act aggressively and disrespectfully to children who have lesser abilities would be influential. This is not surprising, as the moral development of these kids is nowhere close to being complete. Children are often interested in playing with those who are similar to them in appearance. This phenomenon becomes especially pronounced in the teenage years when the desire to "fit in" or "belong" gives rise to group subcultures. In my teenage era (1970s–1980s England) groups clustered around different music styles (rockers, punk, mods), fashion styles, and preferred methods of transportation. Sports are not much different—in fact, in North America it is a subculture in itself: the jocks. Regrettably, to be fully accepted as a jock requires a high level of athletic competence. Children who have difficulty in sports may not wish to be identified as a jock but just want to play a game that they like. Children who deviate from the norms of group behavior are more likely to be rejected.

Seconds Out! Play Sports!

My teammates at my rugby club certainly didn't know what to make of me! I would show up to practices on a bike my grandma gave me, complete with the shopping basket hanging on the front. I really liked that bike as it was easy to carry my equipment in. My dad couldn't drive me to games or practices, so I needed to cycle everywhere. We couldn't afford brand-new equipment, so I made do with shirts passed on by the coach. I even bought my rugby boots secondhand at a garage sale. For a while I had the nickname "Seconds," as in secondhand. I hated that name, I really did!

Does Athletic Skill (or Lack of It) Influence a Student's Popularity?

It is likely that we all have memories of children in our PE classes who had poor athletic skills. Ask yourself, were they the most or least popular children? The chances are these children were marginalized. A lack of athletic success does reflect well on a child's popularity; sadly, the converse is also likely to be true. Children are attracted to other kids who are outgoing, have good conversational skills, excel in valued activities such as sports, and are lavish in dispensing praise and approval.

Not a Fading Memory

My memories of school sports are not great, to be honest. I was always lapped in the fitness run. I couldn't kick the soccer ball with any accuracy, or make a lay-up, and I was always the last to be picked for each game. No one ever wanted to partner with me. Why would they? I was useless.

Friendship and Sports

Research has shown that children consider sports as a significant way to develop friendships. Weiss and Duncan (1992) suggested that emotional support for athletes, the affirmation of their athletic ability, and the promotion of self-esteem were important reasons for a child to participate in sports. Companionship, loyalty, and intimacy are important motives for participation. Research has suggested that lonely children are likely to be less active than children who have well-developed friendships (Page, Frey, Talbert, & Falk, 1992).

Friendship has also been recognized as a very important component of girls' participation in sports (Duncan, Boyce, Itami, & Puffenbarger, 1983). Companionship was considered to be more important than a game's outcome for girls ages 10–15 years. Clearly, if we want to build on a child's interest in sports, we need to acknowledge that friendship and social opportunities are meaningful sources of motivation. A sports culture that excessively emphasizes performance and competitive outcomes may actually undermine some athletes' main reasons for participation.

Research has shown that children who are either neglected or rejected by their peers are more likely to engage in solitary play and be at risk for internalizing disorders such as anxiety or depression (Rubin, 1985). Children who are completely rejected (and on an ongoing basis) have been found to be at risk of aggression from other children (Coie & Kuiper-Schmidt, 1983).

Smith (1999) reported that young athletes (middle school age) who indicated that they had a close friend in the sport were more likely to embrace challenges and be physically involved than athletes without a close friend. McNeal (1995) noted that interaction in extracurricular sports provides "fringe" students with connections to students who have a positive outlook on sports. It also helps these children to find a venue of access to the more popular members of the school population.

Final Thoughts

Children with poorly developed skills often experience peer rejection and difficulties in their social and emotional development (McKay & Keyes, 2001). Research has confirmed what we have long observed in our school clubs and sports organizations: Peer culture can either articulate effective inclusion and the acceptance of athletes with challenges or promote exclusion (Corsaro, 2003; Fernie, Kantor, & Whaley, 1995).

CHAPTER 5

Using Sports to Promote Character and Acceptance

A sports culture that is based on inclusion will require its proponents to role model a broad range of virtues that reflect good sportsmanship and character. This chapter looks at some of the programs that promote these qualities; it will also examine the responsibilities of parents as the advocate, mentor, or role model for their child.

Connection Between Character Development and Sports

It has long been recognized that there is a strong connection between character development and sports. For centuries, sports have been used as a tool to shape the desired qualities of a nation's youth, and schools were traditionally the forum for delivering these programs. The Spartan warriors of ancient Greece used schools (actually military training camps) to impart the values of courage and honor, things they believed would be critical attributes in battle. The famous private schools of England—Eton, Harrow, and Rugby—integrated sports and military drill to promote the qualities that the British army required. The famous quote, "The battle of Waterloo was won on the playing fields of Eton," suggested that sports built the leadership skills and virtues of courage, strength, and perseverance; ironically, Lord Wellington—general in command of the British army at the battle of Waterloo—did not play sports at Eton (Sage, 1998, p. 15). General Douglas MacArthur also recognized the role that sports played in developing leadership: "Upon the fields of friendly strife are sown the seeds that on other fields and other days will bear the fruits of victory" (U.S. Military Academy, West Point Admissions, n.d.).

A different view is that "Sports don't build character, they reveal it" (famed basketball coach John Wooden), while some researchers have proposed that character must be "taught rather than caught" (Hodge, 1989). Some research has revealed that sports programs that emphasize the development of sportsmanship and sound moral development can enhance a young athlete's character (Gibbins, Ebbeck, & Weiss, 1995), although Shields and Bredermeier (1995) cautioned that sports can sometimes produce socially undesirable characteristics.

How Do We Teach Character Development and Good Sportsmanship?

When educators design their curriculum, they include an academic component (i.e., the skills they plan to teach their students) and what is termed a *hidden curriculum*. The hidden curriculum includes things like courteous manners, compassionate and empathic behavior, and so forth. The teacher then establishes acceptable norms of behavior in the classroom and acknowledges students that follow or exemplify this approach.

Sports coaches should have a hidden or character curriculum included in their overall program design, as well. Many coaches solely focus on developing the skills of the athlete, but they are also instrumental influences in shaping the character of the athlete. What kinds of qualities should the coach be promoting and modeling?

A Character Curriculum

The great Greek philosopher Aristotle reflected on the nature of character and stated, "We are what we do." He believed in the importance of virtues and how they can shape our behavior. Aristotle understood that the development of character would be best achieved through the application of pragmatism and wisdom. How does this apply in this context? Themes such as acceptance of differences, compassion, and understanding are central in this book, and coaches can promote these values by choosing athletes who role model these desired behaviors. Here are some practical examples:

• Coaches should be encouraging emotional self-control in their players. As the execution of many sports skills deteriorate when an athlete loses control of his or her emotions (e.g., nervous or angry shooting from the free throw line in basketball, failing to concentrate in a fast-moving game), enhanced self-control will only benefit the athlete.

• Perspective taking is another important character skill; sadly, it is one that is poorly developed in professional sports. Coaches and players may disagree with the referee's decisions, but respecting and accepting the right of that person to make a decision about the game is necessary if the game is to stay cohesive.

- Traditionally, sports coaches have chosen team captains based on athletic performance. The "Great Man" idea of leadership is well suited to a confident and athletically precocious child, but it does not necessarily follow that this person can unify a team and help everyone feel valued. If we are trying to teach prosocial behaviors (politeness, helping, good listening, compassion, and so forth), the coach may wish to choose Captains of Character. The coach could reward a player who demonstrated a particular virtue by giving him or her the captaincy for the next game.

Can You Be Highly Competitive and Character Driven?

Is it possible to be highly competitive and yet be character driven? Sports are full of people who are contradictions. I have met some of the world's greatest athletes; some have been very polite, modest individuals who become intensely focused on the competition. After the game or race, they revert back to their humble self. I have also met athletes who, by virtue of their God-given talents, believe they are superior in every way. I have witnessed some of these "sports princes" pompously parade in their arena, unconcerned about their rude behavior. Many sports use codes of conduct to emphasize fair play and provide a moral compass that participants can use to orient their behavior on and off the sports field. These codes allow athletes to be competitive and yet respectful. Here are several examples:

- The Canadian Fair Play for Kids program expected participants to respect the rules, respect the officials and their decisions, respect their opponents, give everyone a fair and equal chance to play, and maintain control of oneself at all times.

- The Sport for Peace program (Ennis et al., 1999) is centered on developing a sense of team community and building trust, respect, and responsibility.

- The American Pursuing Victory with Honor and Character Counts (Josephson Institute for Sports Ethics, www.josephsoninstitute.org) programs have been successful in promoting the values associated with good sportsmanship.

- In a Fair Play program (Butler, 2000) basketball players attended a workshop and discussed appropriate values that should be conducted on the court. Teams could earn bonus points for good sportsmanship, and this was factored into the team's league standing. It was reported that sportsmanship improved significantly.

- The United States Lacrosse Association has employed an interesting technique to try to control both player and crowd behavior. Actions that a referee or official considers objectionable—insulting, rude behavior—result in the fan or player being given a Sportsmanship Card. This card asks the person to "honor the Game" and "rethink your actions." It goes on to state that "your current behavior is contrary to the high level of sportsmanship that is expected. This event may be terminated if your conduct does not improve." The Lacrosse Association (www.USlacrosse.org) has noted significant reductions in problematic behavior.

If coaches and sports organizations wish to promote an inclusive sports participation philosophy, they will need to role model behaviors that reflect these values. I have detailed two possible approaches that can be used to state the values that promote acceptance: a code of rights and responsibilities and a code of sportsmanship.

A Code of Rights and Responsibilities

- Everyone has a right to participate in the sport.
- I have the responsibility to let everyone play.
- Everyone wants to be accepted in this sport.
- I have the responsibility of making all participants feel welcomed.
- Everyone has the right to learn.
- I have the responsibility to listen, try my best, and not interfere with the learning of others.

A Code of Sportsmanship

- To win the game is desirable, but playing for fun and enjoyment is just as valuable.
- I will treat all other participants (players, parents, coaches) with respect.
- I will not cheat.
- I will not lose my temper.
- I will avoid the negative criticism of teammates, coaches, referees, and opposing players.
- I will not blame teammates for mistakes or a poor team performance.
- I will not "trash talk" and taunt my opponents.
- I will congratulate my opponents after a game.

Whereas sports organizations may make every effort to teach and role model good sportsmanship and character-based development, ultimately the young athlete with challenges will be required to embrace the help that is offered and use it, not as an emotional crutch, but as a springboard to self-reliance. That may be an advanced skill for some children—and one that requires a degree of personal maturity—however, this is where their parents and coaches can be most effective in providing role modeling and support.

Life as a 12-Year-Old All-Star

When I was 12, I joined a soccer team that was meant to be for young boys in our village. When I attended the first practice I only recognized a handful of the players;

most of them were from the city (10 miles away). The coach had decided he was going to create a "super-team full of All-Stars" (his exact words). These "All-Star" players came to each game with their "All-Star attitudes" and "All-Star parents." Screaming at each mistake, pouting when they were substituted, were typical behaviors. On several occasions their parents had to be restrained from assaulting the referee or each other. The coach had created a monster and it attacked itself. The coach's decisions were constantly challenged, and several players—apparently not getting the respect that their superstar status deserved—were pulled from the team. I never played one full game; apparently my specialty was coming on with 5 minutes left.

"Beyond the Lip Service"— Role Modeling Appropriate Behavior

Respect, responsibility, self-control, and *equal opportunity* are easy words to type on this page, but can be a lot harder for young athletes (and sometimes their coaches) to enact when emotions are running high. In some situations on the sports field, excitability trumps rational reasoning, and the player behaves in a manner that is completely out of character. It is incumbent on the coach and parent volunteers to model the aforementioned values, not just when things are going their team's way, but especially when the outcome does not appear to be favorable. This does not mean that parents or coaches cannot be emotionally involved in the competition and participate in the excitement that is generated in a thrilling game. The important thing is to retain a strong sense of context.

Good Manners—but Only if We Win!
As a referee of adult soccer, I have noted that after most games the winning team shakes my hand and the losing team generally walks away in apparent disgust. The loss of the game is my fault!

Few people will dispute that children are influenced by the actions of others; indeed, psychologists have long recognized that observation and mimicry are important skills in the formative years of the child's development. The desire for acceptance and recognition prompts children to copy the actions of other people. If the behavior is appropriate, this becomes a rewarding experience; the action achieves its desired purpose, and this reinforces the validity of the action. However, the pressures of conformity in group social situations can sometimes prompt children to behave in inappropriate ways, such as taunting a child who is less able or less popular. The modeling and sharing of this inappropriate behavior invariably contributes to the exclusion of the child with challenges.

The connection between sports ability and peer acceptance is well documented (Kunesh, Hasbrook, & Lewthwaite, 1992; Weiss & Duncan, 1992) and shows that young athletes who are more likely to be popular than children who are less able. Children learn from their peers; from a family social network (parents, siblings, extended family members); and, in the athletic context, from their coach.

How will the children with various challenges find acceptance in competitive social environments? Undoubtedly some of these children will be included by virtue of their strength of character and a culture of acceptance actively promoted by peers, parents, and the sports organization. Where this support is limited, the child may struggle and the importance of social support, role modeling, and mentoring becomes evident. Parents, teachers, and coaches can promote diversity, and they need to recognize that they have an influential role in the promotion of the unconditional acceptance of children (Manning, 2000). This is important, not just for sports, but for the overall well-being of the child. Saracho (2002) has reported that students struggling with peer acceptance will often require adult support in the classroom. This is not surprising; issues that arise on the sports field do not always stay on the field but translocate into the classroom and even the family home.

Research has recognized the importance of parent modeling and the reinforcement of positive behaviors in encouraging children to participate in sports (Brustad, 1988). Children's perceptions of their parents' level of interest in their sport are predictive of children's initial and sustained involvement (Greendorfer, Lewko, & Rosengren, 1996). If a young athlete perceives parental pressure to be low, he or she is likely to have a higher degree of enjoyment (Brustad, 1988). Furthermore, parents who role modeled a healthy interest in sports and held positive views of their child's participation were influential in the child's developing sense of athletic competence (Brustad, 1996).

> The most valuable and useful character traits that will prepare their children for success arise not from extracurricular or academic commitments, but from a firm grounding in parental love, role modeling, and guidance. (Ginsburg, 2007, p. 187)

If sports organizations want to have effective collaborative relationships with parents, they will need to define an appropriate role for them to take. Parents do want to get involved in their child's education (Hoover-Dempsey & Sandler, 1997), but often they avoid participating because they believe they may not be welcome in the environment, or they feel they do not have the skills to be of help. Unfortunately parental involvement in sports is not always positive. A study of 154 high school sports coaches revealed that difficulties with parents was probably one of the most challenging issues they had to deal with (Gould, Chung, Smith, & White, 2002). A survey study of junior tennis coaches reported the view that 36% of parents hurt their child's tennis development (Gould, Lauer, Rolo, Jannes, & Sie-Pennisi, 2004). Parental pressure has been identified as a significant source of anxiety for young athletes (Scanlan & Lewthwaite, 1984). When parents were found to be demanding, expecting a high level of performance and excessively involved in their child's athletic endeavors, the child experienced heightened states of anxiety.

How to Design an Effective Role Modeling Program

Demonstrate the behavior that you wish to see. Effective role modeling does not expect the coach to be able to execute the skills that younger, fitter, and more flexible bodies can achieve. It does expect the behavior to be ethical, respectful, and inclusive. People who work with young children are in a position of authority and can be very influential. Coaches and teachers should never underestimate the impact that positive and negative behavior can have on these young minds.

Here are some tips for designing an effective role modeling program:

- Don't expect from the students behavior that you are not prepared to model yourself.
- Discuss with the athletes what kind of values are desirable. Build the conversation around sportsmanship and virtues that promote healthy competition balanced with acceptance and inclusion.
- Communicate to the athletes and parents the standard of conduct that you expect to see. Some organizations ask parents and athletes to sign contracts in which they agree to abide by defined standards of conduct.
- Have the athletes identify appropriate ways to deal with transgressions of these agreed standards. *Note:* It is inadvisable to use the sport (or other physical activities) as a punishment. We want to inspire children to continue in sports, not to associate it with a negative experience.
- Understand the developmental stages of the children and build a value system that is achievable.
- Recognize that children are not complete individuals. Their sense of moral reasoning is still developing and the children will make mistakes— behaviors of lying, cheating, and being mean to others will occur. Some of these issues may have emerged out of the frustration experienced by the child from being excluded. Compassion and understanding combined with education ("this is why this problem happened") are important skills in the coach's role modeling duties.
- Make sure coaches and parents do not belittle the efforts of children in the group.
- Create an environment that allows a particular talent or interest of the child to be acknowledged and showcased (Wohlwend, 2005).

**When It Comes to Role-Modeling, Parents
Need to Use Their Head, or Not, as in this Case!**
The Summer Soccer Camp was in full swing and dozens of young boys and girls were running all over the field chasing balls. A conversation was struck up in a

group of parents proudly watching their children play. The dialogue went something like this: "Did you see the World Cup [of soccer]? It was a great game, France versus Italy. What about the incident where Zidane [the French soccer player] was dismissed from the game for head-butting the chest of a rival?" Another parent commented, "I didn't have a problem with Zidane's actions. He should never have been sent off the field; he was only defending himself." The other parents were bemused and refrained from commenting; that remark did not merit a response.

Later that day the son of the lady concerned was severely reprimanded by the sports camp leader for—you guessed it—head-butting an opponent (age 10 years). No doubt his mother condoned his actions. The very next day the son was expelled from camp for violently punching another child. Young children internalize the messages that we give them; it is incumbent on us to give them words and ideas that allow them to enjoy sports and respect others—clearly, this did not happen in this case!

How Enabling Parents Can Limit the Development of a Student's Athletic Potential

It is reasonable to understand that almost all parents want the best for their child. It is also the role of every self-respecting parent to protect his or her child from harm. Harm is interpreted as something that threatens a child's well-being; however, it can also be translated by some parents as anything that is denied to their child on and off the field. Some parents take the view children's self-esteem is damaged by anything that is denied to them; the parent then feels compelled to take up this issue with the coach, or even worse, with their child's peers. An unfortunate consequence of such enabling behavior is that the child can quickly learn to adopt inappropriate conduct in the full knowledge that the parent will leap to a vigorous defense if the child's conduct is reprimanded by the coach or teacher.

> The central struggle of parenthood is to let our hopes for our children outweigh our fears.
> —E. Goodman

An enabled child usually makes excuses for boorish conduct, and parents can externalize responsibility by blaming somebody else, such as the coach, the referee, the mistakes of other athletes, and so forth. An overprotected child is micromanaged from the sidelines of the sports field rather than being allowed to play the game. It seems that almost every decision is dictated by the vocal demands of the parent.

Empowered children are those whose parents have taught them self-monitoring and self-discipline skills. The parents will encourage their child from the sidelines but refrain from comments or criticisms that diminish the child's decision making.

The Value of the Struggle

Experiencing difficulties in sports can be seen as valuable. While struggling to achieve our goals initially may be frustrating, it can be an experience that conveys important life lessons and teaches the value of perseverance, courage, determination, and so forth.

This does not mean that we are trying to protect children from all forms of setback, defeat, or disappointment. I believe that coaches should use these setbacks as teaching tools to help their athletes learn how to overcome obstacles. Immunizing children from these downturns provides a sterile experience and denies them the opportunity to grow. The value of the struggle is the struggle itself; if the solution were easily attainable, there would be no sense that we have defeated something that we thought would get the better of us.

Promoting Resilience

Sports clichés encourage athletes to rise above setbacks and draw on qualities of toughness and resilience—"when the going gets tough, the tough get going." But what does it mean to be resilient when you are a young child, facing challenges and lacking confidence? Is it really "all in the mind"?

The development of resilience requires the individual to effectively regulate his or her emotions. An all too common sight in sports is watching a team unravel when a referee makes a decision—usually at a critical point in the game—that places the team at a disadvantage. Resilient individuals (or teams) accept the decision and focus on the next phase of play. Individuals with poor emotional regulation fail to contain their anger or frustration and can be cautioned or ejected from the game. Emotional regulation is understandably inconsistent in many young children, and they require the support of a responsible adult to role model their emotional responses. Coaches play a critical role in showing their athletes how to conduct themselves in the various outcomes of the game. A good reference on this topic is the Penn Resiliency Program (PRP; see the Appendix for contact information) based at the Positive Psychology Center at the University of Pennsylvania. The Center has developed a series of lesson plans that help guide teachers and coaches as they work to develop the resilience of their students.

Ways of promoting a young athlete's resilience include the following:

- Role model and recognize behavior that demonstrates good emotional control, especially in tense situations.
- Promote a sense of realistic optimism.
- Expect your athletes to be empathic. If they are not, role model how empathy can be used to promote positive relations and emotional resilience.

- Encourage your athletes to study the nature of the problem and help them identify practical ways of finding acceptable solutions. Don't just tell them to "suck it up, kid!" Further reading on the topics of causal analysis and attribution theory will help coaches develop skills to assist their athletes with this kind of reflective practice (Heider, 1958; Weiner, 1992).

Final Thoughts

Accepting people who have differences requires strong role modeling from coaches and parents. While compassion and understanding are important features of a program that supports the inclusion of students with differences, they should not be used as emotional crutches that reinforce a culture of victimhood. Rather, the development of young athletes' emotional resilience is an important part of supporting their authentic participation in sports.

Understanding and Teaching Students with Differences

Understanding the characteristics of a child's challenges and utilizing his or her strengths allows the coach to design a program that meets each athlete's requirements. In Chapters 6–17, you will read about various disorders, challenges, or learning styles that can inhibit athletic performance. The information presented comes with an important caveat: *Remember, a little knowledge can be both a useful and a dangerous thing!* The technological age has given the general population access to information that was traditionally the domain of professionals who had received extensive training. Now you can type various medical symptoms into an Internet search engine and derive a possible explanation for the malady. However, many (if not all) medical, psychiatric, or psychological conditions require correct interpretation of symptoms and cross referencing with the individual's personal medical history. It has become too easy to play the role of amateur physician, and this carries a myriad of risks. Knowledge of the symptoms of ASDs, ADHD, obesity, learning challenges, and so forth may help parents pursue a diagnosis, but I cannot emphasize enough that an accurate diagnosis can only come from a recognized professional (likely a pediatrician) in the field.

It is unrealistic to expect coaches to suddenly become experts in all the challenges that children face, but a working knowledge of the issues specific to certain disabilities and conditions can certainly help the coach meet the child's programming needs. Although sports do have therapeutic value, the information presented here is not meant to provide therapy, nor should coaches assume that they are therapists. Many children with challenges have an individualized education program (IEP) and may be working closely with an aide (if they are in a school setting). If the child does not have an aide, the coach is advised to form an effective relationship with the rest of the educational team and the parents to encourage a candid and respectful information exchange about the child's needs. Sometimes, having a mentor to shadow or guide this child through a practice session helps to achieve the desired goals. Coaches and parents wishing to further develop their knowledge in a particular area are advised to contact societies dedicated to disseminating information about the particular challenge, many of which are included in the Appendix.

Using Labels to Describe Our Differences

There is nothing more painful than a label. Many of us can recall difficult moments in our lives when we were called stupid or ugly by our peers. With these memories as a personal context, it is understandable that many parents are fearful of their child being labeled. Is the terminology used to define the challenges of children a label or a description? This question can invoke powerful emotions, as many people are opposed to the stereotypical connections made with the words that describe various challenges. Mention the word *autism* and many people think of the film *Rain Man*. Use the word *obesity* and many people think of the person as being lazy and not interested in sports. There have been times when "disabled" terms such as *retard* and *spastic* have been used as pejoratives.

The word *disability* is typically used to describe the difficulties that can accompany a mental or a physical challenge. One of the inherent—stereotypical—assumptions is that the disability applies to skills and capabilities well beyond that which the word was intended to describe. The term *disability* also suggests that the child is "without ability," which, of course, is completely erroneous. Many people with disabilities have skills or aptitudes far beyond that of a typical person.

Labels and descriptions are often very poor at conveying an individual's strengths. Advocates for children with challenges want as much normalcy in the child's life as possible; this is understandable and admirable. However, some conditions consume the lives of families, and parents can easily suffer a loss of perspective. There have been cases of parents becoming zealots, arguing that the social acceptance of their child will be achieved only if words such as *disability* are thrown out. These individuals view these labels with suspicion; they believe that discrimination is folded within the words. Ironically, some moves toward "politically correct descriptions" of people with challenges have created a countermovement. Deaf people now prefer to be known as the Deaf (Padden & Humphries, 1988), and the National Federation of the Blind is refusing to acknowledge terms such as *visually challenged* or *hard of seeing* used to describe blindness.

Does Nature Overcompensate?

A gross stereotype about children with special needs is that they are not capable of making significant contributions in sports. Even a cursory study of high-performing athletes reveals that some of them had to overcome challenges with learning, behavior, and so forth. Michael Phelps, a winner of 14 Olympic gold medals (more than any other athlete in the history of the Olympic Games), experienced difficulties with ADHD. His mother enrolled him in swimming as a means of helping him find a purpose and focusing his energy. American soccer player Tim Howard has a diagnosis of Tourette syndrome, but this is not something that influenced his performance when he competed as a goalkeeper for Manchester United and other top soccer teams. Basketball players Magic Johnson and Jason Kidd, track athletes Carl Lewis and Bruce Jenner had recognized learning difficulties but still managed to achieve some of the very highest levels of athletic achievement.

There are individuals acquired disabilities as a result of accident or illness, but their life story quickly dispels the notion that they are "without ability." Many people think of running a marathon as a remarkable feat of endurance, and the thousands of participants in the great races—New York,

London, Boston, and so forth—can attest to the muscular soreness that accompanies their successful completion. Can you imagine running a full marathon every day with only one leg? Terry Fox, a young Canadian, is regarded as a national hero. Despite losing his leg to cancer, he decided to run across Canada—one marathon distance each day—on a mission titled "The Marathon of Hope." He wanted to raise awareness of cancer and raise money for a cure. He had a disability perhaps by definition, but he possessed a remarkable spirit and determination that marked him as an incredible athlete. Sadly, Terry died before achieving his goal, but his memory and legacy are celebrated by runs all over the world that raise money for cancer research and cure.

There is also a school of thought that suggests labels are demeaning to the individual and fail to see the person's spirit and soul (Armstrong, 1998). The argument is that "educators have lost sight of what makes each student a fascinating person" (Armstrong, 2001). These arguments may carry some validity if the teacher or coach accepts the *deficit paradigm*, that is, the view that the child has a number of problems and limitations rather than positive traits. I think that clear terminology, used appropriately and with the view of clarifying the child's needs, will help the teacher to design effective programs that foster inclusion, awareness, and respect for differences and help to preserve the dignity of the individual.

How to Use this Information

Helping children with different challenges starts with gathering information that describes the child. Parents who want to see their child fully involved in sports not only need to advocate for their child, but also need to help prepare the school or organization to receive the child. It is not fair to sit back, let both the child and coach falter, then become highly critical. A bit of groundwork can lay the foundation for successful inclusion of the child in a program. The school or sports organization needs to learn the following information from reviewing the child's educational records and getting to know him or her:

- What type of challenges does this child face?
- How severe are these challenges?
- What type of experiences has this child had in sports?
- Does the child require an aide to help him or her participate?
- What skills should the child work on first?
- How well does the child interact with other children?

Most modern societies have laws that protect confidentiality and place restrictions on the gathering and use of information. Parents are required to give written consent to sports organizations to release this information to coaches. It is important that coaches use this information discreetly, as some parents do not want the public to know that their child has challenges; this must be respected. If the coach and the parents decide that the other athletes will be more accepting if they understand the child's challenges, the coach will choose a forum where this information can be discussed.

Difficulties with Sports as Part of Typical Physical Development

Parents are aware that children develop at different rates. They may recount baby stories that tell us when their child first walked, talked, kicked a ball, and so forth. Not surprisingly, these milestones are achieved very early for some children and very late for others. It is not uncommon for some parents to become concerned when their child has difficulties in sustaining interest in sports, or perhaps forming friendships, or mastering simple skills. There is also a tendency for parents to benchmark their child's progress with the performances of a successful child. Their child's lack of physical aptitude may be met with dismay. And yet research has shown us that success at a young age is often a reflection of precocious physical development rather than pure talent. Physical development also doesn't follow the scenario that we assume will unfold if the parents have special talents. I know of two parents—both Olympic athletes—who have a child that has yet to show any interest or aptitude in sports. Reassurance is important for all concerned parties. These parents need to understand that their child will make progress. The child just needs to receive coaching, support, and opportunities to participate.

Which Sports Are Appropriate for Children with Challenges?

Sports should be an enriching experience for all children. For children with challenges, some sports are beyond their capabilities. We should create a system that allows them to participate and find success, not to set them up to fail. We want all children to retain their dignity and be respected and accepted. The guidelines offered here are not intended to stereotype or limit a young athlete's choices. As mentioned in the paragraph titled "Differentiation," a child's readiness and preferences should be the primary consideration in choosing the most suitable activity.

Obviously, some sports are more suited to the needs of these children than others. A student with an ASD and with heightened sensitivity to sound, for example, may find the noise generated by bouncing basketballs too intense. For another person with an ASD who has a different sensory sensitivity, basketball may be just fine.

A Template to Help Coaches Match Differentiation Strategies and Coaching Techniques with a Student's Needs

The following chapters introduce various challenges children face when they participate in sports. After the characteristics of the challenge have been described, you will find a template or checklist that recommends how you can effectively support a child with that challenge. These checklists have four sections:

Assessment—Teachers or coaches are not asked to be psychologists or pediatricians and attempt to diagnose what they observe. Assessment in this context refers to gathering appropriate information, often in consultation with the parents, about the child's interests, motives for participation, attitudes to the sport, and so forth. An understanding of any unique needs the child has then allows the coach to design an effective sports environment.

Designing an effective sports environment—The child's learning style and the way that his or her challenges manifest themselves may shape the manner in which the environment is designed. For example, a coach working with a child with cerebral palsy would consider the environmental temperature, as this can exert some influence over the child's muscle elasticity. A coach working with a child with an ASD should consider if the child has sound sensitivity and how ambient noise in the gym (e.g., bouncing basketballs, shouting students) might affect this child.

Coaching/teaching techniques—Recognizing that students will have many different styles of learning and interests requires the coach to be able to draw on an inventory of coaching methods. Some coaching/teaching techniques are clearly more beneficial than others for students with unique needs and learning styles. For example, a child with an ASD often benefits from having a teacher who makes lots of eye contact, speaks clearly, and doesn't use jargon. A child having difficulty processing information is supported by a coach who uses different learning aids (visual techniques such as Boardmaker) to clarify expectations.

Differentiation—Coaches utilizing principles of differentiation in their instruction balance the needs of the individual with the practical demands of a group. This section recommends various techniques and methods of organization that help a coach meet the needs of a broad range of participants. Each challenge is connected to the key words of differentiation: *interest*, *process*, and *content*.

CHAPTER 6

Teaching and Coaching Children with Different Athletic Abilities and Learning Needs

Effective teaching and coaching requires that we understand the underlying processes of how students learn. We want our athletes to learn how to play the game, to learn the life lessons that emerge from their participation in sports, and to learn how to respectfully interact with others. Parents concerned that their child seems to be struggling or underachieving should be reassured that there are many ways to learn. With so many ways to learn, how can a teacher or coach be effective in supporting all students in their learning?

Experienced teachers and coaches understand that their athletes do not always fit an easy template for teaching and learning. It would be very convenient if all athletes learned in the same way, at the same speed, and had the same interests, but that would make teaching dull and dreary. Thank goodness for the spirited child, the athlete who doesn't fit the mold, or the child with unusual interests. This is the person who may be challenging to teach, but who may provide you with some of your greatest rewards as a coach. Taking reluctant or disinterested learners, helping them to develop their athletic potential, and motivating them to overcome personal obstacles can be very satisfying.

This chapter discusses how you can build a learning environment that respects many different learning styles and utilizes some of the principles of universal design and differentiation.

What Factors Should You Consider When Designing the Learning Environment for Your Athletes?

In an article titled "Invitations to Learn" (Tomlinson, 2002), Tomlinson proposed five principles that make learning (and in the context of this book, participation in sports) irresistible:

- Affirmation
- Contribution
- Purpose
- Power
- Challenge

Tomlinson stated, "The impetus to learn generally does not come first from content itself, but rather because a teacher has learned to make the content inviting" (p. 6). A good sports coach can make the most uninviting activities seem exciting, and so everyone wants to participate. The converse is equally true: A poor coach can take a sport and turn children off it forever. Being an effective coach is a complex task that requires not only a sound knowledge of the sport, but also (and more importantly) excellent "people skills." The best technical coaching knowledge is useless if the coach can't relate effectively to the athletes. The principles of affirmation, contribution, purpose, power, and challenge are important concepts that a coach can use to help student athletes. These principles are described in the next sections.

Affirmation

Everybody wants to feel valued and recognized for doing something well. From the infant who looks at a parent for reassurance to the child who wants to please the teacher; from the teenager who wants to be liked by peers to the adult who wants to feel valued by the boss, recognition and affirmation are important. Sports are generally acknowledged as an important vehicle for conveying these feelings in young children. When our athletes feel valued (*affirmed*) for their contributions, their sense of connection to the team and their reasons for playing are strengthened.

Coaches are powerful agents in conveying words and actions that either help athletes to feel valued or that contribute to anxiety and insecurity. We know that athletes who feel socially isolated and insecure are likely to withdraw from sports. A coach who is committed to developing all athletes—and not just the motivated and talented ones—considers practical ways to affirm the efforts and achievements of marginalized children. Some approaches are remarkably simple, perhaps a kind word of encouragement or an empathetic ear when frustration shows. The coach might recognize the athlete in the club newsletter (the "Employee of the Month" approach is often used in business to fulfill the same purpose) or give the young athlete some important responsibilities followed by praise in front of the team or classmates for completing the task well.

Contribution

The significance of the athlete's *contribution* varies according to his or her skills and natural abilities—the right sporting culture honors these contributions and builds on the athlete's confidence. It is critical that coaches understand the developmental stage of their athletes and how this relates to their capabilities. Imposing activities suitable for adults on young people is pointless—the children fail not through lack of effort or desire, but simply because they are not ready yet.

Tired and Broken Wings

My son's baseball team brought in a pitching coach to conduct a workshop. About 50 kids between 8 and 12 years old attended. After the introductions, the coach had them circling their arms for 30 minutes. I'm not exaggerating. This so-called expert aggressively prowled through the group barking directives about being tough, saying if you wanted to be a great pitcher you had to have strong arms and the belief that you could do anything. As these kids started to become fatigued, he repeatedly yelled: "Suck it up, kids, fatigue is for wimps!" He may have been an expert with the major leagues, but with these young kids he didn't have a clue.

Purpose

If the activity has no clear sense of *purpose*, athletes, especially those with a marginal interest, do not feel motivated to participate with great enthusiasm. How can a coach convey a sense of purpose? Matching the choice of activities to the motives of the athletes helps to make the sporting experience meaningful and authentic. If the activities don't appear to be relevant, the young athlete can rightly ask, "What was the point?"

Power

Attaching importance to a young athlete's actions—either in practice or in a game—gives that child both *power* and responsibility. Research supports the view that when students take a role in decision making, their sense of responsibility and value increases (Mahoney, 2000). For example, in a traditional approach to coaching a soccer game the players are expected to follow the game plan and instructions as directed by the coach; under an authoritarian coach, there is no room for other opinions or dissent. A different approach is to draw on students' leadership skills by guiding them through a decision-making process. The coach might pose questions such as, "This is where I think we are making mistakes. What do you think? How should we approach our game differently?" Engaging the athletes in considering their roles as active decision makers helps to build their confidence, their sense of leadership, and their sense of power and importance.

Challenge

Many athletes participate in a sport for the *challenge* it provides. They may ask the question: "How do my skills measure up against those of other athletes?" For challenges to be meaningful and motivating (as opposed to restricting and potentially humiliating), they need to borrow from the principles of goal setting. Two goal-setting techniques have proven particularly helpful in creating an inclusive environment for children with disabilities or other challenges. *MAPs* (*Making Action Plans*; Falvey, Forest, Pearpoint, & Rosenberg, 1997) is a technique that is used to help individuals, their parents, and organizations collectively decide what goals children should pursue in their athletic and academic development. Another technique is *PATHs* (*Planning Alternative Tomorrows with Hope*; Forest, O'Brien, & Pearpoint, 1993). A goal (a dream) is set; then a series of processes are developed to help the child achieve the goal. The recognition of the child's strengths is critical in this planning process.

Universal Design Principles of Teaching Sports to People with Different Needs

The principles of universal design have been used to help create a learning environment that is well suited to all learners. The principles incorporated in this method were initially developed by architects to help increase access for people with physical disabilities into the buildings they were designing. These principles, applied to children participating in sports, include the following:

Inclusiveness: The term *inclusiveness* refers to recognizing the value of including children with all ranges of needs and abilities in society (and in the context of this book, in sports).

Physical access: The term *physical access* refers to whether the young athlete with physical challenges can access the sports facility. Sometimes young athletes face structural barriers. Physical access has traditionally focused on wheelchair access, yet sensory modifications (e.g., the brightness of gymnasium lights, poor gym acoustics—things that can overwhelm people with an ASD) are seldom considered. This book does not make recommendations on how to reduce structural barriers, as that information goes beyond the scope of this book.

Delivery modes: This principle considers what the best instructional methods are to teach these young athletes. This chapter looks at differentiation as an educational practice that can increase the learning capabilities of all children.

Interaction: This principle looks at how successfully these children interact with others. As children with challenges are often marginalized, this principle prompts us to find ways of improving their success in building relationships.

Feedback: Using information to build skills and relationships is a key part of universal design. This chapter looks at different methods of giving feedback.

Other principles for effectively teaching children with special needs include the following:

- Least restrictive environment
- Pragmatism
- The preservation of dignity
- Creating a culture of acceptance
- Accommodation
- Modification

Teaching children in the least restrictive environment is a principle that has been enshrined in federal law relating to people with disabilities. Please refer to Chapter 2 for more information on least restrictive environments.

Pragmatism Rules the Day

Learning is an adaptive process; some days we may be more attentive to verbal methods of instruction, other days we may be more receptive to bodily/ kinesthetic methods. Coaches and teachers should realize that instructing young children is a dynamic and flexible process—an art, not a rigid construct or a precise science. What might be effective today may not work tomorrow. Being prepared to change a lesson because it is just not working for your athletes is part of coaching pragmatism.

More Principles for Designing a Sports Environment

When designing a sports environment for students with special needs, it is important to keep the following principles in mind.

Preservation of Personal Dignity

The preservation of personal dignity is an important principle when designing a sports environment for children with special needs. Placing children with special needs in a sports situation where they are clearly going to fail, where they will be overwhelmed, and where they will possibly be humiliated is not social justice or equal opportunity. It just undermines the dignity of the individual.

Creating a Culture of Acceptance

Much of this book is written with the common theme of creating a culture of acceptance, but it is important to reiterate here. Coaches and teachers are encouraged to consider their approaches to team and activity development and how all students can be included. It is important that the adult in charge model the kind of behavior he or she expects of the students and encourages participation by all.

Accommodation of the Sports Environment

To meet this principle, the coach changes some feature of the practice to help an athlete with needs, but the overall expectation for this athlete is the same as for every other athlete. The coach may provide this athlete extra time to prepare, or have the athlete work in a smaller group, or perhaps work with a mentor or peer buddy.

Modification

Modification refers to changing the activity in such a way that the performance outcome is reduced. Perhaps the athlete is given equipment that moves slower or in a manner that allows this athlete to have an increased chance of success. I have used balloons in badminton to help some athletes accurately connect with a moving object. I have changed the rules of a game so that students with special needs have a greater chance of making meaningful contributions.

There are three aspects of a young athlete's involvement in sports that influence the effectiveness of teaching accommodations or modifications, according to Newell's (1984) model of constraints:

- *Structural issues:* for example, the young athletes' physical status and abilities
- *Functional issues:* for example, the athletes' behaviors in sports (Are they timid or aggressive? What is their attitude toward sports? What is their motivation?)
- *Sports environment issues:* for example, the sports facilities, their accessibility, how the coach matches the child's needs to the environment, and so forth

The interplay among these factors will help the coach determine the area in which the athlete needs greatest support.

Using Multiple Intelligence Theory for Coaching Student Athletes

Gardner (1983) classified learning styles (or intelligences) into eight areas or types of learners: verbal/linguistic, visual/spatial, bodily/kinesthetic, interpersonal, naturalist, intrapersonal, logical/mathematical, and musical. Coaches, teachers, and parents may identify the child's preferred learning style by reviewing the characteristics outlined in the next sections. It is important to note that Gardner emphasized that these learning styles can be interrelated and that these preferences may change over time (i.e., they are not fixed, life-long preferences).

> I have always believed that the heart of the MI perspective— in theory and in practice—inheres in taking human differences seriously. (Gardner, 1995, p. 208)

Verbal/Linguistic Learners

These are students who seem to learn best through listening and speaking. As the predominant style of coaching is verbal instruction, students with this preferred learning style often thrive. An athlete with this style of learning demonstrates a keen interest in discussion or debates.

Visual/Spatial Learners

An athlete with strengths in this learning style likely has a well-developed visual memory that recalls details (especially if prompted by the coach) of past performances. These students benefit from the use of images to teach them. A coach who uses drawings (on a clipboard or whiteboard) will have more effect than using words to explain a concept. Children with an ASD and children with recognized ADHD have effectively used visual schedules to help them understand a sequence of events.

Bodily/Kinesthetic Learners

Bodily/kinesthetic learners seem to learn best when they have lots of opportunity to move, manipulate objects (these are the students who always want to touch things), and generally be energetic. These young athletes have a tough time sitting still listening to long-winded coaching instructions. They are better served by watching visual demonstrations and moving around.

Interpersonal Learners

Interpersonal learners learn through their interactions with others. These students get along well with others and are strong candidates for leadership opportunities. Athletes with this preferred learning style thrive in group learning situations and are noted for their contributions in discussions. Cooperative learning strategies (discussed in later chapters) are effective teaching tools for athletes with this learning style.

Naturalist Learners

Naturalist learners observe how systems work and then decide the best way to succeed in those situations. These students may be considered quiet and passive participants when in fact they are just learning in their own style. Given time and confidence from their coach, they may become more vocal.

Intrapersonal Learners

Intrapersonal learners are quiet and reflective individuals who often prefer to work alone. Athletes with this learning style are attracted to individual sports where a degree of self-awareness helps to define their performance. For example, long-distance running requires a great deal of patience and personal comfort in solitude. As a distance runner for many years, I have found that intrapersonal learning is the dominant style for many of the athletes that I have met. How can you teach someone with this style? You set them the task, let them work at achieving their goal, and be available as a coaching sounding board. Perfectionism can be associated with this learning style, and although it may further motivate the athlete, it can also be a source of anxiety if things do not work out.

Logical/Mathematical Learners

Logical/mathematical learners like to apply reasoning to problems and use numbers whenever possible to increase their understanding. These learners often are fascinated with club and sports statistics. Athletes with a preference for this learning style respond well to coaching challenges that require them to think abstractly or apply reasoning to technical problems. For example, a coach might ask an athlete to analyze the movement patterns of a top athlete, then introduce principles of biomechanics (movement of the body in the context of sports). After discussion and thought about these principles, the coach might then ask the athlete to analyze his or her own movement patterns and identify areas for improvement. I have used this approach effectively—with modifications as required—with many athletes, some of whom have a learning disability.

Musical Learners

Musical learners respond well to musical patterns. These learners often gravitate to fine arts activities, especially those that incorporate rhythm: dance, rhythmic gymnastics, and so forth. Athletes with this learning preference respond to coaching that disseminates tasks through auditory means: good old-fashioned "tell them what to do"!

What Are "Entry Points"?

Inspiring young athletes to make a strong connection to their sport may take a number of approaches. A traditional if not stereotypical method is for the coach to stand in front of the athletes and to dispense wisdom. Howard Gardner has suggested that the teacher (coach) may find other ways to engage students through what he terms *entry points* (Gardner, 1999). Like motives (as discussed in Chapter 3), entry points are personal ways of participating (or entering) into an activity, discussion, or play.

Foundational Entry Point

A foundational entry point is where the student is introduced to the vocabulary or philosophy that underpins a topic. When I teach track and field to my students, I provide historical context through discussions about the ancient Olympic Games. I use the terminology that describes the various skills and explain how the sport has evolved over the years.

Aesthetic Entry Point

An aesthetic entry point is where the child experiences the sensory features of the concept and is encouraged to explore what that means. Although that may sound difficult, it is actually quite simple. For example, a child is asked to do a distance run. Discussion after the run focuses on how the body responded (heart rate increased, breathing increased, the body started to sweat, and so forth). The discussion can then lead to other fitness concepts and help the child to increase understanding of the body's potential.

Experiential Entry Point

The experiential entry point is where the concept that is being taught is linked to the child's previous experience. The coach may ask athletes, "Have any of you ever tried shooting the ball with this technique?" or "Have you ever seen a gymnast twist and turn through the air? Perhaps you have seen this on television?" The coach is inviting experience sharing, and this may reassure, build confidence in, or encourage participation by hesitant athletes.

Narrational Entry Point

A narrational entry point is where the athlete is introduced to a concept through storytelling. For example, a child may not be particularly athletic, but the child is so intrigued by stories about the ancient Olympics, with its rich imagery of warriors participating in foot races, that he or she may decide to give the sport a try.

Logical-Quantitative Entry Point

The logical-quantitative entry point uses scientific approaches to understand a particular question. For example, I introduce gymnastics to my students (Grades 4 and 5) by discussing some principles of biomechanics: the use of levers, how center of gravity affects balance, and the application of momentum to complete a skill. I ask the children questions that build on their understanding of these principles; they then have the opportunity to work on various skills—advanced for the club gymnast, introductory for the child lacking confidence.

Risks and Benefits of Using Multiple Intelligence Theory

> Schools should cultivate those skills and capabilities that are valued in the community and the broader society (Gardner, 1998, p. 66).

The ideas encapsulated in Gardner's theory can provide teachers and coaches with a better understanding of how their students learn. However, these ideas are meant only to give indicators of preferred learning style. These ideas do not state that the child exclusively learns in this one way. It also does not mean that people do not have elements of other styles in their learning profile. Research with gifted children has shown that these children often have exceptional abilities in a number of areas, and they can use different learning styles to develop their interests (Rogers, 1986; Silverman & Ellsworth, 1980).

In his book *Five Minds for the Future* (2006), Gardner identified the importance of "the respectful mind." Gardner described the attributes of this way of thinking as "an awareness and appreciation for differences among human beings and human groups" (p. 3). This approach resonates with the central theme of this book: the promotion of inclusion and the acceptance in sports of people with differences.

What Factors Can Restrict a Student's Learning?

Sometimes children do not learn, or they do not appear to be enjoying an activity, not because of the style of teaching or coaching, but because environmental factors are interfering. In this section, I consider just a few of these issues: the influence of temperature, sound, and time of day on children's involvement in sports.

Temperature

Children are sensitive to extreme temperature. They produce more heat per body mass than adults. Children also sweat less than adults, and this places them at risk for dehydration and other heat-related injuries (Falk, Bar-Or, Calvert, & MacDougall, 1992). Dehydration also increases the levels of ACTH, the stress hormone, which interferes with the learning process (Yair-Bar, Urkin, & Kozminsky, 2005). Coaching children in very hot conditions requires a commonsense approach. If it is blazing hot, you should not demand high effort, intense focus, and excellent performance from young children without providing them with an abundance of rest and fluid replenishment.

Sound

Some children are sensitive to sound, and this can interfere with their learning. Difficulty in calibrating the strength of sensory input (in this case the auditory sense) is a characteristic exhibited by some students with an ASD and a sensory processing disorder. Heightened sensitivity to the sounds created by ambient gymnasium noise can be very stressful for some of these children. A child experiencing such sensory overload reacts through behaviors: Some children may scream, some may become aggressive, and some attempt to reduce the overstimulation by removing themselves from the source or blocking the sound out by placing their fingers in their ears. Such situations are clearly not compatible with effective learning. There are also children who may crave loud sounds to adequately stimulate their auditory mechanisms; these children are hyposensitive.

Time of Day

Assumptions are often made by teachers about the best time for student learning. Prime-time teaching is generally recognized as taking place in the first few hours of the school day. The reasoning is that students are rested, alert, and more likely to sustain their focus on challenging material. This logic may hold true for some children (especially in the primary years), but we must always recognize individual variance. Some children are the proverbial night owls and learn better under conditions that respect their natural biological rhythms. Coaches, parents, and teachers should be aware of changes in sleep patterns that occur in puberty. The increase in hormones during puberty influences the release of oleamide, a chemical that causes drowsiness and adjusts the sleeping patterns of teenagers. They are able to stay awake longer, but find it difficult to start the day (due to the high levels of oleamide in the early morning). Several schools have experimented with later start times for the school day (9:30 a.m.) and have found that student absenteeism dropped and academic performance increased (Kalish, 2008). Coaches—especially coaches of teenagers—should be mindful of the challenges faced by teenagers in attending early practices. It would be easy to criticize the athletes and suggest their tardiness is a reflection of poor commitment, when participation is being inhibited by a neurochemical event.

What Type of Curricula Should Coaches Teach?

When young athletes show up to play sports, we want them to learn so many things. We want them to learn about themselves and thus develop their character. We want them to learn how to play the game and improve their skills. We want them to learn how to get along with others. These themes are articulated throughout the curriculum. Educators have defined several types of curricula: the active, hidden, and functional curricula.

Active Curriculum

The active curriculum is something that is transparent and obvious to parents and athletes. Coaches make it clear what they are teaching and what they hope to achieve. Coaches and teachers need to articulate to athletes and parents how they plan to design the curriculum in a manner that will challenge and support all students in the group.

Hidden Curriculum

The hidden curriculum sounds sinister, but it actually refers to the goals that a coach or teacher hopes will be developed indirectly from practices and competitions. Teachers and coaches tell inspiring stories of hope, courage, and perseverance in the hope that their athletes will take these messages and apply them in their lives. The coaches role model appropriate behavior (excellent sportsmanship) with the goal of having their athletes recognize the importance of such behavior.

Functional Curriculum

A functional curriculum (Hutchinson, 2002) has been shown to be an effective way of supporting the learning needs of children with developmental disabilities. This approach sets goals and skills that will help the child succeed in and out of an educational (and in our context, sports) environment. This functional curriculum is delivered in a context that can be considered the most enabling environment (Hutchinson, 2002). Not only do children with special educational needs require a curriculum structured with appropriate accommodations and modifications, but they also need their coach to exercise sound and thoughtful leadership in the hidden curriculum to promote a culture of acceptance.

How Can Coaches Teach Students Who Have a Broad Range of Sporting Abilities?

There are many teaching techniques available for coaches. It should be acknowledged, however, that these teaching techniques are not generic prescriptions that are dispensed with the expectation that they will work for every child. It would be easier if they were; the coach could use the exact same teaching technique for all athletes. Some children might flourish with this kind of learning support. However, it is likely that the child who cannot easily kick the ball or follow complex instructions would struggle with a generic teaching strategy. Whatever technique you decide to use, ensure that you match this technique to your students' unique needs and interests.

Differentiation on the Sports Field

The word *differentiation* is a classic piece of educational jargon that has been created to describe how various methods of instruction are used to help people learn. The definition of *differentiate* refers to an individual's unique response to the environment as he or she grows and develops. Tomlinson and Allan (2000) stated that differentiation "is an approach to teaching that advocates active planning for student differences in classrooms." Although it is an awkward word, differentiation brings profound benefits for athletes taught by its multifaceted methods. Content, process, and outcome form the key concepts at the core of differentiation—fundamentally, differentiation is something that recognizes that children learn in many ways. Differentiation is an approach to teaching and coaching that

- Challenges all children with age-appropriate and skill level–appropriate content
- Welcomes student choice and new ideas
- Uses different methods of grouping athletes to bring out the best in them
- Focuses on the child rather than the coach

Differentiation is an approach that is "open to acceptance rather than judgment, and so [it is] 'psychologically safe' for risk-taking, creativity, and individuality" (Maker & Nielson, 1995, p.10).

Designing a Sports Practice Using the Principles of Differentiation

As a coach, you make decisions about what to teach by assessing the learning styles and needs of the children that you will be working with. You take this information and decide how to balance the content so that it enriches your talented children and supports those who need extra help. You consider the athletes' physical, emotional, and social readiness, as some are more advanced than others. These issues also factor in the design of your practice. Then you decide how to teach the material (the process). To be effective in teaching the process, you then consider the learning styles of your athletes as individuals, and decide how these will fit into a method that also develops the team.

You understand that your athletes have their own interests and goals for a practice, remembering that many young children prefer to scrimmage (actually play the game) rather than repeatedly execute drills. Finally, you convey performance expectations to your athletes (the outcomes/product of the practice).

The Key Words of Differentiation
Assessment—Content—Readiness—Process—Interests—Learning Profile—Outcomes

Assessment: The Starting Place for Differentiation

The question of when a child is ready for sports was discussed in an earlier chapter. Assuming that the student, parent, and coach believe that this student can safely participate, issues of how to differentiate instruction emerge.

Many factors influence how we learn. These factors can be consolidated into four key areas (also known as domains):

- The affective instructional domain
- The social domain
- The movement domain
- The cognitive domain

Gathering information about the students in these areas helps teachers or coaches build a profile of the capabilities of the students with whom they are about to work. This assessment information may come from their own observations; from formal, published assessments; or from conversations with parents and previous coaches. But the best source of information is actually talking to the students. The following suggested questions may help to guide your assessment practices.

The Affective Instructional Domain

This domain considers the state of motivation of the child and his or her attitude toward learning.

- What are this child's interests?
- What are his or her reasons for participating in the sport?
- What does this child hope to achieve?
- Is the child ready for the skills that form the core of the program, or does he or she need additional time or practice to bring those skills up to a certain standard?
- Is this child highly competitive, or does he or she prefer passive involvement in this sport?
- What are realistic goals for this child?

- Is the content age-appropriate? I have observed too many coaches using adult practices and imposing them on young children; ironically, these activities might work with modifications.

- Each child will have already had different experiences in sports. Did something happen to this child in a previous experience that might explain his or her reluctance to participate?

- What level of parental support does the child receive?

The Social Domain

The social domain assesses the child's skills in social and group situations. It assesses confidence and emotional resilience.

- How does this athlete respond in social situations?

- Is this athlete a good team player or does he or she prefer solo situations?

- Is this athlete a risk taker? Taking healthy risks is an essential part of play, sports, and general learning, but some children prefer to stay well within their comfort zone. These children do not progress at the same pace as children who are prepared to challenge themselves.

- Is the group homogenous in skill level, or is there a broad range of children with different needs?

- How emotionally or socially resilient is this athlete? Children with poorly developed physical and social skills are at risk of marginalization and require structured support from the coach. A confident and capable athlete may want an engaging and challenging style of coaching.

The Movement Domain

This is an area where the coach gathers information that helps to determine the level of physical skill of the athletes. Questions to consider include the following:

- Which athlete has advanced skills and requires the program to be modified to ensure continual challenges?

- Which athlete requires a lot of extra support to ensure success with some of the basic movement patterns?

- Are there any athletes who need different equipment (e.g., different sizes of balls to help promote coordination and control)?

The Cognitive Domain

Bloom (1956) identified six catgories in the cognitive domain of learning: Knowledge, comprehension, application, analysis, synthesis, and evaluation. Coaches and teachers are encouraged to ask parents for information to build their understanding of how each child on the team learns in this domain. Coaches also need to assess the group dynamic and learning capability. Some of the questions that could be asked include the following:

- Do the members of the team have a wide range of social skills, emotional needs, and cognitive abilities?

- Will the members of the team be capable of learning and participating without too many modifications or accommodations?

> Assessment should be used as a tool for growth, rather than pointing out mistakes (Tomlinson, 1999, p. 10).

The list of assessment questions could be endless. Essentially, you want to develop an understanding of each child so that you can design a program to support and enhance all of your students' potential.

Assessment Is Ongoing

The assessment process does not end once the coach has started to work with the children. The purpose of coaching is to help all children make progress and reach their goals. How do you know when that has happened? How do you measure that progress? A differentiated learning environment recognizes the progress that children have made and adjusts or defines new goals to ensure the children are continually challenged. I have observed some coaches not allowing their athletes to progress to new challenges until the majority of the group has "caught up."

The methods of assessment do not have to be complicated or time-consuming. An observant coach can see that a child has mastered a skill or has a clear understanding of a concept. More formal assessment practices have been designed, but skill and caution must be used in interpreting the results.

Use Caution When Assessing Skill or Fitness

Test results in physical education classes and sports can often reflect states of motivation in children rather than indicate actual progress. A few years ago I conducted a fitness test with my 20 Grade 4 students. I asked them to run a 1 km time trial and insisted that they give me their very best effort. Their times were recorded and when asked, they all reported that they could not have run any faster. One week later we repeated this exercise. This time, I told them that if they beat their previous time they would all receive "house points." The greater their improvement, the more "house points" they would receive. Every single child improved his or her time, with the slowest children improving by as much as a minute. Had they improved in one week? Did the first test evaluate fitness or reflect motivation?

I have met coaches who have used performance data to hold back a child who is capable of a much higher level. For example, a basketball coach used free throw tests (10 throws) to assess readiness for the introduction of other skills. One child, who happened to be a talented athlete, did not perform very well on this test, and so the coach decided he wasn't ready for the next level. This phenomenon is well understood by classroom teachers of gifted children. The assumption is that these children should be gifted in all areas, and if they happen to perform poorly on a test, they are not given the curriculum challenges that they need. So what assessment techniques work well?

Using Self-Assessment and Peer Assessment

Self-assessment is used to help students recognize their strengths and areas of additional work. The coach presents a number of skills or concepts and asks children to rate themselves: Do they think they have an excellent, mediocre, or poor mastery of the skills? This technique must be used carefully; children with very low self-esteem may convince themselves that they have nothing to offer. Conversely, talented children may determine that they have extraordinary skills and do not require coaching. The coach needs to act as a filter to bring perspective to self-assessment.

Peer assessment is a technique in which the coach allows teammates to give one another feedback on their skills or performances. This technique needs to be well managed by the coach to prevent any bullying remarks. I have placed children in pairs or triads and asked them to comment on specific aspects of the performance.

Three Stars and a Wish

To keep a positive tone in peer assessment, I use a technique that I call Three Stars and a Wish. The peer is asked to give a friend three items of positive feedback (three stars). For example, "I really liked the way that Gary dribbled the ball. I think he had good control of the ball. I could tell he was really working hard, etc." Then the peer gives a wish: "I think that Gary needs to practice dribbling with both his left and right feet." The purpose of the assessment is to give the child information that helps him or her to develop confidence or identify areas for improvement. As with self-assessment, the coach needs to ensure this technique is used in a positive manner.

The Five Most Difficult First

The Five Most Difficult technique, adapted from Roberts and Roberts (2001), requires children to demonstrate five of the most difficult skills that the coach wants to see mastered. Those children who struggle with such skills may need additional instruction and practice; children who have already mastered these skills are clearly ready to learn more complex skills. Remember, the purpose of this assessment is not to publicly humiliate a child, so if it is apparent that a particular child is not ready for advanced challenges, there is no need to have the child assess him- or herself using this technique.

Create a "CW" Chart

A "CW" chart is a goal-setting and self-evaluation technique. Students are asked to write down (or have a scribe write for them) what they *Can* do in the context of the sport they are about to play, and also to describe their strengths in this sport. They are then asked to write down their goals and what they *Would* like to do. The coach can use this information to further develop understanding of the children's readiness and needs in the sport.

Keep Assessment Practical and Manageable

The intention of assessment is to help guide the coaches' decisions, not to burden coaches with a huge amount of paperwork or data that they cannot use in a meaningful way. Although teachers in academic subject areas are required by law to do assessments and keep data, often physical education teachers or coaches are not. Use the suggestions above and throughout this book as a guide to your coaching. The goal is to get to know your student athletes better and provide coaching and instruction that ultimately benefits everyone.

Using Differentiation Teaching Techniques to Help Students and Develop Your Team

Once you have assessed your athletes, what are you going to teach them, and how are you going to organize the material? Consider the following questions:

- How will the coach introduce content complexity?
- Will the skills be varied according to the needs of the athletes?
- Will the practices be organized around a particular concept or skill set?
- How will the coach structure the content to offer enrichment?

Tiered Assignments

Education in the classroom uses the technique of *tiered assignments* to deliver complex material in a variety of ways (Coil, 2004; Davidson & Decker, 2006; Heacox, 2002; Tomlinson, 2003). All the students study the same material, but they pursue assignments not only with different levels of complexity but also in a way that reflects their interests. In applying this technique in a sporting context, a coach might be working on soccer shooting skills with the task being to shoot a bouncing ball accurately and powerfully. After learning the skills, the group may be sent off to practice; some athletes may decide to practice volleying the ball, others may wish to work on a half-volley (the ball hits the ground once, then the student kicks it in). Some students may wish to shoot a ball that is bouncing toward them, others a ball bouncing away. The principle is the same, but the practice context allows the athletes a choice and allows them to work on areas where they feel they will receive the greatest benefit. The jargon of differentiation terms this *product choice*.

Compacting

Compacting is another differentiation teaching technique in which the teacher or coach initially assesses the athlete's skills. The coach may then modify the skills to be taught or decide the athlete has surpassed that challenge and needs to move on to something more complex. The effectiveness of the instruction, especially for high-ability athletes, will increase with streamlined practices.

Anchoring

Anchoring is a technique in which the athletes are given the opportunity to practice activities and skills of their own choice (almost like free play) once they have completed the work the coach assigned. Using this time appropriately gives the coach a chance to help an athlete struggling in a particular area while allowing other athletes to reinforce skills or challenge themselves with new skills.

Content Modification

In a differentiated learning environment, the coach or teacher allows the content of the practice to be modified. It is a misconception that children who have difficulty with a particular task should be given something else to do. Content modification is a principle that ensures the child does the same task as everyone else, but the way it is instructed or delivered is molded to the child's needs. Principles of modification can include the following:

- Give the child larger or smaller equipment that allows improved visual tracking

- Use equipment in which the speed of an object (e.g., shuttle, ball) can be adjusted

- Create rules that allow a child who is poor at anticipating or making quick judgments to be more involved in the practice or game. For example, children who are poorly coordinated might be playing basketball. The rule in that circumstance might be: Everyone on this team must be allowed to dribble or pass the ball before the other team is allowed to vigorously defend. If you want to practice a particular type of shot, the rule is that the only shot allowed is a lay-up, and so forth. Adapting the rules can greatly benefit children in need of extra practice or support.

- Give the children more time to practice their skills
- Design challenging and achievable goals around this modified practice
- Modify the way that you teach the child. Children with various sensory impairments (e.g., visual, hearing) may be fully capable of meeting the performance expectations as long as they are taught in a manner that understands their sensory challenge. Modifications for children with sensory impairments are discussed in the next chapter.

> There may be no best way to teach, but there may be a best way to teach particular content to particular learners. (Rink, 2001, pp. 123-124)

Using Differentiated Learning Processes to Organize Students and Effectively Facilitate Learning Opportunities

Having considered the issues around what you are going to teach or coach, the next step is to determine how you will deliver this content. How you organize your students and athletes can effectively facilitate or limit their learning opportunities. Issues to consider in differentiated learning processes include the following:

- How to organize the learning
- How to determine the pace of the learning
- How to organize your athletes into effective learning groups
- How to create practical ways of giving your athletes some choices

Organizing the Learning

If you want to engage your athletes at all levels, you need to ensure that they are highly active. This sounds like common sense, but some coaches spend too much time instructing and do not give the children enough time "doing." When organizing your practices, try to structure your activities so that one activity seamlessly follows the next. Considerable time can be lost setting up the equipment, choosing groups, and explaining the activity. With planning, you can build your practices around a particular setup (cones being laid out on a field in a particular order, and so forth), and then your athletes will not have to stand around waiting for you to finish setting up.

Determining the Pace of Learning

It is important for coaches and teachers to assess the skills of the athletes on a fairly regular basis. Here are some things to remember when determining the pace of students' learning.

Acceleration/Deceleration

If the athlete has mastered the skill and is ready for greater challenges, the coach must move that athlete forward and increase the degree of challenge to match the pace of learning. Conversely, the pace of learning may need to be slowed if some athletes need extra time to master the skills. Failure to do so will result in the athletes becoming bored and possibly disruptive.

Variable Pacing

When reviewing material that is already mastered, coaches and teachers should be able to progress fairly quickly. This allows more time to be devoted to tasks that require deeper thinking and challenge.

Organizing into Effective Learning Groups

There are many ways to organize student athletes into effective learning groups. Some ways to organize students include providing independent work, encouraging leadership skills, providing flexible organized or randomized grouping, using whole group coaching, and working with team captains to explore leadership opportunities. These topics are discussed in the next sections. A case study example about using flexible grouping in a PE classroom is also provided.

Whole-Group Coaching

This is the most traditional method of coaching instruction—the classic "one size fits all." The organization of some activities does not readily lend itself to a differentiated learning approach; for instance, the effectiveness of a play in a team sport may require the coach to issue instructions in a uniform manner. It is when this technique is the only teaching instrument the coach employs that it can become inappropriate for different learners. Athletes may also be clustered into groups according to their readiness for particular skills.

Independent Work

The coach may decide that the athlete needs to work on his or her own. This decision should never be punitive. The talented athlete may be sent off to practice a challenging skill before being brought back into the group. A child requiring remediation might also benefit from this arrangement. If the athletes become used to this type of coaching (individualized programs that intersect with team coaching), they will not think it is unusual when a teammate is sent to practice some aspect of his or her skills. Independence is important as excessive parental, peer, or coaching intervention can actually undermine the child's purpose and motivation. Believe your athletes can achieve, and they may surprise you by how much they can do.

Athlete Leadership

The development of leadership skills can be an important aspect of participation in sports. A stereotypical idea about sports leadership is that the team captain is usually the most talented, confident, and assertive student. This ties into the notion that leadership is somehow the reserve of the elite and will not likely be found in a student who lacks athletic competence. My view is that all students are capable of exercising leadership, especially when leadership is viewed as acts of contribution and service rather than something that is self-interest based (i.e., the view that a good leader is someone who gets the team what they want). Coaches are encouraged to design leadership opportunities for all their athletes, not just the talented and confident students.

Flexible Grouping

Sometimes children may have excellent skills in one area, but significant weaknesses in another. This is often the case with a gifted child who also has a learning disability. In *flexible grouping* the teacher creates groups of students working together based on student strengths, needs, and interests. There are a number of advantages in this approach: Flexible grouping helps to develop a sense of community, break down cliques, and foster inclusion. Having created the groups, the coach may wish to start with some activities to warm up the children to the concept of the flexible group; ice-breaking activities can be competitive or just relationship building. The purpose is to build the idea that each person is one of the team, and everyone will play a role in the successful completion of the task—that could be a long-winded way of saying that a relay race needs each member of the team to run.

Flexible grouping is effective when the group size is more than three and less than six or seven. The coach needs to establish the rules that govern the group behavior—essentially, everyone shares and has a turn. Sometimes the coach may decide to use flexible grouping to bring together students with similar learning preferences. Other times, students with different learning preferences may be clustered; the coach then sees how students view a problem and its solution from different perspectives.

Example of How Flexible Grouping Can Be Used in a Physical Education Classroom

When teaching gymnastics, it is not uncommon for me to have students who can barely master a forward roll while also having sports club standard gymnasts capable of complex somersault routines. I mix the children into clusters of mixed abilities and then teach the theme for the class; perhaps it is a brief discussion on the mechanics of levers. We talk about the speed at which a short lever moves and contrast that with the speed of a long lever. We discuss how rotation is created and controlled. The athletes who have more advanced skills demonstrate a range of skills, from very simple to complex. The groups are then sent to another area of the gym and work on the skills that challenge their particular capabilities. I move around the groups ensuring not only that the students are on task but also that each athlete is being challenged. The athletes who have more advanced skills take a leadership role and support the athletes who are less advanced in their gymnastic skills.

Performance Grouping

Talented children must have their needs met as much as children with special needs. Using performance grouping, these young athletes are placed in groups where they can receive acceleration and enrichment. *A cautionary note:* Use this technique with care and consideration; I suggest using it sparingly. The teacher in the introductory story of this book (the "Dregs" versus "Stars" story) might have argued that he was using performance grouping. It is the manner in which this technique is applied that determines its effectiveness. If it challenges the capable but is used to demean less able athletes, it must be avoided. Framed appropriately, it can help talented children be challenged and support students with different needs.

Matched Grouping and Random Grouping

These are two different methods for organizing your athletes into learning groups. The coach may decide to create a group based on a whole range of criteria; these may include ability (as already discussed), matching the individuals whose learning needs are comparable. Sometimes the coach may need to group children to prevent behavioral disruptions from occurring. Random grouping is self-explanatory. The coach may assign the kids a number (from a sequence that repeats; for example, 1, 2, 3, 1, 2, 3); all the children with the number 1 are grouped and so forth.

Guiding Team Captains in Their Leadership Development

Team captains have traditionally been used in sports to lead and inspire the performances of teammates. This sporting talisman is usually considered to be one of the best players and usually has a confident personality. Children dealing with difficult challenges in their lives are seldom chosen to be a team leader, unless the coach or teacher creates opportunities for all athletes. One method to promote leadership is to have captains identified for something other than athletic skill. The coach might choose a virtue that the team needs to develop—courage, perseverance, effort, and so forth—and then select an athlete who role models this virtue. Reward this captain with a valued and meaningful club tradition; for example, "The captain of the practice gets to choose our first game."

Problems can arise when a coach allows captains to select teams during practices; invariably the most successful or popular children are chosen first while children with fewer abilities are left to the end. I find it quicker and less rancorous to choose the teams myself; this not only avoids the stigma for a child who thinks "I am always the last to be chosen," but it also allows the coach to match teams on abilities, avoid certain player pairings that may cause conflict, and so forth.

Creating Practical Ways of Giving Your Athletes Some Choices in Their Activities

Some practical ways of giving athletes choices in their activities include providing coaching centers and providing athlete-centered activities, such as choice boards.

Coaching Centers

A coach may decide to have a number of different learning areas in which the athletes can work. The skills can range in complexity; the athletes can work for however long they need before they move on to the next skill. This technique (or structure of organization) allows children with challenges to practice without showcasing their difficulties in front of their peers. It also provides talented children a chance to work on skills matched to their abilities. The students can rotate through the centers in a controlled fashion—for example, "You have 15 minutes at each station"—working as individuals or in groups. This presents the coach with a good opportunity to match children in mixed ability groupings.

Athlete-Centered Activities

In athlete-centered activities the coach develops themes that are focused on the children's interests. The coach may gather ideas from the team on what to do during the practice before designing it. This may include providing enrichment activities for the more advanced young athletes.

Choice Boards

Using choice boards is an example of an athlete-centered activity. Different activities are written on cards and posted on notice boards (or simply written on a whiteboard). The athlete chooses which activity to work on for that part of the practice.

Example for a Running Fitness Class

45 minutes long, for Grades 4/5

Activity 1: Choice of warm-up activities

10 minutes group jog, 10 minutes aerobics in the gym, 10 minutes on the exercise bike, or 10 minutes of tag games

Activity 2: Running workout

10–15 minutes of speed play (also known in distance running as fartlek) on trails, 2 times 5 minutes of 200 meter fast, 200 meter slow on the track, or 10 minutes sustained fast running on the road

Activity 3: Running game activity

15 minutes of Capture the Flag (A popular running game widely used in PE classes)

The essence of this choice board strategy is that the athlete has some choice in the activity. One criticism of such techniques is that they are impractical; they may dilute the group and reduce opportunities for team instruction and cohesion. Certainly athletes younger than 11 years old may only need a few choices (and simple ones at that). This technique is particularly effective with older students who are more self-reliant.

The Products (Outcomes) of Differentiated Instruction and Coaching

In a differentiated learning environment, athletes are consistently being challenged and supported in a manner that personally resonates with their preference for learning. Outcomes that you may observe include the following:

- Increased willingness to participate
- Visible enjoyment
- Increased confidence
- Healthy risk-taking behavior (e.g., students start to participate in physical activities they previously might have avoided)
- Increased attention and concentration
- Improved social relationships

Tomlinson (2002, p. 7) noted, "Students are more apt to become competent adults if they learn to develop their strengths as well as their weaknesses." When an athlete's interests and areas of confidence are starting points, he or she has a stable foundation on which to develop the learning process. The benefits of such an approach are considerable; these student athletes start to view themselves as more capable, and achievement levels rise (Tomlinson, Callahan, & Lelli, 1997).

A Differentiation Checklist

Assessment

❑ What prior experience does this child have in this sport?
❑ What can this child do now?
❑ What are this student's goals for participating in this sport?
❑ Assess with the Five Most Difficult technique.
❑ Create a CW chart.

Design

❑ Determine the complexity of your material. Is it pitched at the right level for your students?
❑ How will you alter your content to enrich your talented or support your developing athletes?

Readiness

❏ Is the child ready for the content that you plan to teach? Draw on the assessment information and determine the child's physical, social, emotional, and intellectual readiness.

Determine the Pace of Learning

❏ Will you teach the content at a steady pace, allowing for difficult concepts to be practiced?

❏ Will you use the class to rapidly review material already covered?

Organize Your Athletes

❏ How will you organize your athletes to help them learn the content of your class?

❏ Is the class structured for independent learners or a group clustered by performance level?

❏ Will you teach the session to the whole group or a group designed by random selection?

Choice in Activities

❏ Are choice boards or coaching centers effective techniques of differentiating your material?

Products of Differentiation

❏ What would you like to see from the class?

Final Thoughts

Being an effective coach is not just a function of having excellent technical knowledge of sports or of physical activities. Being able to understand your athletes' preferred learning styles and interests and then designing the content to meet their needs significantly increases a coach's potential for effectiveness. Differentiation is not just a piece of educational jargon; it is practical and embodies the noble purpose of helping all students to learn and develop their skills to ever higher levels.

CHAPTER 7

Effective Teaching Tips and Coaching Styles

C oaches and teachers can exert a significant effect on the development of young athletes. Their effectiveness is shaped not only by their technical knowledge (content) and their ability to positively interact with other people, but also by their skill in applying principles of pedagogy (teaching). This chapter explores some of the teaching techniques that can be used to support all learners as they participate in sports.

Rosenshine's Six Components of Effective Teaching

There are many ways to teach. Effective teaching is not a prescription but rather the flexible application of a number of themes. Rosenshine (1986) synthesized much of the research on teaching effectiveness into six basic steps:

- *Review*—The coach starts the practice with a discussion and demonstration of the skills or concepts that were practiced or introduced at the last session.
- *Introduction of new material*—If the coach feels the athlete or group is ready for new skills and concepts, these skills are introduced in a manner that is both challenging and supportive.
- *Guided practice*—The coach asks questions to ascertain if the athletes understand the task (concepts). The athletes then start to practice the skills.
- *Feedback*—The coach provides feedback on the athletes' performance of the skill.
- *Independent practice*—The coach encourages the athletes to pursue some independent practice. This may be something that they can do at home or at school during recess, and it is tailored to meet each child's needs.

- *Review progress*—The final step is for the coach and athletes to review the progress. Is the work sufficiently challenging? If the skill has already been mastered, the coach must enrich the program. If not, it might be necessary to change the independent practice drills or simply to keep practicing.

What Is the Role of Information Feedback in Learning and Coaching?

Children create an understanding of their sports abilities via the information that they receive from other people. Coaches and parents play a critical role in an athlete's perception of competence—it is this that forms the foundation of self-esteem. A child who consistently hears the message that he or she is not valued or competent will develop a self-image that reflects this message; the converse is equally true.

Providing information about progress and performance has been termed *feedback*. How it is structured determines its usefulness. A coach can shout out a series of instructions but, although that is feedback, if the athlete just tunes the coach out, the information is irrelevant. It may also be that the athlete does not respond well to verbal cues or has a hearing impairment, so the coach must take care to deliver meaningful feedback to each student. The key features of the feedback process include using specific feedback, using feedback directed at something that the athlete has the power to change, using appropriate timing, using "profound simplicity," and using the correct perceived tone when talking to athletes.

Using Specific Feedback

A coach who asks for greater effort runs the risk of not being respected when the athletes feel they are already trying as hard as they can (that request is too general). Asking for increased effort in the way a particular skill or tactic is being performed is a targeted request that is not dismissive of the efforts the athletes are already making.

Using Feedback Directed at Something the Athlete Has the Power to Change

Feedback directed at something that is within the power of the athlete to change is especially important for young athletes who have challenges or disabilities. These children may have difficulty sustaining continuous effort or executing the requests from the coach. Giving guidance and encouragement based on achievable goals challenges the child while at the same time maintaining his or her dignity; this is a good use of coaching feedback.

Using Appropriate Timing

Parents and coaches almost intuitively understand the value and the importance of a teachable moment. When a child dashes out in front of traffic, the best moment to teach is immediately, not days later! However, some situations are better learned after a period of personal reflection: The athlete who has just finished a race and is clearly exhausted does not require an immediate debrief. The application of common sense in the timing of delivery feedback is needed—it is not a complicated sports science.

Using "Profound Simplicity"

There is a tendency for some sports coaches to overinstruct their athletes. The freedom to play, explore, and innovate is the essence of creative movement; a coach who provides too much information on how to play the sport (the tactics and strategies) can overload the athlete. The cliché "analysis-paralysis" seems applicable in this context; the overloaded athlete spends so much time trying to adhere to the coach's requests that he or she performs poorly. More effective is using the concept of *profound simplicity*. This means the athletes understand what is expected of them, and the coach allows them to perform without constraint.

Using Correct Perceived Tone

Voice tone can be modulated to convey many feelings ranging from anger and sarcasm, to kindness and understanding. Some young athletes may like a convincing voice tone that inspires them to exert more effort. Other athletes may be deterred by a voice tone that is aggressive and demanding. Coaches should choose their voice tone wisely. The power of the tone of voice should not be underestimated, especially with students who have fragile personal confidence.

How to Use Praise and Recognition

Coaches who use praise appropriately can maintain the motivation of their athletes and also optimize learning opportunities. Praise that is used to excess becomes devalued; a lazy kick of the ball combined with lethargic effort is not "excellent effort," and the child may treat such a comment as a joke. Effort requires some energy and enthusiasm, combined with a desire to complete the task; children receiving appropriate recognition and praise value these comments because they have earned them. Other practical techniques to give children recognition include the following.

Give Athletes Responsibilities

Give athletes in need of a boost some important responsibilities. Students often want to help out and love having a job.

Engage Each Athlete in Conversation

Engage each child in conversations about his or her life. Not only does it help to develop the child's relationship with you, but it also reassures the child that you genuinely like him or her. This is an important issue for a child who consistently feels disregarded by the coach and therefore may drop out of the sport.

Use Incentive Programs

Find ways to reward effort and commitment. Stickers, ink stamps, badges of recognition, certificates, and special honors can all be used to show athletes that their efforts are appreciated and valued.

Recognize Each Athlete Personally

Personal recognition from the coach can help to increase the sense of attachment and accomplishment the athlete will feel. Public recognition, whether by posting something in the club newsletter or by honoring the athlete's efforts in the debriefing after a competition or practice, can be helpful. Family recognition is also an important way to strengthen the child's feelings about participating in the sport.

Use Rituals

Rituals are a very important part of a sports culture and can promote inclusion and acceptance. The coach can create his or her own rituals, which will soon become cherished and much desired by the athletes. Following are some examples of rituals that I have used.

King/Queen for the Day

The coach may wish to designate an athlete the King/Queen for the Day. With this title comes a certain privilege; maybe it is choosing a game, being the team captain, or leading a valued ritual of the club.

Receive a Knighthood

At the end of a practice, I choose an athlete to receive a knighthood. The athlete steps forward, kneels down, and is "blessed" by a magic wand. The other athletes applaud. It is plain silly, but the young children love this ritual. I keep a record to ensure that all the athletes receive this "honor."

Break the Record

I used to have my athletes compete in a practice to beat a previous "record." The record was anything that I could think of: the number of athletes who showed up for a Wednesday practice, the best time ever for someone not being caught in a game of tag, the record for the quickest person ever caught in the game of tag, and so forth. At the end of the practice, we would celebrate by having a selected athlete (again, on a rotational basis) come forward and break one of my much cherished vinyl records.

Use the Sandwich Technique

Coaches have used the sandwich technique to help athletes identify errors in their skills. The coach praises some aspect of the child's performance, offers some technical advice aimed at improving the execution of the skill, and then finishes the feedback with another positive remark. The idea is that the child does not view the process as criticism but as a learning opportunity.

Recognize Efforts

One of the more important principles of coaching young athletes, especially those with challenges, is to recognize the effort that the athletes have made, more so than the actual outcome.

Use Wiggling Finger Answers

Many students may know the answer to a question. Rather than acknowledging just the fastest thinker (or the most vocal), the coach can use Wiggling Fingers. Quite simply, the coach selects a student to provide an answer or demonstrate a skill, and then says, "Everyone who knows this answer or can demonstrate this skill, wiggle your fingers." This technique gives all students a chance to indicate that they understand. After a while, the students will wiggle their fingers without solicitation from the coach.

Practical Teaching Tips for Students with Special Needs

The principles of differentiation previously discussed can be effective for all children; however, children with special needs may need additional support to facilitate their learning. Here are a few practical tips to supplement your coaching techniques.

Outline Expectations

Coaches should outline their expectations for their athletes in clear and simple language. Many sports have developed their own language and to the uninitiated, phrases such as "shake and bake" (in basketball) or "nutmeg" (in soccer) may seem nonsensical. Coaches should try to avoid jargon and clichéd communication if at all possible.

Use a Peer Buddy

Sometimes young athletes are too shy or nervous to ask for help or clarification of what is expected of them. One suggestion is to have a peer buddy support them by quietly reminding or guiding the student once the activity has started (Carter & Hughes, 2008).

Use a Routine

Coaches are encouraged to use a routine that is consistent and understood. My athletes know they can have free play with the equipment until the coaching is ready to start. We then proceed with the instructional period, followed by the activities. The different instructional tools are then selected and employed—perhaps it is a choice board or a visual schedule. Although this structure may seem like common sense, the routine is especially important for young athletes with different needs and learning challenges.

Use Visual Signals

Getting and keeping your athletes' attention can sometimes be difficult, especially if they are energetically involved in activities. Whistles are traditionally used, but this may not be appropriate for children with severe sound sensitivities. Visual signals can be used, such as placing your arm up in the air to tell students they must stand still and listen. With a short amount of practice, the students can become skilled at recognizing this signal, and the coach no longer needs to strain his or her voice to be heard.

Give a Time Line

Children with difficulty sustaining attention benefit from being told that the instructional period is short and defined. For example, the coach could say, "Give me your attention for 20 seconds. Right, this is what I want you to do. Everybody understand?"

Schedule Transitions

Children with challenges can experience difficulty moving from one activity to another. Transitions can be improved if the child is given notice that a change of activity is coming. Using a countdown approach is also helpful; for example, I use a 1-minute egg timer to help the child understand that a change is about to occur. Acknowledging and rewarding a successful transition (for a child that has difficulties in this area) is important for communicating your recognition of the child's effort.

Incorporate the System of Least Prompts

Incorporate the system of *least prompts* (Dunn, Morehouse, & Fredericks, 1986) into your teaching style. When helping a young athlete tackle a particular challenge in sports, by all means employ the support strategies that will help the child, but also encourage the child's independence and work toward achieving the goal. Sometimes, too much support is offered (i.e., too many prompts), and this may actually undermine the child's efforts and make him or her stand out in front of peers. Certainly support students, but realize that students do not need or desire an "educational crutch."

Use Brailling

Brailling is a technique used when a child with challenges feels the coach or peer successfully complete the task. This is not necessarily something used for people with sight impairments; for example, a young athlete with poor arm coordination for running may hold the coach's arms as the coach demonstrates correct technique. Not only observing but also "feeling" the correct movement pattern helps the child learn what is expected.

Use the TARGET Approach

The acronym TARGET (Epstein, 1988) has been used to teach children with different needs. This approach helps give children a sense of competence and mastery, thus reinforcing the underlying principles of intrinsic motivation. The acronym TARGET stands for the following process:

Task—The coach creates different ways to make the skills and activities fun and challenging for the athletes.

Authority—The coach allows the athletes to help choose the activities.

Recognition—The athletes receive acknowledgement, either in private or publicly, for their effort and achievements.

Grouping—The coach changes the way the sports program is structured by grouping athletes by skill level, mixing genders, mixing skill levels, and so forth.

Evaluation—A young athlete is encouraged (or directed by the coach) to evaluate his or her own performance, rather than compare him- or herself with the performance and achievements of others, to enhance intrinsic motivation.

Time—Athletes given sufficient time to practice and develop their skills are likely to retain their interest in the sport.

Teaching Tips for When Things Don't Go Well

Some children compensate for a lack of success in sport by behaving in a manner that attracts recognition from their peers. Coaches know them as the class clowns, the children who "goof around" and disrupt the practice. Perrenoud (1991, p. 92) has described many of these children as being "imprisoned in the identity of a bad pupil and an opponent." Children with learning disabilities and other special needs may have diagnoses or related problems that include exhibiting challenging behavior from time to time. There is a robust literature about behavioral interventions, which is too lengthy to cover in detail here. The following list is meant to be a simple reference for coaches and teachers. For those students with significant problem behaviors, consider consulting with a member of the education team or the child's parents. The inappropriate use of discipline strategies with children who have special needs carries the risk of damaging their confidence and their sense of connection to the sport.

There are many techniques that can be used to help maintain a sense of discipline and order in a sports program. These techniques do not have to be harsh or punitive. All sports organizations and schools have rules about conduct. These rules help to shape the identity of the group and communicate what is expected from its members. The consistent application of rules to all student athletes and clear consequences for their transgressions helps to maintain an appropriate standard of conduct. A coach who makes up rules and then applies them unevenly creates uncertainty for young athletes as they are not sure where they stand.

It is important to place rule making in context. Children make mistakes, and educating them about their errors rather than punishing them is a far more effective way of helping them learn. Preemptive discipline planning is better than reactive sanctioning of behavior. Outlining the rules and expectations is a good starting point. Have an agreement among all participants of your group's shared values: "This is what we stand for; this is what we can expect from others; this is what will happen if we break these codes." This is especially important if your program has a number of children with special needs. Incorporating the knowledge covered in this book will help coaches to avoid situations that lead to disciplinary problems. Children who are enjoying their sport, who are participating in a sports environment where they feel valued and respected, and who are kept busy do not need to resort to inappropriate behavior to gain recognition.

Following are some examples of appropriate disciplinary techniques.

Positive Reinforcement

Positive reinforcement is a valuable tool to encourage excellent behavior. Praise for appropriate actions received from influential people in the student's life (parents, teachers, coaches) can increase the likelihood that this student will continue to behave in this positive manner.

Behavioral Contracts and Contingency Contracts

Behavioral and contingency contracts are documents prepared by the coach (or parent) that state what the child will or will not do. The child needs to be sufficiently motivated to keep such a contract—just writing a list of expectations is not always effective. A clause that states what the child gets if he or she does as asked gives the child a goal to work toward.

Proximity Control

Using the technique of proximity control, the coach brings the athlete close so that the athlete can be quietly reminded to focus effort on what is required.

Preventive Cuing

The coach uses a signal that is recognized by the athlete (and only that athlete) as a signal to refocus. For example, it could be tapping the wrist three times with the fingers.

Traffic Light System

Children who are very poor at interpreting social cues (e.g., not knowing when to stop a particular behavior) benefit from the traffic light system. Coaches could keep three small cards in their pocket: red for stop, orange for warning to stop, green for go. If the coach anticipates a particular problem developing, covertly showing the card "cues" children about the appropriate behavioral response.

Lava-Busters

This is a visual technique that can help a child try to regain some self-control. I have a laminated picture of a volcano spewing lava posted on a wall. When a child has trouble with anger, he or she is invited to choose a Lava-Buster. The child can go to the picture of the volcano and choose a laminated card that "cools the lava." These options can include going for a drink of water, visiting the school goldfish tank and then returning to the gym, and so forth. Essentially, the idea is to allow the child to remove him- or herself from a potentially confrontational situation, regroup, and then return to class "cooler." Obviously, you have to decide if this technique will work for the particular child. I knew one teacher who used a Lava-Buster, and the child used the opportunity to go home.

As a Last Resort: Time-outs, Planned Ignoring

Each of these interventions should be used sparingly, and if a child is exhibiting any kind of extreme behavior, consider a consultation with the child's teacher or teaching team. A time out is an effective tool when the student is becoming frustrated (perhaps by a perceived injustice) and is struggling to appropriately calibrate a response. Without the time out, the child's emotional self-control may deteriorate and evoke behaviors that exacerbate the difficulties.

Planned ignoring is used when the coach recognizes that a child's particular behavior is inappropriate; the coach instead focuses on something more positive that the athlete could be (or is) doing. There are unavoidable times when a situation may require the complete removal of the child from the situation (e.g., sending the child to the office or home). Students with significant behavior problems may have a specific behavior intervention plan that the coach or teacher can consult.

Finding the Right Coaching Style

Some coaches prefer to sit calmly on the sidelines studying the game and considering how they might adjust their tactics or motivate their players. Other coaches are vociferous and seemingly engaged in every single play as if they are trying to micro-manage the movements of their players. The coaching style that works for some athletes may be totally inappropriate for a different group. Which is the most effective style? Are there certain types of coaching a young athlete with challenges or disabilities should avoid?

There are a number of different coaching styles, which can be condensed into three categories: transmission coaching, transaction coaching, and transformational coaching.

Transmission Coaching

Transmission coaching is when the coach stands in front of the group and dispenses wisdom. Teachers have termed this approach "one size fits all," but that is probably a bit simplistic. There are undoubtedly autocratic coaches who instruct their athletes with expectations that they are obliged to follow. Some of these coaches insist that they are not to be challenged, and athletes are expected to stay within the game plan. Certainly some athletes respond well to this approach; however, I would argue that a child who is at a developmental stage behind his or her peers or has special needs (learning or physical) will find this technique to be a mismatch. Compassion and empathy are qualities that are not likely to be found in coaches who aggressively employ this coaching strategy.

Transaction Coaching

Transaction coaching encourages an exchange of views between the athlete and coach. Some coaches are reluctant to engage in this type of coaching style because they believe this will undermine their authority. If the coach believes that his or her power and control over the athletes is at the core of a successful program, it is almost certain that this will not be a useful technique for our diverse young athletes. An emotionally secure coach, one who is not threatened by the opinions of others, or a coach who welcomes input and uses it to strengthen respect and acceptance will find this technique beneficial.

Transformational Coaching

Transformational coaching challenges and develops all aspects of the athlete's makeup: physical, social, emotional, intellectual, cognitive, and so forth. Employing all of these areas into a sports program promotes acceptance, skill development, and personal confidence of a child with special needs.

> Whether sport is constructive or destructive in the psychological development of young children greatly depends on the values, education and skills of adults [that coach them] (Martens, 1993, p. 42).

Coaching Styles to Avoid

There are also some coaching styles that parents of children with special needs may wish to avoid. These prototypes of coaching styles are described in the following sections.

"The Perfectionist"

This kind of coach is demanding and likely unforgiving of mistakes. This coach is probably happy when things are going the team's way, but could be prone to fits of anger when decisions of the referee, or outcomes in the game, appear unjust. This coach may make statements such as, "You'll need to try harder."

"The Commander"

This kind of coach likes to be in full control and does not want contributions from athletes or parents. This individual could be quite insecure and compensates by aggressively asserting him- or herself in situations where he or she can exert control; working with young children is the perfect environment in which a coach can bully without contest (unless called to account by an astute parent). Statements such as, "I'll give the orders; you follow them," form the essence of this kind of coach's instructional approach. Benching a player for being outspoken, talkative, or disruptive has been a common method used by coaches to gain compliance. Certainly, team cohesion requires respect for the coach's position and respect for his or her experience in guiding sporting activity. However, this approach is one that stresses absolute compliance with and obedience to the coach's demands. This style of coaching has been shown to be counterproductive to athletes with fragile self-confidence (Kohn, 2005). These students invariably learn to fear the coach and eventually dislike the sport.

A Fading Whistle

As a soccer referee in the local leagues, I have had experience with youth coaches (both teenage girls and boys) who prowl the sidelines, scowling at each decision that goes against their team. They berate the way I manage the game and express outrage when a goal is scored against them. Decisions against their team are externalized; for example, it is the fault of the referee or the result of a perceived injustice (a foul). I wish I could say that this is the behavior of just a few coaches, but I am increasingly seeing this become more prevalent. Sometimes I wonder if what I do is worth it. Who wants to be constantly shouted at?

"The Passive Coach"

This individual may offer no words of encouragement and may generally have low energy. Although this coach may be technically proficient, there could be too much emphasis on instruction and an absence of fun in practices. Children need to have dynamic interactions with their coaches to stay motivated and excited about the sport; however, the passive coach may rely on the children to be self-motivated.

"The Cheerleader"

You can hear the cheerleader on the sidelines. This coach makes lots of noise, which may not be a bad thing if it is all positive and supportive of the athletes' efforts. However, when the "noise" becomes critical of athletes (or opponents), becomes argumentative with refereeing decisions, or becomes abusive, this coaching style is inappropriate.

"The Expert"

If you become involved in sports, you will encounter "The Expert." This type of coach is noted for being inflexible, opinionated, and potentially aggressive. This coach believes that his or her experiences in sports make him or her eminently more qualified than you. "The Expert" uses this view to justify biased decisions, especially in areas such as team selection or athlete playing time. When "The Expert" is a parent, he or she is a difficult person to deal with. This kind of parent might harass the coach (or worse, the young athletes), contradict the coach's decisions in front of the athletes, criticize the tactics or philosophy of the program, or undermine the coach with a gossip campaign to other parents. "The Expert" is not likely to easily be persuaded into another view, so organizations must outline a plan for preventive action. Many clubs provide guidelines for parent conduct and on occasion ask parents to sign contracts agreeing to abide by these guidelines. Persistent transgressions can be dealt with by suspending or expelling a parent.

What Are the Skills Needed to Be an Effective Coach?

First, you have to have a sound grasp of your material. If you don't feel comfortable with some aspects of coaching—whether designing the program content or managing people—either bring in technical expertise (another coach or advisor) or take some coaching courses. Coaches are encouraged to be confident and secure enough to acknowledge that they can always learn more about their sport. Sports knowledge—especially in science—is ever changing, and some of the ideas that may have served them well in their playing days might now be completely outdated.

This book has identified some of the coaching myths and stereotypes that inhibit the successful inclusion of children with challenges. Your willingness to engage in ongoing education and to critically reflect on your own coaching methods ensures that you remain an effective coach for all children. Coaches are the leaders of the team and their role often extends beyond that of strategist. Many children look to their coach as a mentor, especially during troubling periods of childhood development. One study found that 96% of young athletes reported that their coach played an important role in influencing their behavior compared with 65% who said it was their teachers and 55% who said it was their parents (Deshaies, Vallerand, & Guerrier, 1984).

The reputation of an effective coach often precedes him or her. This coach is noted for his or her good humor, kindness, clarity of thought, and respectful conduct. Parents may overlook weakness in a coach's technical knowledge if the coach is kind and considerate. The converse is equally true: A coach with excellent knowledge but a ruthless, demanding manner of athlete interaction will struggle to be respected—especially by the children who find sports difficult.

Coaching is not an easy task. Difficult situations with other parents were frequently identified as a source of stress for coaches (Strean, 1995). Parent coaching volunteers without any experience of the sport may have difficulty not only with structuring appropriate learning environments, but also in dealing with "sideline sports critics" such as "The Expert," discussed in the previous section. Coaches in successful sports programs report the value of having a mentor in helping them make an ongoing commitment to sports (Bloom, Durand-Bush, Schinke, & Salmela, 1998).

So how can we train sports coaches to develop their skills in respecting children with differences? The seminal work in this area was the development of the coaching effectiveness training program.

Understanding What Kids Need

Mr. Jones was my favorite teacher. One moment he would be serious and everyone would carefully listen to each word he spoke; then he might throw in a joke or a really interesting story. Then it was back to work. He really brought the best out of me; he understood when I needed to be pushed and the times I needed to be reassured. Looking back at my school days, I realize that Mr. Jones was probably a teacher ahead of his time.

Coaching Effectiveness Training

Coaching effectiveness training (CET), a program developed by two psychologists, Frank Smoll and Ronald Smith (1979), downplays the importance that adults attach to children's competitions. It is a program that asks coaches to consider how their behavior might influence the athletes in their charge. CET recognizes that children want to please adults, so part of the underlying message promoted in this program is that a lack of success in the traditional sense (winning) does not diminish how the coach feels about the young athletes. CET praises children's efforts and states that success is not the sole domain of winning. This is an important message for children who are struggling to develop their skills and find acceptance from their peers in the sports environment.

Five Key Principles of Coaching Effectiveness Training

First, the coach must create the sports environment with norms of behavior that respect the strengths and needs of all participants. These norms will be the moral compass that helps to guide the students' behavior. Coaches can be influential figures in the minds of young children.

Second, role modeling positive behavior is an important principle of CET. If the coach models discriminatory and hostile values, the athletes will believe that he or she sanctions behavior reflecting these norms. Coaches should not expect from athletes what they are not prepared to role model themselves. An important question for parents to consider is whether the coach teaches these young athletes how to respectfully handle success and gracefully cope with defeat.

Next, CET recommends that athletes become involved in the decision-making processes. Some of the principles of differentiated instruction invite children to decide the pacing and focus of their practices. Allowing kids who have a fragile confidence to choose a manner of participating that they perceive as being safe is certainly preferable to coercing them to play in an overwhelming context. Athletes being coached by someone who received CET reported having lower levels of anxiety (Smith, Smoll, & Barnett, 1995).

Fourth, the CET program asks coaches to create a sports culture that promotes respect, fun, and personal achievement rather than emphasizing the outcome. Research suggests that these programs have produced lower athlete attrition rates (Barnett, Smoll, & Smith, 1992). They also significantly raise the self-esteem of all participants; children with the lowest ratings of self-esteem showed the greatest increases under this program (Smith, Smoll, & Curtis, 1979).

The last principle is the positive reinforcement of effort and behavior. Positive reinforcement and behavior (respectful of the stated norms of the group) help the athletes develop their sense of trust and connection to their coach and the program. What might this achieve? A research study has shown that coaches trained in CET had more athletes returning to the sport the following year (95%) compared with a rate of 74% of returning athletes for coaches not trained in CET (Barnett et al., 1992).

Coaching Expectations and Athletes with Challenges

Research in education has long pondered the significance of a teacher's expectations of a child's academic performance. The *Pygmalion effect* (Rosenthal & Jacobsen, 1968) was a term used to describe the idea that a teacher's beliefs about a student (even if the beliefs were erroneous and based on inaccurate information) would lead the student to change his or her behavior based on the teacher's expectations. This self-fulfilling prophecy has damaging consequences for children who are not expected to achieve to a desired standard.

Coaches working with children who have various challenges have to overcome the stereotypes, the myths of incapability, and the misinterpretations of these athletes' motives for participation if they wish to effectively coach these children. Having low expectations for children with challenges has often been used as an excuse to deny them authentic opportunities.

Even if the coach does hold positive expectations for all athletes, these expectations must not be fixed. In the *sustaining expectation effect* (Weinstein, 1994), the athlete's performance plateaus because the coach did not adjust his or her expectations of the athlete's capabilities even though the athlete had made progress.

Expectations are communicated to the athlete through task assignments, the feedback given by the coach, peers, and parents. The quality of the athlete–coach interaction also powerfully conveys expectations for the athlete. This returns us to one of the key themes of this book: A coach who sets a positive tone, creates a rewarding culture, provides authentic experiences, values all children, and believes in helping them to fulfill their potential avoids the pitfalls associated with low athlete expectations.

One Mistake Is One Too Many for Some People

The soccer team we were playing had traveled all day to get to our field. The game was close and one of their players had a great chance to score. He fumbled the ball at his feet and made a mess of his shot. The coach—who had been shouting aggressively throughout the whole match—went absolutely berserk. He immediately substituted the player and ranted about how he had let the side down and that a kindergarten kid could do better. The player looked like a balloon that was suddenly burst by a sharp pin. The coach just would not let up; he shouted that this player might as well take his boots off and throw them away. I can't imagine what the long journey back home was like for that player. I doubt it was fun. It's hard to believe that coaches are allowed to treat players like that.

Story from a Newly Qualified Elementary School Teacher

From the very first day of kindergarten, children seem to become their most excited when it is time for their PE class. PE is synonymous with fun. Who wouldn't love running around outside with friends playing soccer or going for a jog around the school? Every child loves to run and play outside, right? Unfortunately, not all children share the same passion for physical activity. Growing up in a school that prides itself on remarkable coaching and winning sports teams can be difficult if you struggle with your weight. I have had a weight problem all my life and have never felt more aware of it as when I was attending school.

Getting changed in front of everyone, struggling through countless laps around the field, and having to do fitness tests with the class athletes were some of the hardest moments that I encountered growing up.

This is not to say that PE was never fun for me. Like almost every person I know, I love having fun. I love to play. If I could play in every class at school I would be in heaven. For those PE classes where the teacher incorporated fun and play into the lesson I was in heaven and would exhaust every ounce of energy from my body running around the pitch having the time of my life with my friends (while at the same time being completely oblivious to the fact that I was doing physical activity—something I usually feared!). With a fun PE lesson planned and a multitude of different activities scheduled I was able to successfully partake in classes at the same level of my peers who were much fitter and more athletically versatile than I was. This wonderful integration and differentiation seemed to slowly disappear as I aged, and I found that as I got older, teachers seemed less inclined to keep the fun and play in fitness and would much rather have everyone doing the same thing (regardless of ability and confidence).

It was clear to me at the high school level that we were no longer in PE to have fun but to keep fit or, in some cases, just lose weight. How does this feeling in a child motivate them to try their hardest in each class? I can tell you it doesn't. It pushes them even further away from physical activity and continues to bring fear and self-consciousness into the child. I feel that it is important to focus on integration and differentiation in PE so that every child is given a chance to shine.

Success can be found in the smallest of personal victories and PE can be an amazing place to foster this theme.

Final Thoughts

The teaching techniques discussed throughout this chapter can be effective if they are matched to the student's unique learning style or preference. Utilizing multiple ways to instruct, praise, and reinforce the class's efforts is critical in reaching every student. Coaches and teachers are encouraged to develop relationships with students and engage in discussions with the student and parent as to what works best for the individual. This collusion increases the likelihood that each student develops a lifelong interest in sporting experiences.

CHAPTER 8

Sports for Young Athletes with Physical Difficulties and Coordination and Mobility Challenges

T he movement patterns that accompany many sports require the athlete to utilize speed, skill, strength, flexibility, balance, and coordination. Difficulties in any one of these areas can compromise the efficiency of movement and present a challenge to the athlete to overcome this issue. This chapter discusses some of these challenges and makes recommendations to coaches and teachers for supporting these athletes' participation.

Coordination Difficulties

A lack of coordination in movement has been a source of frustration for many children and teenagers. Most of the activities that form the core of traditional sports programs require some degree of coordination; indeed, success in any skill ranging from a simple forward roll to a basketball lay-up needs the synchronizing of voluntary movements in an efficient manner. Sadly, 6% of school-age children will likely be diagnosed with a developmental coordination disorder (Missiuna, 1995; Smyth, Anderson, & Church, 2001). Students with movement difficulties were reported to have lower perceptions of athletic competence than students without such difficulties (Skinner & Piek, 2001). The term *ataxia* has also been used to characterize clumsiness and an unsteady gait. It is not uncommon for clumsiness to also be symptomatic of learning difficulties such as dyslexia.

Catch Me if You Can!
I couldn't catch! I was always getting hurt in PE. I broke my arm once, wrist twice, and suffered countless abrasions from falling on the playground. It became a bit of a standing joke in our family: "What's he going to hurt today?"

What Characterizes Good Coordination?

Good coordination can be observed in athletes demonstrating most of the following skill sets:

- Balance in both static activities (being still) and in movement
- Speed of reaction—starting, turning, stopping, and accelerating
- Spatial orientation—awareness of the changing environment in relation to one's own movements or position
- The ability to differentiate movements by feeling and applying the correct amount of tension or speed
- Precision, fluency, and control of rhythm and important elements in coordinated movement

Poor coordination can be observed in a child who has problems in gross motor coordination (e.g., jumping, hopping, running, walking) and fine motor coordination (e.g., tying shoelaces, manipulating pencils, and so forth). A young athlete with poor coordination is usually quite easy to identify. This is the child who often falls over in games of tag or who fails to successfully execute a simple sequence of skills. If the soccer task is to control a bouncing ball, then dribble and shoot at the goal, this young athlete will be the one who completely misses the ball or shoots so wide of the goal it becomes a throw-in. This may seem funny to teammates, but it is a source of embarrassment to the athlete and could be the result of a legitimate disorder. It should be noted that children with difficulties in coordinated movement report lower levels of perceived social support and have greater levels of anxiety than peers without movement difficulties (Skinner & Piek, 2001).

A sports coach needs to identify whether the young athlete has general (i.e., overall) coordination difficulties or sport-specific difficulties. A developmentally appropriate sports program should incorporate skills that develop the general coordination of movement before working on sports-specific skills.

When working with a young athlete with coordination challenges, it may be helpful to do the following:

- Introduce the skill that will be practiced. Discuss it verbally and demonstrate it visually by using different media, such as Boardmaker images or film clips.
- Practice the skill in a stable environment. A stable environment is one that is safe for the participant. For example, a stable environment would be a place where the student will not be ridiculed by peers and will not have time restrictions.

- Practice the skill with emphasis on increased fluency and precision (if possible).

- Practice the skill in different situations. Learning new skills in a constantly changing environment challenges the body to make adaptations (and thus improvements).

- Provide lots of praise and positive feedback at each stage. Give information that can help the athlete improve the skill, but provide practical tips as well.

There are no quick fixes when dealing with coordination challenges. Lots of practice, encouragement, sound goal setting, and mentoring will help these athletes improve. Coaching the child with poor coordination can be challenging; despite your best instructional efforts, this child may repeatedly fail to successfully complete the task. It can be frustrating, but the child who is giving his or her best effort can find it demoralizing to perceive the coach's frustrations; thus it is important to be positive and supportive. Finally, children with coordination difficulties (beyond that which is typical for a young child) should not be rushed into competitive sports; repeated failure may undermine the child's motives for participation.

Cerebral Palsy

Cerebral palsy is a permanent condition caused by damage to the area of the brain that controls movement and posture. It is often characterized by difficulties with muscle control, poor balance, muscular weakness, plus challenges with speech and the control of facial movements. Cerebral palsy can be caused by difficulties during fetal development (possibly from substance abuse), during birth (oxygen deprivation), or maybe as a result of serious head injury during infancy or infection (meningitis) (Geralis, 1991; Murphy, Yeargin-Allsopp, Decoufle, & Drews, 1993).

Children with cerebral palsy can have a broad range of intellectual abilities. A coach should not assume anything about a child's abilities until reviewing his or her records and getting to know the student as an individual. Some children with cerebral palsy can have very well-developed intellectual abilities and are capable of significant academic achievements.

There are essentially three different types of cerebral palsy: spastic, athetoid, and ataxic. The degree of muscle tone determines the movement and control the individual has. In spastic cerebral palsy tension in the major muscle groups creates erratic, jerky movements. Muscles with very little tension create limp athetoid movement. Ataxic movement patterns are a mix of tense and limp muscle control and are characterized by poor coordination. Cerebral palsy does not necessarily affect all major muscle groups. Hemiplegic palsy affects the limbs on one side of the body. A quadriplegic condition affects all limbs, and paraplegic affects the lower limbs. Some people with cerebral palsy may also exhibit dystonia, characterized by repetitive, twisting movement patterns, or hypotonia, characterized by extremely poor muscle tone, poor reflexes, and difficulties with breathing.

How to Design a Sports Program for Students with Cerebral Palsy

As with all the conditions discussed in this book, the starting point is always gathering information. Build a picture of your student's needs; try to understand his or her interests and physical capabilities. For students with this particular physical challenge a coach needs to assess how mobile the child is, which will determine the choice of activity. About 70% of people with cerebral palsy (Morrell, Pearson, & Sauser, 2002) experience chronic pain in their joints, spine, hip, and so forth. Thus, activity choice may not necessarily be guided by the athlete's interests, but by a more pragmatic desire to limit or control pain. The stereotypical assumption might be that if exercise is difficult and even painful for children with cerebral palsy, they would not want to participate. The social benefits of inclusion have already been discussed, but there is much research that supports the strength benefits of participation in exercise programs for children with cerebral palsy (Damiano & Abel, 1998; Darrah, Wessel, Nearingburg, & O'Connor, 1999).

Important Considerations When Coaching a Student with Cerebral Palsy

Sports participants with cerebral palsy often have to expend significant levels of energy to create movement. Research has shown that children with cerebral palsy can use up to 3 times the amount of energy when walking as children without this condition (Norman, Bossman, Gardner, & Moen, 2004). The coach should recognize this effort by structuring adequate rest periods based on each child's abilities.

One of the ways a human body responds to stress is by increasing muscular tension. This can compound the source of the disability for children with cerebral palsy. It is essential that this child feels comfortable and accepted in the sports environment. If not, the resulting tension can increase the spasticity of the muscles and make the movement pattern even more challenging.

Poor muscular control can also limit a child's speed of reaction to sports implements (e.g., balls, shuttles). This can make manipulative skills (throwing, catching, kicking) difficult; however, these challenges can be overcome by modifying the activity and the equipment. Tactile objects that do not easily roll away, such as beanbags, scarves, or Koosh balls, are excellent in helping this child learn to catch. Covering balls and a large paddle (table tennis bat, tennis racquet) with Velcro is a useful way of helping children with cerebral palsy learn to catch and manipulate objects.

Swimming and Cerebral Palsy

Swimming conveys significant benefits to a child with cerebral palsy, because the buoyancy helps to relieve pressure on the joints. Strength building can also be achieved by utilizing ankle and wrist weights while in the water.

There is a curious paradox that coaches should note when it comes to swimming. Water temperature brings different responses from children with cerebral palsy. Shivering in cold water usually makes muscles tense, whereas warm water relaxes them and allows them to function at optimal efficiency (irrespective of the individual's abilities). When a child with cerebral palsy becomes cold, this may increase muscle tension and, thus, the spasticity. Those with spastic palsy perform better in a warmer swimming pool. Ironically, the poor muscle tension associated with athetoid cerebral palsy means that a swimming pool with cooler temperatures is better suited to this child. The cool water may create some increased muscle tension and improved movement control. An excellent web site for resources on cerebral palsy can be located at http://www.ucp.org.

The Wheelchair Sports Movement

People who have paralysis have many opportunities to participate in sports. The *wheelchair sports movement* is impressively developed, provides many competitions (e.g., the Paralympics), and conducts research and development to help increase access to sports (and its enjoyment). These organizations are powerful advocates for participants and help to both increase public awareness of the challenges facing participants and, more important, celebrating their capabilities and successes. Coaches and teachers requiring information and resources in this area can visit http://www.paralympic.org.

The choice of sport best suited to a young athlete with paralysis should consider the degree of physical challenge. Some wheelchair sports can be operated under the power of the athlete, and endurance events such as basketball or rugby are all viable options. Some young athletes may require a motorized wheelchair to propel them, but they still have the chance to play in team sports. Static sports such as archery, lawn bowling, or cue sports (pool or snooker) are also options for athletes who are not suited to kinetic sports. Winter sports offer some intriguing possibilities; specially designed skis and wheelchairs have given some athletes who use wheelchairs the chance to participate in skiing and ice hockey.

There may be a need for athlete advocacy or some accommodations or modifications to the program, but essentially the teaching techniques and coaching strategies for athletes who use wheelchairs are really no different from the coaching of athletes without disabilities.

Sports for Students without Limbs

It is not common for a coach to encounter a young athlete who has lost a limb. Amputations in children are usually the result of disease (usually diabetes) and have an occurrence rate of 46 per 100,000 people compared with 5 per 100,000 due to trauma (Dillingham, 2002). Thus children are too young to have accumulated the long-term damaging effects of disease. Being born without a limb is termed *limb difference* and has an incidence of 25 per 100,000. Again, it is not a common occurrence. But for the few children who are without limbs, sports can still be a meaningful and desirable part of their overall development.

What Issues Does the Coach of a Student with an Amputation Need to Consider?

An athlete moving an amputated limb uses a lot more energy than someone who is able bodied. People who have an above-the-knee amputation use 65% more energy to walk at a casual pace than someone with healthy limbs. A person who has two above-the-knee amputations expends almost three times as much energy to match the pace of a friend without this challenge (Gaily, Gailey, & Sendelbach, 1995). Thus, these young athletes tire much sooner than their peers. It makes the achievement of Terry Fox, who ran one marathon (26 miles) every day for 143 days, so remarkable (see the introduction to Section II). Although his attempt to run across Canada to raise funds for a cure for cancer was sadly curtailed by lung cancer, the Terry Fox Foundation has raised over $400 million.

Prosthetic limbs give the athlete a range of options that can allow for full participation. The mechanics of movement and the design of the prosthesis is an advanced science; the coach does not need to understand how such devices work, but encourage information sharing with the athlete and parent to design appropriate activities. Once a few modifications or accommodations are made (which are specifically designed for the athlete), there is very little difference between a child with a prosthesis and typical young athletes. What is most important is that students feel included with their classmates and encouraged to participate fully whenever possible.

A Checklist to Help Students with Physical Challenges to Participate in Sports

Assessment

❑ Determine the motives for this child's participation in this sport or activity.

❑ Identify the child's strengths and interests.

❏ Determine what activities work well with this child.

❏ When the child encounters difficulty in physical activity, how does he or she respond? Does the child experience fatigue or frustration, or does the child display a sense of resignation?

❏ What medical conditions threaten this child's safe participation in sports?

Example: Atlantoaxial joint (neck joint) instability in children with Down syndrome can make gymnastics (forward rolls) potentially life threatening.

Designing a Safe Learning Environment

❏ Is the sports playing surface safe and appropriate for this child?

❏ Can the activities be presented in a manner that is challenging, safe, and gives the child a sense of control?

Example: Modify the activity by skill complexity, time allowed to complete the event, the way the equipment is used, and so forth.

Coaching Techniques

❏ Use the assessment information to mold your coaching style around the child's physical capabilities.

❏ Challenge and support the whole child. If the student cannot physically execute a particular skill or task, challenge him or her intellectually or provide responsibilities that signify importance and belonging.

❏ Role model compassion, understanding, and acceptance.

Differentiation Strategies

❏ What are the child's interests?

❏ Is there a particular style identified in the multiple intelligence nomenclature that best describes the way this child learns?

❏ Will the coach's predominate style of teaching meet the needs of this student?

❏ What is the child's readiness for increased challenge? Does this child need more time to develop core fundamental skills? If those skills are in place, can this child work with his or her peers on complex tasks?

❏ How will the coach present the content of the program in a manner that best suits this child? Consider the flexible groupings, choice boards, and so forth.

Final Thoughts

Athletes with physical challenges can have a highly visible presence in a sports environment. To promote the inclusion and full acceptance of athletes with these challenges, coaches and peers need to understand and be sensitive to the difficulty this person may be experiencing.

CHAPTER 9

Sports for Young Athletes with Attention-Deficit/ Hyperactivity Disorder

C hildren who have consistent difficulties in managing their behavior often attract the attention of observers. Harsh judgments that label these students as bad people and also question the quality of the parenting they receive can exacerbate the difficulties of behavior regulation. Such judgments likely ignore the possibility that an underlying condition may be contributing to these behaviors. This chapter focuses on attention-deficit/ hyperactivity disorder (ADHD) and discusses its influence on a student's learning and behavior in sports.

Attention-Deficit/Hyperactivity Disorder

ADHD is perhaps one of the most widely known disorders. This disorder may also be one of the most misunderstood. It has been popularized by articles in magazines, web sites articulate weird and wonderful theories about its origins, and it is discussed on radio chat shows. ADHD has provided a bonanza for the "snake-oil" salesman offering all kinds of cures for this condition. Ask the layperson what ADHD is and he or she will describe behaviors using terms like *inattentive, disruptive, argumentative,* and *impulsive.*

Parents, informed that their child will not sit still in class and is struggling to learn, too often conclude that the child has ADHD. A similar self-diagnosis is given to the teenager who acts impulsively and without thinking of the consequences of his or her actions, or the adult who cannot concentrate for more than a few minutes. ADHD is often viewed as something that the individual can control with more self-discipline. The suggestion is that an

uncooperative student lacks this self-discipline and must be deliberately sab-
otaging efforts to help him or her. Children with this condition are exhorted
to try harder to sit still. Teenagers are told to be more "responsible" and sanctioned for any transgressions. The adult is told to improve work concentration skills or risk a poor performance evaluation. The truth is, ADHD is a
recognized and serious clinical condition, and those affected by it sometimes
endure a lifetime of interventions and medication to manage it.

What Is Attention-Deficit/Hyperactivity Disorder?

The American Psychiatric Association (2000) has identified three areas that
are needed to meet a diagnosis of ADHD:

• Inattention, which must be age inappropriate

• Hyperactivity, characterized by excessive fidgeting and having difficulty
  in playing calmly

• Impulsivity, a tendency to act without age-appropriate judgment

A study (Pastor & Reuben, 2008) on the prevalence of ADHD noted that
9.5% of boys and 5.9% of girls have received such a diagnosis. It is more than
likely that coaches and teachers will have athletes who have this condition
to some degree. As with many of the conditions discussed in this book, a
diagnosis of ADHD is seldom straightforward. The symptoms may vary with
intensity, frequency, and duration. It is also possible to have an ADHD diagnosis but with a predominance of some characteristics more than others. Two
subtypes are widely used: hyperactive-impulsive predominance and inattentive predominance. A young athlete with a diagnosis of ADHD can manifest
many more symptoms than not being able to sit still (hyperactivity) and not
being able to concentrate (inattention).

How the Executive Function System of the Brain Is Connected to Attention-Deficit/Hyperactivity Disorder

Increased understanding of ADHD has emerged from studies of the executive functioning system, which is located at the frontal and prefrontal areas
of the brain (Brown, 2000). Understanding this system's functions makes it
clear how impairment can present significant challenges for someone with
this issue.

The executive function system of the brain is responsible for inhibi-
tion, persistence, planning, motor control, and social fluency. Some research
(Sieg, Gaffney, Preston, & Hellings, 1995) has suggested that in those with a
diagnosis of ADHD, this region of the brain has decreased levels of cerebral
blood flow compared to that of people without an ADHD diagnosis, thus
accounting for impairments in the skills that it controls.

The compliant young athlete is easy to teach. This athlete simply does the things the coach asks. Conversely, athletes who have a degree of dysfunction in this system of the brain struggle to suppress impulsive ideas that come into their head. You may hear questions such as "What were you thinking?" as the child is remonstrated for an inappropriate behavior—but it is quite possible that the athlete was not thinking (i.e., weighing actions and consequences) at all. These young athletes may also have difficulties in applying self-regulation of arousal; they may become "hyper" and unable to bring themselves "down," much to the chagrin of coaches or parents. Difficulties with moral reasoning are not uncommon for someone experiencing challenges in this system.

Organizing and Planning Activities and Sustaining and Regulating Attention

Difficulties with these skills present ongoing challenges in this athlete's development. Sports activities that last lengthy periods (e.g., soccer games) prove taxing. An athlete with ADHD who makes mistakes—as a direct result of being inattentive—can attract criticism from teammates and coaches. This young athlete can be perceived as not being interested in the game. Coaches and peers are more likely to be understanding (or forgiving of errors) if the athlete carries a visible challenge. When the challenge cannot easily be recognized and is misunderstood, the athlete's errors are criticized as a lack of effort or application (Barber, Milich, & Welch, 1996).

Coordinating the Management of Emotions

Young athletes with dysfunction in this area may have poor frustration tolerance, and this can have a significant impact on their ability to learn. Wisdom in learning from life's experiences can come from different sources; we often learn as much from our failures and setbacks as we do from our successes. The lessons learned from a situation guide us as we either repeat the task or try something new. Excessive frustration, anger, or loss of confidence not only impairs our judgment, but also prevents us from taking healthy risks or developing our skill set. Children noted for their inability to manage their emotions quickly establish a reputation and are then considered volatile, explosive, unpredictable, and so forth. This leads them to be marginalized and possibly excluded.

Selecting Sensory Information

Some children with impairment in this system manifest their challenge by being overwhelmingly excited. This athlete is described as "bouncing off the walls" and can disrupt the instructional time. Other children with the same diagnosis may experience a lack of sensory stimulation.

Using Working Memory

Working memory is a very important role of the executive function system. Working memory is the temporary store that allows us to execute a coach's instructions and refer back to him or her if we need some clarification. A child with impairment in this area has difficulty maintaining ideas and drawing on them as required. This can certainly inhibit the child's progress as increasingly complex patterns, for example, team sports tactics and skills, are introduced. The difficulties with working memory may also be responsible for other challenges such as having a poorly developed sense of time (the athlete always arrives late for practice) and not being motivated by longer term goals. This athlete requires learning support techniques to strengthen working memory.

Challenges that Can Accompany Attention-Deficit/Hyperactivity Disorder

ADHD is often accompanied by other challenges as well. Here are some statistics about challenges that can accompany ADHD:

- Forty percent of children diagnosed with ADHD are also likely to have an anxiety disorder (Tannock, 2000).

- Twenty-five percent of children diagnosed with ADHD have a learning disability (Tannock & Brown, 2000).

- Sixty-four percent of children diagnosed with ADHD may also experience Tourette syndrome (*MMWR*, 2009).

- More than 60% of children diagnosed with ADHD also have oppositional defiant disorder (Barkley, 1998).

Children with ADHD are likely to have social challenges. They can be poor at perceiving social cues (Stormont, 2001), and they are likely to experience significant social rejection because of this (Guevremont, 1990). Difficulty in following the rules of social behavior further compounds the effects of this social rejection (Barkley, 1997).

Differences Between Girls and Boys with Attention-Deficit/Hyperactivity Disorder

ADHD can be manifested by a cluster of symptoms of varying intensity, and these symptoms may express themselves at different ages and in different ways for girls and boys. In general, boys seem to be more susceptible to impulsive and hyperactivity symptoms at an early age—which may explain why more boys are diagnosed with ADHD than girls. For girls, inattention seems to be the dominant symptom, and unlike boys, who externalize their responses, girls are more likely to internalize their difficulties (Gershon, 2002). Girls may become quiet, develop perfectionist tendencies, and exhibit anxious behaviors. ADHD seems to take longer to be identified in girls and causes them to "suffer in silence" (Quinn & Wigal, 2004, p. 2).

Using the SMART Approach for Helping Children with Attention-Deficit/Hyperactivity Disorder

Stereotypical interventions to various disorders and challenges focus on what the child is not able to do rather than valuing the strengths the child may have. Nylund (2000) addressed this topic in his intriguingly titled book *Treating Huckleberry Finn*. The SMART approach suggested by Nylund has a different focus than the goal-setting usage (discussed in Chapter 3); it is a series of steps that help redefine the perspectives of a child with ADHD. The SMART approach stands for separation, mapping, attending, reclaiming, and telling. The ideas behind this approach are explained in the following sections.

Separation

In separation, the effects of the ADHD are "taken" away from the child. In this approach students receive counseling to help them consider, and then believe, that the ADHD is something that does not describe who they are. This is a person-first approach: The characteristics are separated from the person.

Mapping

During mapping, teachers, parents, and the child discuss how ADHD influences the child and the family. The idea is to put a "human face" on the condition and understand the extent of its influence on the student.

Attending

In attending, the parents and coaches interpret the unique way that ADHD affects the child. This is an important point, because not all children exhibit or experience the same characteristics of this challenge.

Reclaiming

Reclaiming refers to parents and coaches encouraging the child to focus on his or her special qualities. They all agree that the child is so much more than a few symptoms that characterize the ADHD.

Telling

Everyone supporting this individual is encouraged to share the positive view and the contributions that this young athlete can make.

Useful Teaching Techniques if You Have a Student with Attention-Deficit/Hyperactivity Disorder

- Use visual signals to help the child self-regulate behavior.

- Use proximity control. Keep the student who needs support close to you so that you can help him or her to self-regulate behavior.

- Develop a hand signal system (e.g., get the child's attention and tap your finger on your side to let the child know that he or she is starting to become disruptive or lose focus). Such systems allow the coach and student to communicate in a quiet and nonhumiliating way.

- Use visual schedules to map out the plan for the practice. This helps the athlete with ADHD make transitions from one activity to the next.

- Avoid phrases such as "You must take more responsibility!" Taking responsibility for our actions is almost a buzz phrase. Certainly we want to teach children good decision-making skills; however, making rash and impulsive decisions without careful consideration of the potential outcomes is a characteristic of ADHD. Immediate reinforcement helps the child with ADHD stay on task, remain motivated, and learn from errors of judgment (Douglas, 1983).

- Positively reinforce compliant behavior.

- Use a peer mentor to clarify the activity.

- Encourage open communication with parents or social agencies.

- Keep the instructional content relevant and not too detailed. Many children with ADHD have difficulty sustaining thoughts in active working memory. For example, if you tell a child with ADHD what to do with a long explanation, the child may have forgotten what to do by the time that he or she starts.

A Ticket to Ride . . . Somewhere!

I once had a young athlete who had both ADHD and the learning disability dyslexia. He would travel to our practices on the city bus; unfortunately for him the number 37 bus and the number 73 bus always seemed to arrive at the same time, and he would frequently get on the wrong bus. He would arrive late at our practices to a sarcastic chorus of "He's done it again!"

Practical Class Expectations for Students with Attention-Deficit/Hyperactivity Disorder

A traditional practice in school PE programs is to assess students by assigning a percentage of their overall mark for having and wearing the correct gym clothes and arriving on time for the start of the class. Difficulties organizing class materials and having poor time management are symptomatic of the challenges faced by children with ADHD. Some coaches still choose to discipline their athletes for forgetting; that principle is the same as a classroom teacher disciplining children because they cannot learn a concept! Not having the proper gym clothes has no connection to learning and should not appear in a report card about a child's progress. Rather than disciplining this child, provide learning support structures. Develop an individualized schedule or prompt so that the child has a reminder of how to prepare for class; have some spare gym clothes for the occasions when he or she forgets, positively recognize the times the child remembers, and so forth. Assign the child a mentor (perhaps a classmate) who will help him or her to arrive in class or at practice on time and prepared.

A Checklist to Help Students with ADHD to Participate in Sports

Assessment

❑ How does the ADHD manifest itself in this child?

❑ What exacerbates this condition?

❑ What strategies work well with this child or need to be avoided?

❑ What are the child's interests and strengths?

❑ What areas of the child's development are in need of extra support?

❑ How does the child respond to mentorship?

Note: The list of questions could be lengthy. The key point here is that the better your understanding of this child's needs, the easier it will be for you to design a sports environment that will create the opportunities for success.

Designing the Sports Environment

❑ Create a learning environment that minimizes distractions.

❑ Prepare the child for smooth transitions from one activity to the next. This can be simply done by explaining what the process (activity) will be and what the expectations for this student will be.

❑ If the problems emerge during unstructured times, have a plan to restrict these situations. This may be as simple as ensuring supervision or making sure that the child has responsibilities to carry out that preclude opportunities for mischief.

❑ Work with the student to identify "triggers" for him or her and help design instruction and activities to avoid them.

❑ Decide how a child with impulse control difficulties will interact with the equipment. Will the equipment be used safely and appropriately or in a potentially harmful manner?

Coaching Techniques that Work Well with This Child

❑ Consider the length of your coaching instructions; try to be as succinct as possible.

❑ Develop refocusing strategies (perhaps a visual cue) for the children who have difficulty reconnecting with the activity once they have been distracted.

❑ Use a peer clarifier to assist in idea maintenance. As some students with ADHD have difficulties storing in active working memory the directions just given to them by the coach, the consequences of forgetting (or not executing the task) can be ameliorated by having a peer to remind them.

❑ Use visual schedules to support your coaching style.

❑ Be a positive mentor.

❑ Support children experiencing behavioral difficulties by being a calm, but firm authoritative figure. They will respect fairness and consistency but likely have no regard for shouting or hostility.

Differentiation Strategies

❑ Ensure the content is varied, challenging, novel, and appealing to the child's interests. If it is not, the child may become distracted and start to respond to impulsive and disruptive thoughts.

❑ Flexible grouping is an important technique for a child with ADHD. The teacher can assign activities to groups that will support this student. Teachers and coaches know that pairing certain students together may invite impulsive or reactive behaviors, and so some preventive organizing of practice groups is helpful.

❑ Match the child's intellect and physical skills with peers who can both support and challenge the child.

❑ Choice boards help children who have difficulties with active working memory to clarify or remind themselves of what the activity requires.

❑ Anchoring and scaffolding are important techniques that allow children to build on the success they are experiencing. They may serve to reinforce positive developments in the child's self-esteem.

Final Thoughts

The strategies recommended in this chapter are most effective when the coach or teacher works in partnership with the parent and athlete. The student may already be aware of the difficulties and able to identify the triggers for his or her behavior. Asking the student "What works best to help you cope?" and then presenting some of the strategies mentioned in this chapter will help to develop skills of self-regulation.

CHAPTER **10**

Sports for Young Athletes with Tourette Syndrome

Some of the challenges faced by our young athletes are invisible. Perhaps it is a specific learning disability that no one might ever notice in a sports context. Maybe the challenge is a sensory issue or a hearing impairment. Whatever the issue, athletes in a sports group can be educated to be understanding of the challenge. Sports are certainly more challenging for people who have Tourette syndrome. The characteristics of this syndrome are not only visible, but they can be intrusive and very disruptive in a sports learning situation. When these characteristics are not understood by the coach, teacher, or athlete's peer group, they can attract ridicule, which, sadly, can actually increase the severity of the symptoms.

Tourette syndrome is a disorder with a prevalence of 3 per 1,000 boys and 1 per 1,000 girls (Scahill, Bitsko, Visser, & Blumberg, 2009). This syndrome primarily manifests itself in tics. These can be physical movements known as motor tics, with the most common being eye blinking and shoulder shrugging. Vocal tics, such as throat clearing, making grunting noises or unusual sounds, and echolalia (repeating something that was just said) are most common. The greatest frequency of tics occur between the ages of 8 and 12 years (Leckman, Zhang, & Vitale, 1998). Coprolalia (shouting out swear words or other inappropriate comments) is the stereotypical view of Tourette syndrome, but this only affects about 5%–10% of people with the syndrome (Singer, 2005).

What Causes Tourette Syndrome?

Tourette syndrome has been recognized as having a genetic origin (Walkup, Mink, & Hollenback, 2006), and also seems to be connected to the dysregulation of key neurotransmitters: dopamine, serotonin, and norepinepherine

143

(Debes, Skov, & Hjalgrim, 2008). Tourette syndrome is a treatable condition (but not curable), with the drugs haloperidol or clonidine being used to control the tics. There are side effects to these medications: drowsiness, a "dulling" of thought, and weight gain are quite common. Behavioral interventions typically focus on relaxation and biofeedback techniques, while habit reversal is a technique that has been reported to reduce the incidence of tics (Himle, Woods, Piacentini, & Walkup, 2006).

People who are not knowledgeable about Tourette syndrome assume that the individual just needs to exercise more control to stop the tic from happening. Many of the motor tics are caused by involuntary muscle movements and are beyond conscious control. Some tics can be suppressed for a while, but when they are finally released they are usually intense.

Tourette syndrome is a challenging condition for it can also have secondary characteristics: About 50% of boys and 30% of girls with Tourette syndrome have ADHD. It is difficult to treat the ADHD in people with Tourette syndrome with stimulants (e.g., Ritalin, which is a common medical intervention for ADHD), as this has been shown to increase tics. Learning disabilities are also found in people with Tourette syndrome. Tics can be very tiring, and this can influence learning. Also, the medications used to control tics can lead to drowsiness and thus reduced learning. Perseveration is a characteristic of Tourette syndrome; the sufferer can find him- or herself in a loop of constantly repeating thoughts or actions. Awareness of what is happening increases stress and tension, with more tics following. Loud noise (e.g., clapping hands) has been shown to stop perseveration. Obsessive-compulsive behaviors, anxiety, and speech problems, such as stuttering and inappropriate sexual behaviors (touching), are also characteristics some individuals with Tourette syndrome may experience.

Teaching and Coaching Strategies for Children with Tourette Syndrome

The parents of a child with Tourette syndrome need to make careful choices of athletic activities. Many sports, by virtue of their design, are both exciting and stressful, which could increase the frequency or severity of tics. The child, parent, and coach should consider which environments creates too much tension (and increases the number of tics) for the athlete. Following are some teaching and coaching strategies for children with Tourette syndrome.

Help the Athlete Control His or Her Level of Stress

Coaches are advised to help the athlete control his or her level of stress by encouraging the use of self-monitoring strategies. It is likely that the athlete with Tourette syndrome will be able to identify the type of situations or interactions that increase the expression of tics. Some sports activities require a young athlete to perform with a high degree of athletic competence while under significant pressure. For example, a poor performance from a baseball pitcher can determine the outcome of the game for the whole team; this pitcher needs to be emotionally resilient in the face of criticism that may occur from this poor performance. Such roles should be avoided if a student with Tourette syndrome finds they increase feelings of anxiety.

Educate Peers About Tics

Educate peers about the potential tics caused by Tourette syndrome. Coaches are encouraged to explain to the other students how tics manifest themselves and how the student with Tourette syndrome feels when the tics happen. Education about a particular condition—whether by the coach or the student—is an important part of promoting acceptance for this child.

Communicate with Parents and Athletes

Ask both the young athlete and his or her parents for updates on the tic. For example, are the tics increasing or decreasing? What are the characteristics of the tics? What supports have been found to be helpful at home or in the classroom?

Use Positive Reinforcement

Positive reinforcement of appropriate behavior is also effective with someone who has Tourette syndrome. Recognizing the student's effort and achievement will help to reduce sources of anxiety, promote acceptance and feelings of self-worth, and thereby reduce (to some degree) the stimulus for a tic.

Encourage Self-Regulation

Encourage the athlete to self-regulate behavior. If he or she is feeling tense or is "about to explode," allow the athlete to the leave the sports environment and release the tic.

Be Prepared to Offer Reassurance

Behavioral issues are likely with someone who has Tourette syndrome. Tics generally attract the attention of onlookers. Sensitivity to the comments and observations of peers can prompt the child with Tourette syndrome to act out with behaviors ranging from anger to aggression, sadness to depression. Coaches should be mindful of such responses and be prepared to offer reassurance to this child. Again, encouraging open communication between the student with Tourette syndrome and his or her classmates is very helpful.

A Checklist to Help Children with Tourette Syndrome to Participate in Sports

Assessment

❑ How does the Tourette syndrome manifest itself in this child?

❑ Work with the parents and classroom teachers to understand what triggers the tics.

❑ How does the child respond when he or she releases a tic? Does the child become embarrassed or self-conscious?

❑ What strategies help this child to cope?

Designing the Sports Environment

❑ Anxiety is often an underlying trigger that prompts a child to have a tic. Although this child has the same interests and dreams as other children, the coach should be mindful of the game situations that might increase discomfort (anxiety). Individual sports—such as badminton, bowling, running, gymnastics, cycling, and swimming—allow athletes to exercise a high degree of personal control over their performance. If they do not perform well, they might not attract criticism from other athletes; this is not always the case in team sports, where a mistake from one athlete might determine the outcome for the whole team. I am not suggesting that all team sports should be avoided for young athletes with Tourette syndrome; a coach who helps this young athlete effectively self-monitor the levels of tension can facilitate the student's successful participation in team sports.

Coaching Techniques that Work Well for This Child

❑ A coaching style that involves lots of shouting may not work well for a child with Tourette syndrome.

❑ Create a visual signal method of communicating that allows the child to leave the situation (e.g., the class, practice) so the tic can be released in private (assuming the child has control over it).

❑ Role model respect and understanding for all students. Don't make fun of the child releasing a tic and do not tolerate teasing by classmates.

❑ Give the child lots of praise and recognition with the goal of keeping anxiety under control.

Differentiation Strategies

❑ Coaches can utilize various differentiation strategies in their practices to help students with Tourette syndrome manage their tension and anxiety levels. Group dynamics and strong personalities within groups can exert a significant influence on the learning of athletes, and it is not always beneficial. Confident young children can sometimes have an imposing manner on the sports field and either directly or inadvertently increase the anxiety of a student with Tourette syndrome. A coach can help manage such dynamics by organizing the practice groups with matching, pairing, and group management differentiation techniques; these can help to reduce the tension for the athlete with Tourette syndrome.

❑ Choice boards can be effective teaching tools for a student with Tourette syndrome. The coach could identify a series of increasingly complex skills or activities for an athlete to choose. If the athlete with Tourette syndrome is feeling relaxed, he or she could choose something that is challenging; alternately, if the anxiety level is high, the athlete might prefer an activity that does not exacerbate feelings of tension.

Final Thoughts

The characteristics of Tourette syndrome can present themselves in unique ways within the individual, thus there is no generic approach to help a students with these challenges. The coach or teacher needs to work in partnership with the student, parents, and aides to determine what works best for this student.

CHAPTER 11

Sports for Young Athletes
with Autism Spectrum Disorders

A utism is a serious developmental disability that affects the communication and social interaction skills of the individual. The severity of this condition can vary immensely, thus creating the need for the term *autism spectrum disorders* (ASDs). Increased media coverage has helped to raise public awareness by drawing attention to the difficulties people with an ASD (and their families) experience. This chapter discusses these difficulties and identifies techniques that can help support students with ASDs participate in sports.

Autism

Before I discuss the characteristics of ASDs and make recommendations to support students, it is important to dispel some popular views about this disorder. The media's increased interest in ASD has not necessarily provided clarity or advanced understanding. I have repeatedly noted how the layperson's understanding seems to default to a Hollywood definition. Dustin Hoffman's film *Rain Man* is erroneously viewed as the stereotypical example of an adult with an ASD. His character, as portrayed in the film, was in fact a savant, someone with truly extraordinary abilities. Such people are rare and unique individuals and do not represent the typical skill set of people with an ASD.

I have also noted instances of parents—and even some teachers—making an ASD diagnosis for their child or student. There will undoubtedly be some symptoms outlined in this chapter that you think describes your student or child. These symptoms should not be interpreted in isolation, and there is a real risk of using this information inappropriately. Autism is a complex disorder, and a diagnosis should only be made by licensed psychologists, pediatricians, and speech-language pathologists all working collaboratively. It should also be acknowledged that this information is not intended to be therapy for the child with an ASD. The information presented here is background knowledge that may help a teacher or sports coach understand some of the difficulties this child may face and be able to plan effective lessons or activities.

What Are the General Characteristics of a Student with an Autism Spectrum Disorder?

The characteristics of ASDs cluster into three areas:

- Impairments in communication
- Impairments in the ability to socially interact
- The demonstration of repetitive (perseveration) or stereotypical behaviors

Each of these areas is discussed in the following pages.

How Prevalent Is Autism?

Rates of autism have been estimated to be 1:150 children. However a recent study by the Centers for Disease Control and Prevention (CDC) (U.S. Department of Health and Human Services), published in *Morbidity and Mortality Weekly Report* (18 December 2009), noted that rates of autism may actually be closer to 1:108 students. The CDC has calculated that 26,000 children will be diagnosed with this condition each year (CDC, 2009).

Communication Issues

The range and skill in verbal communication for children with an ASD is vast. Some children have expressive speech that is fluent and may mask their autism; other children may be nonverbal. Some children with an ASD may have excellent comprehension (receptive speech), but limited abilities to express their understanding with words. It is not uncommon for children with an ASD to use speech only to satisfy a personal need (i.e., they may only talk because they want something) or tell you something. It is much more challenging for such children to use language for experience sharing and expressing interest in something or concern in others.

Students with an ASD may not be very good at understanding facial expressions, gestures, or other forms of body language. As so much of our communication with others is amplified by our nonverbal gestures (some research has suggested that between 80% and 90% of the communication process is nonverbal; Mehrabian, 1968), this places the child with an ASD at a significant disadvantage in social interactions. Students with an ASD may have a difficult time interpreting the signals a sports coach uses to communicate; sometimes they may not even look at the coach.

These communication issues present serious challenges for a young athlete. If the child is nonverbal, some people may assume that he or she does not comprehend the task and is not capable of making a contribution. Students with an ASD also experience difficulties understanding phrases used in common language; they attempt to make literal interpretations of phrases such as "Have you got a frog in your throat?" "Hold onto your hat!" and "What's the matter, cat got your tongue?" Teachers need to take care when using idioms or metaphors when talking with a student with an ASD. Other students are generally not aware of the challenges faced by people with an ASD. These children may be either amused or ridicule the staccato rhythms of the child who is struggling to communicate. Students with ASDs, sadly, have a difficult time being accepted by their peers in sports and other social situations.

Social Interaction Challenges

Difficulty with social interaction is also a characteristic of students with an ASD. These students may appear to display a lack of interest in pleasing people or fitting in. Again, this is problematic for a coach or peer who is looking for some sort of feedback from such a student. The egocentricity and lack of empathy that this student can exhibit is not intended to be a personal slight against other people, but often this is how it is interpreted. Studies have repeatedly shown that few people with an ASD report having friends or stable social relationships with anyone other than their parents (Bauminger & Kasari, 2000). It is a cruel irony that the need for enhanced social skills and the benefits of social interaction are compromised by this disability.

Students with an ASD also may have limited eye contact in their social interactions. Their gaze may be intensely focused on another object, and they may appear to have a "zoned-out" manner. This lack of eye contact contributes to poor emotional referencing, or the inability to interpret the actions or feelings of others. A child will look to his or her parent for reassurance, clarification, understanding, and sharing joy. A young person with an ASD does not emotionally reference the parent (or peers) in the same way a child without an ASD does; this represents a significant challenge for them. A lack of emotional reciprocation—for example, I smile at you, but a student with an ASD does not smile back or acknowledge the nonverbal communication—is also a common characteristic. This student may not be skilled in the nuances and spontaneity of play with other children.

A student with an ASD often avoids playing with his or her peers, preferring a solitary activity in which he or she can control all the variables of the play and turn it (if given the chance) into a static (and potentially repetitive) system. Play is dynamic and requires willing participants who give and take and innovate and improvise; these are skills that are difficult for children with ASDs (Gillberg, 1990; Tsai, 1998).

The psychologist Robert Selman (1981) created a developmental chart that explained how children move through different levels of friendship. The mechanism for this process, he suggested, was the child's perspective taking skills. Young children are initially based in egocentric focused friendship—"You are my friend because you do things for me." With maturity, the child starts to understand how emotions can influence friendship and that trust in another can bring social advantages ("You play games that I like with rules that I agree with"). Between the ages of 6 and 12 years, a typical child starts to engage in reciprocal perspectives; this is when the student is able to view thoughts and feelings from another's perspective (Selman, 1981, p. 12).

Students with an ASD may have very poorly developed perspective taking skills, and this can impede their ability to make friends. Students with an ASD may also have difficulties with social coordination; they can be confused by not knowing how to use feelings of trust and acceptance in play and friendship development.

Perseveration

The general public tends to notice someone with an ASD when he or she is engaged in perseveration. This is when the person repeatedly makes gestures such as hand flapping or makes body movements such as spinning or walking on tip-toes. They may also perseverate by making unusual sounds or repeating certain phrases. These characteristics invariably attract attention and can be a source of ridicule by ill-informed people. Coaches working with a young athlete who perseverates need to work with the parent to understand the best way to help the child. Although the underlying reasons for perseveration are not well understood, anxiety and uncertainty in transitions can trigger this need in the child.

Sensory Issues

Some children with an ASD experience an overreactive response to sensory input (e.g., sounds, smells, touch). These children may be overwhelmed by too much noise (e.g., basketballs bouncing in a gymnasium) or visual stimuli (e.g., the waving of a flag marking the boundaries of a playing field). Even the smell of perfume might overwhelm the children. Consequently, these children can become very stressed and may display what is known as perseveration behaviors. These behaviors can include hand flapping, toe walking, and repetitive rocking movements. But not all children with an ASD share the same sensory sensitivity, and so there are no hard and fast rules about how the child will react to different situations. Parents quickly learn which situations they need to avoid. There are also students who can be "underresponsive," and they may seek activities that provide them sensory input to satisfy a sensory craving.

The proprioceptive and vestibular systems supplement our senses, and these systems can be affected by ASD. The proprioceptive system helps the body orient itself in movement (e.g., somersaulting through the air). Proprioception takes information from all of our senses to form a gestalt, an overall impression of the information. People with an ASD can have compromised proprioceptive abilities, and so they may seek deep pressure activities to amplify their sensory input. Toe walking (walking without putting your heel on the ground), which can be a common characteristic, is an attempt to stimulate the proprioceptive system. Therapists can use elastic body belts to help children with poor proprioceptive systems feel calm and secure. Students with an ASD can also have very poor sleep habits and may benefit from weighted blankets that increase proprioceptive input. The benefits of proprioceptive stimulation can also be developed in swimming. One study noted that stereotypical autistic behaviors decreased when children with an ASD were involved in swimming programs (Yilmaz, Yanarda, Birkan, & Bumin, 2004).

The vestibular system coordinates body movement and balance. Students with an ASD who have compromised vestibular systems seem to have difficulty with changes of body orientation. Playground swings or certain gymnastic activities (e.g., forward rolls, tumbling) can easily overwhelm a child with vestibular system difficulties.

Seizures and Students with Autism

A surprisingly large number of children with an ASD (1 in 4) may experience brain seizures (Filipek et al., 2000), and the frequency and intensity of these seizures will influence the sports options available. Certainly, any sport that carries the possibility of head contact (e.g., rugby, soccer, wrestling) should be carefully prepared for or even avoided. One study noted that seizure frequency dropped if the athlete was involved in physical activity (Durstine & Moore, 2003). Coaches should not be fearful of seizures in children with an ASD, but should use the knowledge (with guidance from parents) to decide which activities are appropriate.

Autism in the Vernacular

Some people with an ASD are starting to call themselves "Auties," people with Asperger syndrome are calling themselves "Aspies," and those who view autism as something that should be cured have been called "Curebies." The idea supported by proponents of this nomenclature is that autism is a type of personality and deserves understanding and acceptance rather than curing. Auties may be offended when they hear the suggestion that they "suffer from autism."

As the father of two sons with an ASD, I can see both sides of these descriptive stances. People who are considered to have high-functioning autism can have strong language skills, they can successfully interact with others, and they can have an independent quality of life. Most people with high-functioning autism likely agree that autism is a clear part of who they are as individuals. Autism makes them unique, and why would they want to change that?

Parents of children with an ASD who are considered to be low functioning may disagree. Some children with an ASD may never speak a word, they can exhibit perseveration behaviors, and they may not function with any degree of independence. Difficulties with toilet training and self-feeding are not uncommon. Teachers or coaches of students with an ASD quickly recognize that the disorder not only manifests itself in unique ways in each child, but that the parents can have differing interpretations of what it means to their child. I would advise teachers to focus on practical strategies that can facilitate the student's full participation in sports and avoid what can be contentious debate about the meaning of autism.

Why Students with Autism May Find Sports Challenging

Along with the sensory and communication issues already discussed, the child with an ASD also experiences difficulty in movement patterns that require coordination. Clumsy physical behavior and poor gross motor skills are typical. Children with an ASD may possess low levels of physical fitness (Auxter, Pyfer, & Huettig, 1997), not necessarily because of physical hindrances, but because the child may lack the motivation to participate. Teenagers with an ASD may spend a lot of time in front of the television or the computer; these are environments that they can control and that require limited (if any) social interaction with other people. The sedentary nature of these activities contributes to poor physical fitness.

Benefits of Physical Activity for Students with Autism

Studies have shown that physical activity offers children with an ASD significant benefits:

- Frequent aerobic activity was found to increase attention span and on-task behavior (Rosenthal-Malek & Mitchell, 1997).
- Physical activity was found to be effective in modifying challenging behaviors associated with ASDs (Elliott, Dobbin, Rose, & Soper, 1994).
- Vigorous physical activities were effective in helping children with an ASD cope with their inappropriate behaviors (Lavay, French, & Henderson, 1997).

- A Japanese autism treatment program, Daily Life Therapy, developed by Dr Kiyo Kitahara, used physical activities to improve sensory integration and vestibular stimulation; this also enhanced coordination. These physical activities also reduced stereotypical behaviors, reduced anxiety, and improved the stamina of children with an ASD (Quill, Gurry, & Larkin, 1989).

- Physical activity that increased the heart rate was found to increase the prevalence of appropriate social behaviors and decrease the inappropriate behaviors (Watters & Watters, 1980).

Teaching and Coaching Strategies for Students with Autism

The parents of children with ASDs need to take an active role in helping teachers and coaches understand the needs of their child. Because there can be such variance in the symptoms of this disorder, it is unrealistic to expect those providing the sporting activities to understand what will help and what will distress the child. Following are some basic guidelines.

Provide a Structured and Predictable Learning Environment

Children with an ASD need a structured and predictable learning environment. Uncertainty is something that can create anxiety, which may produce perseveration behaviors. As some children may exhibit a lack of spontaneity in their play and show limited exploration of new situations, they may also require the assistance of an aide or mentor to help guide them in this learning environment.

Find Out the Child's Interests

Many children with an ASD have interests (sometimes in unusual areas), and this can be used advantageously in encouraging social interactions with other children. Find out what these interests are and use them as rewards for appropriate behavior. The coach should have a number of different activities planned and should change activities so that the child remains engaged.

Use the Task Variation Method

Weber and Thorpe (1992) suggested that a teaching technique known as the task variation method helped children with an ASD better retain information and skills. This technique frequently changes activities but reverts to an important skill every few minutes. Its purpose is to remind the brain that this is something important to learn and remember. For example, in one of my running classes I teach the children a technical point about their sprinting technique: to run with a bent elbow, not a straight arm (as some of them tend to do). We then practice running 40–50 m concentrating on this technical point. We play several running games (chase, tag, and so forth) but return to the technical point if the child reverts to the former straight arm technique.

Use Visual Cues

Children with an ASD greatly benefit from visual cues to help them learn. A coach or teacher may wish to create a visual schedule (a series of drawings or photos) that show the child the sequence of activities. For example, a coach might use a visual schedule to help a child understand how to get ready for gym class using pictures of a child entering the locker room, changing into gym clothes, putting on running shoes, and lining up with classmates. The computer software program BoardMaker (www.mayer.johnson.com) is a very effective tool that generates pictures that help inform or tell a story. As children with an ASD can get stressed over uncertainties and the introduction of new activities, a visual schedule helps to prepare the child for those changes.

Teach in a Brief and Clear Manner

Elaborate explanations and long periods of inactivity are challenging even for children who do not have an ASD. Teachers should introduce concepts in a precise and preferably brief manner. Visual demonstrations of the skills that are expected are a powerful reinforcement of the teaching.

Do Not Make Assumptions

Do not make the assumption that a child with an ASD is not interested in participating in sports, nor capable of learning. When sports are presented in ways that understand their needs, these children are as joyful in their play as other children.

Do Not "Dumb Down" the Lesson

To give children with an ASD a sense of achievement and responsibility, the coach or teacher should avoid "dumbing down" the activity. Set realistic goals and teach the child to ask for help if he or she is struggling.

Do Not Use Emotional Appeals

It is important that the coach or teacher recognize that an emotional appeal to the child for cooperation is not an effective teaching tool. The emotional involvement in an activity of a child with an ASD is generally egocentrically based.

Find Teachable Moments

Teachable moments occur throughout a class, and an experienced coach recognizes this and uses these opportunities to help athletes learn. This is especially important for children with an ASD. Using an emotional experience (joy of success, shared empathy for a child who has been injured) will help this child to develop emotion-sharing skills (something that is poorly developed in children with ASDs).

Become Aware of Sensory Challenges

It is important to have an awareness of the sensory challenges for the child with an ASD and identify a sensory calming area if the child feels overstimulated.
    Here are some sensory control strategies:

- Body belts that wrap around the waist have a calming effect. Squeeze balls, chewies (plastic shapes that the child can chew), and mini trampolines also help the child to satisfy sensory needs.

- Utilize Lava-Busters to help the child decompress from a stressful situation (see Chapter 7 for more information on Lava-Busters).

- Limit surprises. These can unsettle the child and may contribute to perseveration responses.

- Reward success, especially when the child makes a smooth transition.

- Give the child a countdown to transition.

- Use visual schedules to assist in transitions.

- Utilize behavioral modification techniques, for example, tokens, if they are appropriate for the child.

What Sports Are Most Appropriate for Students with Autism?

It is very important that coaches and teachers avoid the stereotypical view that a child with an ASD is not capable of full participation or may have interests only in solitary activities. I have had children with an ASD not only participate in my physical education classes without support or need for any modifications, but also make significant contributions to the success of various sports teams. I have also worked with a child who required the constant support of his aide to help him through each class. The sensory sensitivities of the child is one factor that may determine which sport is well suited to that child. In my experience working with students with an ASD, and with my own sons, activities that allow the athlete to control the pace of the game seem to be more successful for a student with an ASD. For example, the pace of some sports like basketball or soccer cannot easily be regulated by a student with an ASD, and the perceived lack of control (or involvement) may be a source of anxiety. In activities such as archery, swimming, cycling, running, and gymnastics, the athletes with an ASD can regulate their involvement, sit out if they feel anxious, and avoid becoming overstimulated.

A Checklist to Help Students with Autism to Participate in Sports

Assessment

❏ Work with parents and gather relevant background information about the child.

❏ Learn how the ASD manifests itself in this child and develop a plan to support the child's learning and overall development.

❏ What are the child's interests?

❏ What are the child's goals and/or reasons for participating?

❏ Does the child have social interaction difficulties? If so, what are the triggers?

Designing the Sports Environment

❏ Does the child have any sensory sensitivities—hypersensitivity or hypo-sensitivity?

❏ Do you need to adjust the intensity of the gym lighting? Are there activities that will generate too much noise and overstimulate this child?

❏ Is there any sensory calming equipment that you can use to help prevent the child from being overstimulated?

❏ Is there adequate space for the child to move freely? PE held in a small classroom may heighten the anxiety of a child who feels overwhelmed in confined or crowded spaces. Be willing to change aspects of the environment that seem to be agitating the child.

Coaching Techniques that Work Well for This Child

❏ The coach needs to modify voice tone and volume so as not to intimidate or overstimulate children with heightened hearing sensitivity.

❏ The coach can use an aide (perhaps a peer) to act as a clarifier, personal support, and instructional guide for this child.

❏ Short coaching instructions plus lots of modeling behavior helps this child understand what is expected.

❏ A strong use of visual schedules helps the coach convey his or her ideas.

❑ Prepare the child for transitions between activities by using a visual cueing signal (e.g., a finger tap on the child's shoulder means a transition will take place very soon).

Differentiation Strategies

❑ Although many children with an ASD are not only comfortable working on their own, but may even prefer it, working in group situations is very advantageous for learning and social development. Flexible grouping is a useful strategy.

❑ Choice boards designed with lots of visual explanations can provide appropriate activities that allow children to regulate their pace and pursue their interests within the framework of the class.

❑ The content of the activity should be modified to reflect the interests of the child and yet still tie in to the instructional and activity goals of the class. For example, my son loves trains. He is not interested in many games of tag, but becomes animated and fully involved when we play Train Tag, especially when we describe the rules of the game with train terminology.

Final Thoughts

The characteristics of ASD can present themselves in unique ways within the individual, thus there is no generic approach to help students with these challenges. To effectively support a student with an ASD, the coach or teacher needs to work in partnership with the student, parents, and aides to determine what works best for this student.

CHAPTER 12

Sports for Young Athletes with Sensory Impairments

T his chapter identifies techniques that can support the participation of students with hearing or visual challenges. Perhaps the most important point that I wish to convey is that—despite stereotypical and ill-informed opinions—young athletes with these conditions are fully capable of successfully participating if the coach provides modifications (if necessary) in the program.

Sports for Students Who Are Deaf or Hard of Hearing

Whereas some challenges are obvious to the general public, seldom is there any visible sign that a deaf child is experiencing challenges. The difference between being deaf and being hard of hearing is in the primary method of communication that the individual uses. People who are deaf may use visual methods (e.g., sign languages, lip reading) as a source of communication and understanding. Sometimes the deaf person's friend (who can hear) signs the contents of directions or a conversation. Students who are hard of hearing may have a hearing aid to assist them with sound amplification.

Some research states that girls hear significantly better than boys (Cassidy & Ditty, 2001; Cone-Wesson & Ramirez, 1997; Corso, 1959). This research has suggested that most girls have a sense of hearing that is two to four times better than that of boys. The ramifications of this on the sports field are especially significant when coaching girls. Coaches who shout (and who shout aggressively) have a more powerful effect on girls than on boys. As has been mentioned in previous chapters, take care to approach all children in a sensitive, effective manner.

Children who are deaf and hard of hearing can find a lot of success in sports. They are physically able to fully participate. As many sports are very rich in visual cues (e.g., referees pointing one way or another, goal nets used to indicate success), the simple techniques and modifications discussed in this chapter can help these children enjoy sports.

Useful Techniques for Teaching a Student Who Is Deaf or Hard of Hearing

Although it may not be practical to expect coaches or teachers to have a developed understanding of sign language, there are a number of practical methods they can employ to improve their effectiveness with children facing these challenges.

Rely on Visual Cues

A young athlete who is deaf or hard of hearing is going to rely on visual cues for learning. Coaches should complement their verbal description of a skill with a demonstration. This helps children who have hearing impairments and those who learn through visual processes.

Make Eye Contact

The coach should make a lot of eye contact with athletes who are hearing impaired. This will help the athletes understand that the communication is relevant for them. Do not make the assumption that deaf children are excellent lip readers. Lip reading is an advanced skill that can take quite some time to acquire. Some students wear amplification devices. These vary in sophistication from a hearing aid to an FM system that broadcasts directly into the ear of a child wearing a special receiver. This equipment identifies these children as being different and could be a source of teasing from peers if not closely monitored. With the parent's permission, the coach may wish to have a light discussion with the athletes about differences, needs, and how to respect them.

Watch Out for Bullying

Some children who are hard of hearing have a speech impairment. Their difficulty in hearing certain sounds inhibits phonic awareness and presents challenges with tone, pitch, and volume. This may make these children an easy target for bullying, so, again, some awareness and preemptive action on the coach's part may be necessary.

Sports for Students with Cochlear Implants

In 1990 the U.S. Food and Drug Administration (FDA) approved the use of cochlear implants for children ages 2–17 years; by 2009 almost 26,000 students had received these devices (National Institute on Deafness and Other Communication Disorders, 2009). A cochlear implant is a device that is surgically placed in the inner ear and helps the auditory nerve fibers to function properly. This device should not be confused with a hearing aid, which just amplifies sound. Cochlear implants are far more sophisticated. Their technology translates sounds into electrical signals and sends them to the brain's auditory processing center for interpretation.

The internal parts of the cochlear implant are surgically inserted in the mastoid area of the skull, where they cannot be seen. The external part of the device includes a headset with either an ear hook or a microphone to capture sounds, a microprocessor to translate sounds into electronic signals, and a transmitting coil to send the electrical signals to the internal part of the device. Protecting this device during play is important for its continued accurate functioning. Following are a few areas a coach needs to consider:

- Cochlear implants are very sensitive to the influence of static electricity. If static electricity accumulates it threatens demapping, which disables the device (Cochlear Corporation, 1996). The creation of static charges is not uncommon in certain sports activities; for example, bouncing basketballs in dry conditions can create static charges.

- Be aware that some popular synthetic sports garments are prone to static accumulation.

- Physical education items such as parachutes, juggling scarves, vinyl gymnastics mats, and plastic equipment can also accumulate electrostatic charges.

- Preventing the influence of static accumulation and demapping requires the parent or student to advise about helpful practices, such as special straps to electrically ground the device.

- The external components of the device can be removed, but this must only be done with the permission of the athlete's parents.

- The external features of the cochlear implant must be kept dry. Coaches are advised to allow an athlete with this device to wear a hat or hooded rain jacket.

- As cochlear implants are expensive and sensitive pieces of technology, physical activities that require contact (e.g., heading a soccer ball) are not recommended.

A Checklist to Help Students Who Are Deaf or Hard of Hearing to Participate in Sports

Assessment

❏ To what degree is the child hearing impaired? What communication systems does this child use to facilitate hearing (e.g., lip reading, visual signals, amplification systems)?

❑ Does this child have any adverse reactions to loud sounds? Are there sports that provide difficulties due to loud sounds (e.g., the sounds generated by bouncing basketballs, echoes in gyms)? How does this child cope?

❑ Does this child have a cochlear implant?

Designing the Sports Environment

❑ Amplification devices can be effective when used in a contained environment (e.g., the gym), although ambient noise can interfere with the child's auditory discrimination.

❑ Assist and support the child to set the volume control on amplification devices depending on the setting for the activity. These devices can be more challenging to employ in outdoor sports.

Coaching Techniques that Work Well for This Child

❑ Monitor your voice modulation. Don't shout or whisper!

❑ Consider your body position when coaching a child with a hearing impairment and place yourself so that the child can either hear or see your actions.

❑ If necessary, provide a peer to clarify the activity in case the child did not accurately hear or understand.

❑ Role model or demonstrate the activity so that even if the child did not accurately hear, he or she will be able to understand by watching your actions.

❑ Speak clearly, but don't speak down to this child. The child has compromised hearing, not intellectual challenges.

Differentiation Strategies

❑ The use of choice boards is an important differentiation technique for a student with hearing difficulties. This technique allows the student to decide which activity allows him or her to participate in a safe, confidence-building manner. For example, some gymnastics skills, especially those that involve full body rotation (e.g., forward/backward rolls), may knock a hearing aid out of correct alignment. Such activities are not inherently harmful, but a young athlete with a hearing aid may prefer not to perform that particular skill. Choice boards are a respectful way of offering activities to this athlete.

❑ Matching a young athlete with sensory impairments with students who are accepting of differences helps to increase the athlete's feeling of inclusion.

❑ It is important for a coach or teacher to recognize that a sensory impairment is not a learning impairment. This young athlete may well be gifted and have special talents that require enrichment and challenge.

❑ Coaches should ensure they organize the content of the lesson and the pace of learning to meet this athlete's learning needs and not be derailed by any modifications that are used to meet the student's sensory impairment needs.

Sports for Students with Visual Impairment

Visual impairment (which includes blindness) has been defined as "an impairment in vision that even when corrected adversely affects a child's educational performance" (Lieberman, as cited in Winnick, 2005, p. 205). Visual impairment is not a uniform condition but a term that encapsulates a large number of visual difficulties that are characterized by the degree of functionality of the visual system. Some of the terminology that you may encounter includes

- Total blindness—The student cannot perceive any light and likely requires an aide to support participation in sports.
- Partial blindness—The student can perceive some light but may experience problems with rapidly moving objects (balls, shuttles, and so forth).
- Legal blindness—The student has a visual acuity of less than 20/200. Students with this designation may be able to fully participate in regular sports programs but will benefit from some modifications in the design of the activities.

Inclusion mainstream sports activities can be challenging for some children, but coaches should avoid the stereotype that children with visual impairments (or those who are legally blind) are not capable or interested in sports. It is easy to fall into the trap of thinking, "How can a blind child play basketball?" These views must be avoided. Butcher (2002) has reported on the significant benefits of physical education for people with visual impairments. It should be acknowledged, however, that research has also suggested that frustrations and disappointments with the sporting experience can lead young athletes with visual impairments to perceive that physical activity has few benefits (Sherrill, 1998). It has been suggested that students with visual impairments generally have fewer sports opportunities than other students and that many community sports organizations are either unsure how to accommodate or unable to accommodate young athletes with visual impairments (Longmuir & Bar-Or, 2000). That does not have to be the case.

I have taught a student who had the designation of "legally blind" but who was fully included in our physical education program. She could run as well as anyone. She could play basketball but did experience difficulty with depth perception. She enjoyed playing badminton with a very slow-moving, soft ball. These young athletes are well suited to sports in which they can control the speed and direction of movement. Gymnastics, swimming, and running can allow the child to be comfortable with the environment. Fast-moving sports, especially those that require the visual tracking of objects (e.g., badminton shuttles, footballs, hockey pucks) can be more challenging.

Although total blindness may require a sports program to be modified in significant ways, other visual impairments can require very few modifications. In the next section I suggest some practical techniques that you can use to facilitate the participation of an athlete with visual impairments in your sports program.

Useful Techniques for Teaching Students with Visual Impairments

Children with visual impairments often have delays in their overall skill level, so the coach should assess and then determine the skills that will be appropriate for these children. Following are some useful techniques for teaching children with visual impairments.

Use Verbal and Sound Cues

Place greater emphasis on verbal cues to help these children learn what is expected. Sound cues can also alert a child with visual impairments of changes in the game; for example, in a game of tag, the chaser could run with a tambourine to alert the child with impairments of the proximity of the chaser. In the swimming pool devices that emit a special tone can guide swimmers across the pool. Soccer balls and table tennis balls can be filled with small ball bearings so that they emit sounds that help a student with visual impairments track the object.

Enhanced Visual Cues

A coach could use bright tape (e.g., in neon colors) to mark a target or boundary such as lines on a basketball court. For example, a child playing basketball might have some bright tape added to the ball to help him or her track the ball's movement. The tape also might be added to the backboard to help improve the athlete's visual clarity.

Use Tactile Cues

Students with significant visual impairment or total blindness can benefit from participation in swimming. The swimming lane ropes provide a tactile sense of the student's position in the water. To prevent the athlete from swimming into the wall, two techniques can be of assistance. The first uses a water sprinkler one or two strokes before the wall; when the swimmer feels the splashes from the sprinkler, he or she becomes aware of the end of the pool. In the second technique a coach or friend gently taps the swimmer on the head using a bamboo pole (with a tennis ball on the end to soften the impact).

Encourage Running Sports

Running is also a desirable sport for athletes with visual impairments, and they can be particularly successful on running tracks as it is a predictable surface. Running does present difficulties in cross country or road running because the depth perception of constantly shifting terrain can be overwhelming. Assisted running is a technique in which the athlete with visual impairments uses a tether attached to a friend who runs by the side. This requires a degree of trust and practice to be effective. Another technique is having the partner runner forgo the tether and use words to guide the runner.

Use Guided Discovery

Guided discovery is a teaching method that has been shown to be effective for students with visual impairments (Rich, 2000). This technique allows athletes to learn at their own pace in an environment that provides security but also challenge and uses equipment that is appropriate for their skill level.

A Checklist to Help Students with Visual Impairments to Participate in Sports

Assessment

❑ Talk to the child and his or her parents to learn how the visual impairment presents itself and what accommodations the child currently uses.

❑ Does the child have difficulty tracking fast-moving objects (e.g., shuttles, soccer balls)?

❑ How is this child's depth perception? Can the child run on uneven ground, or does running on uneven ground present physical difficulties?

❑ How does the child cope with changes in light intensity?

❑ Does this child use any specialized equipment to facilitate participation?

Designing the Sports Environment

❑ Use the assessment information to modify, where necessary, the sports environment.

❑ Modifications may include dimming the light intensity of a gym or using large sports equipment that helps the child to increase his or her tracking ability.

❑ Use items that move a touch slower than typical equipment; for example, badminton shuttles can move at different speeds.

❑ If the child cannot successfully track the shuttle, use a larger racquet (perhaps a squash racquet). You could even use a balloon just to develop the child's sense of hitting a moving object.

❑ Use brightly colored tape to highlight boundaries in the gym (e.g., to create lines on the floor).

Coaching Techniques that Work Well for This Child

❑ Write instructions on a notice board in large print.

❑ Clarify your instructions verbally, speaking slowly (but not with condescension) and clearly.

❑ Role model compassion and understanding so that the other children accept the difficulties visual impairment presents to this child.

❑ Recognize the effort this child makes to complete the tasks assigned.

❑ Find ways of creating success.

Differentiation Strategies

❑ Organize the content to match the child's visual tracking abilities.

❑ Match the child with children who are positive and supportive. These mentors will be understanding if the child makes mistakes.

❑ Use a CW chart to match the content to what the child would like to achieve (see Chapter 6 for information on CW charts).

Final Thoughts

Promoting the inclusion of students with visual and hearing impairments in sports is very practical and can be extremely successful. A coach designing a program with some of the modifications discussed in this chapter should find that athletes with these challenges will develop fitness, improve their self-esteem, and develop positive attitudes toward sports.

CHAPTER 13

Sports for Young Athletes with Height and Weight Differences

E xtremes in height and weight can either confer a significant advantage or present a significant challenge to a participant in sports. Stereotypical views would suggest that certain physical attributes seem suited to advanced performance in certain sports. It is easy to believe that a flexible young girl might be attracted to gymnastics, or a tall, powerful young boy might be interested in basketball. In the same fashion, it would be erroneous to think that an overweight student has no interest in endurance events, or a small-statured person does not want to play a sport where height is an advantage. In this chapter I hope to dispel some of these stereotypes and convey the view that successful participation in sports reflects the interests of the child and is not limited by physical attributes.

Height Issues

Although there are many factors that determine athletic success, an athlete's height is often considered to be a marker of athletic potential. Athletes with long limbs who move with good coordination and biomechanical efficiency are likely to be at an advantage over shorter athletes. Certain sports offer greater opportunities for success to tall athletes, such as basketball, volleyball, and high jump. Activities that require rapid changes in direction offer a distinct advantage to smaller people, such as diving, gymnastics, and skating.

What Determines a Person's Height?

Physical growth is determined by the release of the hormone somatotropin (also known as human growth hormone). This is released from the pituitary gland centered in the brain and prompts the secretion of other hormones also connected to growth (e.g., IGF-1). Exercise is known to help stimulate the release of these hormones, and eating a healthy diet also helps to maximize the genetic potential for height. Some people have either excessive or restricted growth, and this can have a significant influence on their participation in sports.

Extreme Height

Extreme height is a rare condition, and it is unlikely that a coach will encounter a student with gigantism. This condition, caused by excessive secretions of the pituitary gland, can result in growth to heights of 7–8 feet. For young athletes who are tall and physically healthy, the challenges often emerge out of stereotypes about their interests and capabilities.

Breaking the Mold

I was already 6′2″ by the time I was 14 and like my friends I enjoyed my sport. My teacher wanted me to be a basketball player—basically I was to stand under the net, catch, and shoot. Thing was, I really like running. I can vividly remember my teacher telling me that I was too big to be a runner, and he seemed to go out of his way to dissuade me. I did take up running and actually did quite well.

People make assumptions about tall children; they consider these children to be more developed, advanced, and maybe even more mature just because they look that way. It almost seems incompatible that a young child—who just happens to be very tall—might want to play in the sandbox. The emotional needs of tall children are just as sensitive as those of any other child, and assuming otherwise is harmful.

Dwarfism

Dwarfism is primarily a genetic condition, but dysfunction in the pituitary gland can also be the cause of this condition. There are almost 200 types of dwarfism, and they are characterized by variances in limb length. The most common form is achrondroplasia, with almost 70% of cases having the characteristics of a long trunk and short arms or legs (National Institutes of Health, 2008). The average height for someone with achrondroplasia is around 4′4″. Many of these children have delayed development of motor skills, and they may experience trouble in breathing; this obviously has some bearing on their performance level in sports. However, young athletes with dwarfism are capable of full participation in just about any sport. The most significant challenges they will likely encounter are limiting attitudes and stereotypes.

A Checklist to Support the Participation in Sports of Students with Extremes of Height

Assessment

❑ Is there a medical reason that precludes this athlete's safe involvement in sports?

❑ Does this sporting opportunity preserve the dignity of the athlete with extreme height difference?

❑ Will this student receive an authentic experience by participating?

Designing the Sports Environment

❑ Are any equipment modifications needed to ensure the safety of this participant? For example, does your program have equipment that safely fits this student's size?

❑ Do the activities that you teach need to be adjusted to help this student participate?

Example: In a track and field class, high jump is a popular option, but generally the athletes jump one at a time. A student who is small may be ridiculed when he or she fails even to get close to the bar. Anticipating that this may be a problem, the coach should design some accommodations; for example, have a series of stations that the athletes can rotate through. Have only students who are small work at the high jump station (cluster grouping).

Coaching Techniques that Work Well for This Child

❑ Use an influential figure to role model support and understanding for the difficulties these students may be experiencing.

❑ Make sure you do not make stereotypical assumptions about these students' interests, skills, or motivation.

❑ Involve the students in choosing activities. They know their capabilities and where their difficulties lie.

Differentiation Strategies

❑ Use flexible grouping or cluster grouping when assigning students to various activities.

❑ Use anchoring and scaffolding techniques to build on the confidence and skill set of the student with extreme height.

❑ Skills requiring good coordination can be difficult for some students who have extreme height. The coach may need to break some skills down into their components and have the student practice them separately before trying to combine them into one complex movement.

Body Image Dissatisfaction and Body Distortion

Everybody wants to look good and feel positive about him or herself. It is something in the human psyche that has fueled the fashion, cosmetic, weight loss, and fitness industries as they understand that we are prepared to spend huge sums of money to ensure we look great. In Western societies certain body shapes convey advantage in highly prized careers. We are bombarded with messages that beautiful and successful people are generally lean females (the supermodel) and muscular males (the successful athlete). We are not a culture that particularly values physical bodies that are overweight. In other cultures being overweight (especially for females) is highly regarded. For the Khoikhoi of South Africa, obesity is a sign of beauty; in Zambia, it is a sign of wealth and achievement.

Young children are absorbing the message that you must have a body shape that conforms to an idealized standard. As ridiculous as this message is, its effect is becoming increasingly influential. Research has shown that children as young as 8 years old were already dissatisfied with the way that they feel about their body shape. In this study, 55% of girls and 35% of boys were unhappy with their body shape (Wood, Becker, & Thompson, 1996).

A Breakdown on the Road to the Olympics
Running came easy to me. Every step that I took seemed to bring instant success. I won every sports day, every cross country race, and regional championships. Before I knew it, I was racing at the national level and believed I was on the path to the Olympics. But I destroyed myself. Looking back, I can see how it happened. I was always very light, and that, matched with my talent, contributed to my success. As I went through university I became obsessed with achieving the perfect workout. I wanted only As in my studies. I could only see flaws in my friends. I became exceptionally fussy about my food and would only eat organic pastas, wild rice, and so forth. I started to lose weight but that didn't seem to harm my running. If anything, I ran even better . . . for about 4 months. Then one day I developed a bad pain in my hip. I ran through it but the pain increased. One month later I was diagnosed with a severe stress fracture in both my pelvis and hip. The doctor said that I had driven my body into the ground and it was no longer absorbing calcium. I became impossible to be around and eventually was coerced into receiving some counseling. My perfectionism brought me down. I didn't run in the Olympics.

Inaccurate perceptions of how we look—something that has been termed *body distortion*—can also occur when a child has a poor self-image. Body distortion was found to affect 46% of high school girls. These girls believed that they were overweight when, in fact, only 12% (in this study) were actually overweight (Greenfield, Quinlan, Harding, Glass, & Bliss, 1987).

Distortion of the Facts
I coached a woman who was a triathlete. She ran almost 90 miles a week, cycled 3–5 hours a day, and competed in several Ironman competitions. She hated to be seen in her bathing suit because she believed she had excess fat on her legs. She weighed 115 pounds!

Body distortion and dissatisfaction have both been identified as predictors of eating disorders (Stice, 2001), although they only contribute part of the picture. Other influences may include psychological factors (e.g., low self-esteem, anxiety, depression), interpersonal factors (e.g., difficulties in relationships with others, adverse experiences including marginalization, bullying, excluding behavior from peers), and external factors (e.g., dieting, excessive exercising). All of these factors may combine to contribute to the onset of an eating disorder.

One area that is worthy of further comment is the way that sports are presented to children who are already susceptible to an eating disorder. Many school programs have mandatory participation in physical education—that in itself is not a bad thing. However, the children are expected or coerced into playing traditional sports that emphasize either leanness or profoundly muscular bodies, such as basketball, football, soccer, and so on. The lack of success that these children experience, combined with the low self-image they already have, not only about their sports ability, but also the way they look and feel, increases the potential for them to develop an eating disorder.

Dead Last in the Races on Sports Day

I was born fat—11.5 pounds at birth, to be exact. I was fat in my childhood and was always last in the races on sports day. I was fat in my teen years and this limited my capabilities in the team sports that my parents wanted me to play. I can remember really trying hard to be a good hockey player like many of my friends, but I used to fall down a lot and that hurt. I've had to put up with a load of #**#&! It seems that I have never known anything else when it comes to sports. Hardly the stuff of happy memories, is it? Am I happy with myself now that I am an adult? You do eventually come to a point where you accept the way things are, but I must admit, I wish things hadn't been so tough as a kid playing sports. It's not fair to be considered a joke and a total loser.

Body image dissatisfaction and body distortion can express itself in different ways for each gender. In girls it can be manifested in excessive dieting, anorexia, bulimia, or binge eating. Whereas boys may also exhibit similar behaviors, image dissatisfaction can also be a spur for steroid abuse. Research has shown that young males are increasingly turning to steroids to enhance sports performance and also to alter their sense of self-image. The Youth Risk Surveillance survey of U.S. high schools (1999) noted that almost 5% of students have used steroids—this roughly equates to 500,000 students. Given the very serious side effects that accompany steroid use, this is a troubling issue.

Eating Disorders

Sports do not always attract healthy participants. Sometimes the young athlete can be quite ill with an eating disorder and be in need of support and professional intervention. Two conditions that a coach or teacher may encounter are anorexia nervosa and bulimia nervosa.

Anorexia Nervosa

Anorexia nervosa is characterized by the individual having a distorted body image and a fear that he or she may gain weight. The individual invariably embarks on a ruthless dieting regime, counting calories or obsessively researching the fat content of foods he or she is about to eat. This person becomes determined to lose more and more weight. As is the case with a number of mental health disorders, the individual is often unaware of the personal harm of this illness and may also become defiant toward any attempts to help him or her.

Skipping meals, eating only low-fat foods, undergoing dramatic weight loss, and using dialogue that states a concern for being overweight are also characteristics of someone either approaching or experiencing anorexia. In females, as they start to lose a significant amount of weight, their bodies start to consume muscle mass. Eventually, their menstrual cycle stops. Missing three menstrual periods is an indicator of anorexia.

Anorexia nervosa can become prevalent in young teenagers, with girls being more likely to experience such illness than boys. Preteenagers have also been identified as exhibiting the characteristics of these conditions.

Bulimia

A companion condition to anorexia nervosa is bulimia. Sufferers from this condition eat a full meal and then attempt to reduce their calorie intake by inducing vomiting (something also known as purging). Repeated vomiting episodes have been known to cause dental issues (due to the acid content in the vomit). Sadly, almost 50% of people with anorexia also develop bulimia (NIH Publication No. 93-3477, 1993).

How Do You Coach or Teach an Athlete with a Suspected Eating Disorder?

A coach or teacher's primary responsibility is the safety of the athletes. A coach is abrogating his or her responsibility to the athletes by continuing to coach them (and worse, pushing them hard) when an athlete is suspected of having an eating disorder. Young athletes experiencing eating disorders should be under the care of a pediatrician or other medical professional. Eating disorders are very serious conditions—potentially life threatening—and the coach should only allow this athlete to participate with written guidelines from the doctor. The coach is not a therapist and should avoid the clichéd myths of treatment (e.g., "You've just got to learn to love yourself; then you will be all right").

Research on eating disorders and sports has shown these conditions to be disturbingly widespread. Sports like dance (Hamilton, Brooks-Gunn,

Warren, & Hamilton, 1986), gymnastics (Rosen, McKeag, Hough, & Curley, 1986), and distance running (Katz, 1986; Yates, Leehey, & Shisslak, 1983) seem to attract women who may have a disposition to eating disorders. Burckes-Miller and Black (1988) investigated a connection between bulimia and the attitudes of athletes. Almost 700 athletes were interviewed. Almost 33% of these athletes reported being preoccupied with food; 24% had recurring binge eating episodes; and 15% had a distorted body image. A study of participants at the National Collegiate Athletic Association (NCAA, 1991) level reported that evidence of eating disorders were more likely to be found in gymnastics and cross country running for women and in wrestling and cross country running for men.

It is important to acknowledge that not all children who are thin are suffering from anorexia. Coaches and teachers should not be quick to leap to that assumption. If in doubt, consult with the parents about the child's eating habits, energy levels, self-concept, and so forth. If the parents are forthcoming with this information, it will help you decide just how much exercise is appropriate for this young athlete. Caution is always the best approach.

Sports for Students Who Are Overweight and Obese

Many of the challenges discussed throughout this book are noted for their debilitating influences on children. Our societies have responded by funding research and creating social policies to guide our actions in helping these people with challenges. If a child has difficulties in school, he or she might be given an aide; if a child needs extra time to study, the learning programs can be modified. If parents need some help, there are support groups offering advice and respite. But when it comes to helping children (or adults) who are obese, we are still not sure quite how to tackle this complex issue. Rather than being the exception, people who are overweight and obese are increasingly becoming the norm. Yet very little research or community sports programming exists on how to motivate people who are obese to exercise, how to support their adherence to exercise programs, or how to modify the exercise environment in ways that preserves their dignity and is actually fun.

Obesity: The Raw Data

Obesity is a condition in which the body has stored fat well in excess of healthy limits. Various methodologies are used to define obesity; perhaps the most widely accepted is the body mass index (BMI). The weight (in kilograms) is divided by the individual's height (in meters, then squared). A BMI in the range of 20–25 is considered typical and likely carries low risk factors for disease. A BMI of higher than 30 gives the individual an obese designation.

The numbers of people struggling with obesity mean it is not some fleeting epidemic, but a clear societal trend. Children and adults are increasingly carrying excessive weight, and this is supported by a wealth of statistical data from nations across the Western Hemisphere. The numbers paint a bleak picture for the well-being of a whole generation:

- The Office of Disease Prevention and Health Promotion reported that 33% of people are either overweight or obese (Wright, 2008).

- One study noted that 61% of children (ages between 5–10 years) who are obese have at least one of the risk factors for heart disease, while 27% had two or more risk factors (Freedman, Zuguo, Srinivasan, Berenson, & Dietz, 2007).

- Thirteen percent of American children have obesity (NCCDPHP, 2007), with 30% of 6- to 11-year-olds rising to 50% of 16- to 19-year-olds being overweight (National Health and Nutrition Examination Survey, 2002).

- Data reveal that children who are obese are highly likely to become obese adults (Epstein, Wing, Koeske, & Valoski, 1987), and the risk is highest among children who have two parents who are obese (Dietz, 1983).

- One study of the impact of obesity on the American health system (Wolf & Colditz, 1998) estimated the financial costs to be close to $100 billion.

> Pediatric obesity may shorten life expectancy in the U.S. by 2–5 years by mid-century— an effect equal to that of all cancers combined (Olashansky et al., 2005, as cited in Ludwig, 2007).

- The British Department of Health (2006) has reported that 25% of adults are obese and 66% are considered to be overweight. This report claimed that obesity causes at least 9,000 premature deaths, and the disease added an extra $2 billion annually to health care costs.

- Statistics Canada (2006) noted that 34% of boys and 23% of girls ages 12–17 years were either overweight or obese.

The physical problems associated with obesity are many. They may include stroke, high blood pressure, stress on weight-bearing joints (Blount disease), arthritis, kidney stones, endothelial dysfunction (which contributes to insulin resistance), type 2 diabetes mellitus, and fatty liver syndrome.

The psychological effects connected to obesity are profound: Depression, difficulties with exercise, social stigma, and peer rejection exact a toll on people who are obese. Children who are obese are reported to have a lower quality of life than children who are not (Schwimmer, Burwinkle, & Varni, 2003). Yet a study by the American Obesity Organization (2002) found that only 12% of parents considered their child to be overweight even though actual rates were in the 25%–30% range. This suggests that greater public health education programs are needed to inform parents of the risks associated with obesity. Latner and Stunkard (2003) conducted a study of children ages 10–11 years who were shown pictures of the following:

- A child with crutches
- A "normal" child or typical child

- An obese child
- A child with facial disfigurement

The children were then asked to rank their preferences for friends. The order of their preferences for friends was as follows:

- "Normal" child or typical child
- Child on crutches
- Child with facial disfigurement
- Obese child

The child who is obese was perceived as being undesirable. It is apparent that children with visible physical challenges are at a distinct disadvantage in striking friendships and becoming popular among peers.

Media Stereotypes

Some attention to the way that children who are obese are portrayed in the media is needed if we want to enhance rates of sports participation. Far too many children's films depict people who are obese as the source of amusement when they are on the sports field. The stereotype is for the "fat kids" to be poorly coordinated, more interested in eating than sports, and only capable of falling on their face—much to the amusement of their peers. This view is not likely to enhance a shy and self-conscious child's desire to participate in sports.

Causes of Obesity

Obesity is recognized to be a complex problem with many contributing factors. Certainly, some people are born with a disposition to carry excess weight. Other people may acquire dysfunction in the hormonal systems that regulate appetite. The quality and type of foods that are popular in Western culture can contribute to obesity. The average calorie intake needed to maintain a healthy weight can easily be exceeded by fat-saturated diets. Highly processed foods are cheaper, full of preservatives, higher in fat, and more readily available than fresh and natural foods. When a diet of processed foods is combined with a lack of regular exercise or activity, weight gain—then obesity—is likely.

The Trans Fats Highway

There is a road in a southwestern American city that runs for about 6 miles. It is the main retail drag, and on my first visit I expected it to be lined with furniture stores or book shops. On the first block of this long road were 4 hamburger franchises, a pizza chain, and 2 Mexican fast-food outlets. This constellation of restaurants repeated at the next block—barely 400 m away—and again, and again. Along its length there must have been 30–40 fast-food centers all competing with each other. I saw a sign in one store: "Tuesday: 6 large hamburgers for $1.50." Another sign offered all-you-can-eat fries. The food was cheap, abundant, and encouraged people to eat well in excess of their needs. Initially, I couldn't understand why the sidewalks were nonexistent. It was because no one was walking. People would drive everywhere.

Other risk factors that have been identified in our attempt to broaden our understanding of obesity include a lack of safe opportunities for activity. Perhaps the most disturbing is the strong connection of obesity to poverty. Participation in sports can be an expensive option, and people living in poverty have to face difficult choices when spending their money. Sports policy makers should be mindful of this connection and look for ways to fund children raised in poverty so that they can participate in sports.

This book is about exercise and participation in sports; it does not recommend or endorse dietary approaches to tackling obesity. Treatment programs for children who are obese should be under the direction of a pediatrician or other health care professional.

Creating a Positive Environment that Encourages Participation in Physical Activities

Even though obesity or weight issues affect 30%–40% of people, most sports programs still seem to be catered for the slim and athletically capable. Many of the programs that I have encountered for people who are obese or overweight tend to adopt the "boot camp" mentality with an emphasis on discipline and self-control. As guilt, shame, or embarrassment are the common responses of overweight people when they exercise in groups, they need a more positive, reassuring reason to participate. Sports in the traditional (competitive) sense may not offer what is needed. Activity—especially play-based activity for children—can be more helpful.

Certainly governments are aware of the need for proactive and preventive programs that can work toward reducing obesity. Programs that help children and families change their lifestyles through counseling, diet, and exercise are starting to take effect, as some sources suggest that rates of obesity may have reached a plateau (Sharma et al., 2009). Former U.S. President Bill Clinton has lobbied beverage and snack food companies to keep their unhealthy snacks out of schools. Many cities across North America are starting to ban the use of trans fats in food preparation. In Canada, the British Columbia Provincial Government has mandated that all schoolchildren must do 30 minutes of daily physical activity and has also banned "junk" foods from school cafeterias and vending machines.

Government health promotion policies require willing participants to embrace the goals and directives of the programs. Schools, coaches, and families must take leading roles in this process. The role modeling of healthy eating and exercise habits exerts powerful influences on children. Research has shown that the degree of parental support is an important predictor of an obese child's willingness to participate in sports (Sallis, Prochaska, Taylor, Hill, & Geraci, 1999). A study by Robinson (1999) revealed that when children were told by their parents to cut down their amount of screen time (e.g., computers, television), they lost weight.

Although exercise alone may bring some desired results, combining it with dieting and social and psychological support helps children to lose weight and maintain healthy habits. Research has shown that healthy habits are more quickly learned, more resilient, and longer lasting when they are acquired in childhood rather than adulthood (Wolf, Cohen, & Rosenfeld, 1985).

Motivation Issues Affecting Students Who Are Obese

Motivating a student who is obese to participate in sports can be challenging if his or her previous experiences have been less than positive. It is not realistic for a coach to expect a child who has been ridiculed, has poor self-esteem, and has immature physical skills to be highly motivated and enthusiastic about sports. These feelings can be compounded when the parents coerce the child to join a team in the hope that this will help the child to find acceptance and improved fitness.

Once an attitude about sports is developed, it can be hard to change it, especially if all that the sport offers are painful experiences, both physically and emotionally. It can be difficult for young children who are obese when they come to the realization that success in sports is not going to be easy for them. These children quickly learn that they are always the first to be tagged in a gym class game, or the first to be tackled in soccer. They develop the understanding that no one will pass to them because other students think that they will immediately make a mistake. This is hard to handle. The following questions should be considered:

- Are your coaching methods sensitive to the needs of a student who is obese?
- In what ways do you modify the activity for this student?
- What support systems do you have in place?

Children who are obese should have a mentor, someone who will listen to their frustrations, support their efforts, and praise their successes. This mentor will understand that compassion and dignity in sports activities are key qualities that help to foster a sense of inclusion.

Most of the students who are obese that I have worked with have been realistic about their abilities, and that is an attitude that a coach can work with. These children understand that no magic wand is going to suddenly turn them into a sleek athlete with Olympic aspirations. They want to participate, strike up friendships, be respected, and have fun. If they develop some good skills along the way, that is even better. It is when the child becomes thoroughly frustrated and possibly humiliated that he or she can become cynical; cynicism is a difficult attitude to change. It is easy to fall into a belief system that suggests the child who is obese is not interested in activities that require effort, endurance, or breaking a sweat. Coaches and parents need to move beyond the "You've just got to believe in yourself" approach when working with these children.

Ideally we would like all children to participate in sports because this is something that they want to do; that is, because they are intrinsically motivated. The satisfaction that many children receive can be found in mastering a skill or making a contribution that is meaningful to them. For children who are obese, success in its typical definition (winning) is not likely to be as forthcoming. If their sporting experiences have been less than rewarding (if not painful), it is safe to assume that their intrinsic motivation is low. Many of these children may only be participating because of social expectations ("If my friends are playing in the club, then I guess I should, too").

Coaching and Teaching Strategies for Students Who Are Obese

The techniques already discussed throughout this book are equally applicable here: Having a mentor, modifying the skills of the sport, creating an atmosphere that respects differences produces a climate that increases the likelihood that children who are obese will persevere in sport despite the physical challenges they may experience. Following are a couple more coaching and teaching strategies for children who are obese.

Modify the Sports Program

Modifications to sports programs do not have to be complicated; sometimes all that is needed is more practice or framing the skill in a manner that allows the children to find success relative to their potential. For example, I have students run 800 m on the streets around my school. One of my students who is obese participates and clearly understands that she will not be the first to finish. The activity is presented as a training run, not a race. Each athlete is given a particular challenge: The capable child may be told to run using a specific pacing strategy. A child who is obese may be given the task of beating his or her previous time or perhaps may be given the goal of running 100 paces, walking 30 paces, then running again.

Another competition that we hold is asking the athletes to predict their finishing time for the run. The winner of the race is the person who is closest to the predicted time; thus the young athlete who is obese has as much of a chance of winning this competition as the faster runners.

Use Extrinsic Motivators

It is not shameful to use extrinsic motivators to help mold and support a child's behavior. Psychologists have understood for decades the power of rewards (reinforcers) to change a person's behavior. In a system called token economy, the child works to achieve a particular target and earns tokens that can be collected. Once enough of these tokens have been earned, they can be "cashed in" for a reward. For example, the goal is to have the child participate in 30 minutes of daily activity. The child can choose from a range of activities presented by the coach or parent: a vigorous walk around the school grounds, using exercise bicycles (if available), and so forth. Each session earns a token (a coin or a slip of paper noting the achievement). When the child achieves the realistic target, for example, six sessions in 10 days, the child receives one reward; this is decided ahead of time and ideally should not involve food. Perhaps the teacher allows the student to have a block of free time to pursue an interest or hobby. Inviting friends for an outside (and active) play time is also a good option. Eventually, the coach or parent increases the number of sessions needed to earn a reward.

A Checklist to Help Students Who Are Obese to Participate in Sports

Assessment

- ❑ Has a pediatrician or doctor cleared this child for involvement in sports? If so, which activities are considered most appropriate?
- ❑ What are the child's interests and strengths?
- ❑ What is the child's previous experience in sports? Did he or she enjoy the sport or drop out?
- ❑ What has worked well in the past, and what should be avoided?

Designing the Sports Environment

- ❑ Avoid games or activities that will publicly humiliate this child.
- ❑ Consider what accommodations will support this child, for example, using different equipment, or requiring more time to complete a task.

Coaching Techniques that Work Well for This Child

- ❑ Set realistic goals that are individualized for the student.
- ❑ Recognize and reward effort.
- ❑ Be aware and sensitive in your comments—this child may find sports very difficult!
- ❑ Role model respect and acceptance of all the children in your group.
- ❑ Try to understand the child's motivation for participating, and build your coaching goals around those reasons.

Differentiation Strategies

- ❑ Use choice boards that are designed around the interests and capabilities of the child.

❑ Scaffolding—build your activities around skills that this child is able to perform successfully.

❑ Flexible grouping—place this child in practice groups that provide support, encouragement, and acceptance.

Final Thoughts

Policy makers at almost every level of government—including the President's Council on Physical Fitness and Sports; Healthy People 2010; and various national health, fitness, and physical education associations such as the American Association for Health, Physical Education, Recreation, and Dance (AAHPERD) and the National Center for Physical Activity and Disability (NCPAD)—are leading campaigns to promote health and fitness and to lower rates of obesity. The success of their policies will require support from parents, effective role modeling by teachers, and engagement of students to interest them in physical activity.

CHAPTER 14

Sports for Young Athletes with a Vast Range of Intellectual Abilities

T he successful coaching of a diverse group of learners draws on the principles of differentiation that have been discussed throughout this book. This chapter identifies the characteristics of intellectual challenges and giftedness.

Sports for Students with Intellectual Challenges

One of the biggest challenges is the attitude of ill-informed people. Sadly, the words *retard* or *retarded* have long been part of common language, and they carry demeaning and hurtful connotations. The currently accepted term used to describe people with mental retardation or other intellectual challenges is *intellectual disability*. Just as there are varying degrees of autism or visual abilities or physical size, there are also varying degrees of intellectual disability.

Who Are These Students with Intellectual Challenges?

Whereas IQ scores may help clinicians to define the extent of the challenge, a child is obviously more than a number. This is a child with personality, a child with areas of strengths and weaknesses, a child who needs support and understanding. From timid behavior to overbearing confidence, from poor verbal skills to highly articulate conversation, from excellent sports skills to delayed motor skill development, the child with intellectual challenges can exhibit a vast range of behaviors and does not fit a template (nor a stereotype). The parents, support agencies, and the child must work in partnership to help a coach understand the needs of this individual. In building this profile some familiar themes emerge: What are the child's sporting interests? What physical capabilities does this child have? What is the child's preferred learning style?

How to Coach a Student with Intellectual Challenges

It is important to use assessments to determine the capabilities of a child with an intellectual challenge, handle safety issues appropriately, and avoid risky activities. These topics are discussed in more detail in the following sections.

Use Formal and Informal Assessments

The formal assessment of a child's capabilities will likely already have been done by educational psychologists, counselors, and classroom teachers. This information can be used to produce an individualized education program (IEP), which has specific recommendations to help support a student's learning. PE teachers can access this information to understand the learning needs of the student and techniques that can support learning. It is not realistic to expect a volunteer coach to incorporate the requirements of a child's IEP into a practice. Parents wishing to support their child's involvement in a community sports program can help the coach by sharing relevant information about their child's intellectual capabilities in a manner that is practical and not overwhelming (or discouraging).

Handle Safety Issues Appropriately

There is an inherent risk in all sports activities, and no one can guarantee there will not be the odd scraped knee and occasional broken bone. Some children are natural risk takers, but they usually undertake some decision-making process to help them determine if it is safe to proceed. A child diving into a lake decides if the water is deep enough or looks for traffic while out on a distance run. Children with intellectual disabilities may require some help in determining the risks associated with an activity. Caution must be used in this approach; we don't want to instill fear in a child so that he or she fixates on safety and no longer wants to participate.

Avoid Activities that Increase Risk of Injury

Some activities increase the risk of injury for children with intellectual challenges. For example, children with Down syndrome may have atlantoaxial instability, where the gap between the atlas and axis bones of the neck is larger than normal; the resultant instability places the child at risk for spinal cord compression (and even paralysis). Activities like gymnastics, heading soccer balls, or rugby must be avoided. This example is a reminder of the importance of parents sharing this information with the teacher or a coach.

Use Visual Cues

Children with intellectual disabilities benefit from learning routines that let them anticipate what is likely to happen next. Using visual teaching techniques is particularly effective in supporting these children. A visual cue that some instruction is about to be given helps this child focus. For example, the coach may raise his or her arm high in the air as the signal that directions are about to be given. The coach should tell the students what is expected, then show them (with either the coach or another athlete demonstrating), then help this young athlete.

Modify the Activity as Needed

Poor coordination and difficulties with physical skills often accompany the student with intellectual challenges. This student can easily feel overwhelmed by some of the complex skills that are involved in many sports. To avoid frustration and build confidence, the sports skills should be introduced and developed in small and steady increments.

Change or Overlook Some of the Game Rules

The rules of basketball require the student to move across the court only while dribbling the ball with one hand. Some students catch the basketball and start to run with it in their hands before bouncing the ball (a rule violation known as traveling). Coaches or referees can use their own judgment before calling this rule violation in order to allow the student the opportunity to participate in the game.

Give Students Lots of Time to Process a Request or Consider the Answer to a Question

Students with rapid information processing are usually rewarded with acknowledgement or praise for being the person who answered a question first. Of course, this does not mean that other students did not know the answer. Students with intellectual disabilities may not have information-processing abilities that match the speed of their classmates. The lack of a prompt answer does not necessarily indicate difficulty comprehending the request; the coach should allow the student time to process information.

Give Students a Partner to Support Them and Clarify the Activity

Some students have poor working memories; this means they have difficulty keeping an idea or series of instructions in mind and so are not able to effectively carry out what has been asked of them. A peer clarifier helps remind and focus this student on the assigned task.

Understand the Motivation of a Student with Intellectual Challenges

The student may fail to demonstrate a skill or express no interest or clear understanding of the activity, but this does not mean that the student is not capable. An apparent lack of motivation or an external source of distraction may sidetrack a student with intellectual challenges. The risk is that the coach uses this lack of affect to create activities that are not challenging.

A Checklist to Help Students with Intellectual Challenges to Participate in Sports

Assessment

❑ What is the child's learning strengths or areas of interest?

❑ What are the child's interests in sports and physical activities?

❑ What is the child's preferred learning style?

❑ How does the learning difficulty manifest itself?

❑ What helps this student cope with setbacks in learning?

❑ Does this student require a learning assistant?

Designing a Successful Learning Environment

❑ Does this student require the use of specialized equipment to facilitate learning?

❑ Does this child need more time to process instructions?

❑ Are there ways that the coach can teach the content that draw on the child's learning strengths and avoid the difficulties?

Coaching Techniques that Work Well for This Student

❑ Use simple but not condescending language to explain the activities.

❑ Be consistent when coaching students with intellectual disabilities.

❑ Avoid the use of sports jargon, as this may be confusing for many students.

❑ Children with intellectual disabilities greatly benefit from visual demonstrations of the activity with peers.

Differentiation Strategies

❑ Use the assessment information shared by parents and other education resources (psychologists, special education teachers) to match the content to the child's needs.

❑ Group your athletes with children who are supportive and understanding of errors made on the sports field.

❑ Use choice boards to help build confidence in this child.

❑ Use brightly colored tape on the floor or other field markers (flags, cones) to help this student understand the boundaries of the playing field.

Sports for Gifted Athletes

There are young athletes whose achievements can make us gasp and shake our head in disbelief. These children master advanced physical skills at a very early age. Their coordination, balance, and perceptual abilities are well defined and allow them to compete successfully against students much older than themselves. The words *prodigy, genius,* or *gifted* are often used (or misused, as can be the case) to define their abilities. These descriptors can be qualified by parents stating their child is "profoundly gifted." Assessing a child's abilities—especially in physical development—can be misleading. Precocious or slow growth can mask talent or amplify a child's abilities as gifted, so caution must be used when applying these terms. The accepted number of gifted children in the typical student population is between 3% and 5%, yet many more parents than that believe their child is gifted. This is quite a common phenomenon, because parents want to see the best in their children, and often they do not have a way of accurately comparing their child's abilities with those of someone who really is gifted.

Giftedness has been researched extensively. Although many definitions abound, three themes emerge:

- Gifted children are able to achieve exceptionally high levels of performance (sometimes in more than one area).

- Gifted children can think abstractly, analyze situations, and evaluate outcomes at a high level.

- Gifted children are not always successful. An assumption about giftedness is that a student will automatically be successful in a chosen area, but the anxiety and perfectionist tendencies that often accompany giftedness can prevent the student from being successful.

It is important to make the distinction between a talented athlete and a gifted one. A child who is gifted is said to have superior natural abilities (which may be untrained), whereas a talented child is one who has developed his or her skills to an advanced level. This creates the possibility that our young athlete could be talented but not gifted, or gifted and not (yet) talented (Gagné, 1985). The coaching environment and the support that the child receives from parents are critical in helping the gifted child achieve advanced levels of accomplishment.

What Is the Profile of a Gifted Young Athlete?

When a parent states "My child is gifted," it is often assumed that this "giftedness" applies to all areas of the child's skill set. This is probably one of the most challenging myths that these children face. Many gifted children have age-appropriate skills in some areas and may have difficulties in others. Because success can come easily to gifted children (in some areas), another assumption is that they do not need as much support or guidance as other children. This is erroneous. Gifted children need as much support as any other child. The learning profile of gifted children usually includes a number of areas that create difficulties with coaches or other athletes:

- Gifted children can be very vocal and hold definite opinions on certain matters.

- Gifted children can be perfectionists and are often critical of the performances of others. They can also be highly self-critical, and this has a damaging effect on their confidence (Clark, 2002).

- Gifted children are often good at remembering what they have learned, and they can quickly get bored if the coach dwells on reviewing a particular concept.

- Gifted students can also be prone to anxiety, and this has been shown to inhibit performance (Beilock & Carr, 2005).

- Gifted children like to completely master a particular skill before they advance to the next challenge. This can sometimes hamper the child's progress to the point of distraction. If parents and coaches observe a strong desire for perfection in the child, they should consider this a warning sign that the child needs support and guidance.

Coaches and teachers are undoubtedly familiar with the child who never seems to be paying any attention and who appears disinterested and absorbed in something else. And yet, when this child is asked to repeat instructions, he or she can tell you exactly what you have said. Although this is not uniquely the domain of a gifted child, the ability to intensely concentrate on a number of things is characteristic of a gifted child.

What Kinds of Challenges Do Gifted Students Experience, and How Do They Respond?

The presumption that gifted children have everything easy is a stereotype that restricts the development of these children. Instant success in sports can create the view that this child is generally superior, which can attracts resentment from peers, other parents, and occasionally coaches. A disturbing trend in schools has been the labeling of studious or enthusiastic behavior as "uncool." Boys have faced pressure from their peers to underachieve, to be disruptive in class, and generally to be confrontational to authority. This attitude has found its way onto the sports field. Some children who are gifted have found that success may attract jealousy and resentment. As peer acceptance is an important motive for participation in sports, it is not uncommon for such children to deliberately sabotage their efforts—something that is also termed *masking*—to gain recognition. The underachievement of gifted young athletes can produce behavioral responses ranging from poor performance to quitting the sport.

Sensitivity, stress, and perfectionism are symptoms that may also identify the underachieving gifted athlete. These children can become easily frustrated with setbacks, even though they may be within their skill set to find success. Occasionally the child responds with psychosomatic characteristics such as headaches, broken sleep patterns, lack of energy, and so forth.

Myths and Clichés that Can Hold Gifted Students Back

- "The cream will rise to the top" is a well-worn cliché that can restrict the development of gifted children. The cliché makes the assumption that the child's abilities can overcome challenges and he or she does not need to be nurtured or guided. This is not the only stereotype that gifted children face.

- "The athlete can't perform this particular skill. So much for being gifted!" There are coaches (and some teachers) who believe that a skill must be completely mastered before a child can make further progress. A gifted child may be challenged by a particular skill, but this should not diminish the need for enrichment or acceleration. Gifted children are not necessarily sequential or linear learners; thus, their programs should not be restricted because their mastery of some skills is not complete.

- "I give these kids the same program. The gifted kids will get it, the challenged kids won't!" Proponents of an elitist and exclusive sports environment likely subscribe to this "trickle-down" approach to teaching and coaching. This is when the coach teaches to "the top athletes" and whatever reaches "the bottom" is good enough. Coaches and teachers are morally obliged to help all the children achieve their best. Teaching to the middle (ability wise) is convenient and requires the least amount of planning and effort; however, it carries the likelihood of ignoring children whom you will likely help the most. Gifted children need to be motivated and given special consideration just as much as children with recognized challenges. A differentiated learning environment recognizes the learning needs of all athletes and helps them find personal success.

Teaching and Coaching Strategies for Gifted Young Athletes

Gifted young athletes require enriched sports programs to continually challenge their capabilities. Without this, these children are at risk of being bored and frustrated. The teaching techniques discussed in Chapters 6 and 7 can help these children stay motivated and challenged, but these techniques alone are not enough. Understanding the child's attitudes toward practice and competition, the child's preferences and readiness for these activities, and the way that the child responds to different styles of coaching and learning are important foundations in the program.

Focus the Child's Attention

Coaches of gifted children are encouraged to focus the child's attention, not just on effort, but also on the technical areas of the sport. Because many gifted children operate at an abstract level of thinking, they may be ready to understand and apply some of the underlying biomechanical principles that can hone athletic performance.

Support the Gifted Athlete

Gifted young athletes can be prone to perfectionism. Coaches are encouraged to expect the best from these children. Certainly challenge them, but be sure to support them when they experience setbacks or frustration.

There is an adage in education—"Challenge the strengths and support the weakness"—that is particularly relevant if you are working with gifted young athletes. These children are not likely to be gifted in all areas—and some may actually have learning disabilities. Research has shown that children with learning difficulties are less likely to be accepted by their peers than those with no learning difficulties (Bryan, 1974). So the need for empathy and compassionate coaching is just as important for gifted children as it is for children with other needs.

A Checklist to Help Gifted Students to Successfully Participate in Sports

Assessment

❑ Children who are athletically gifted require as much support as children with difficulties or deficits in their skills. Gifted children have extraordinary skills in some areas and may have immature or poorly developed skills in other areas. Coaches need to find exactly where these strengths or difficulties lie.

❑ Make sure you work with the parent to understand what has worked well in the past and where the child and parent believe support is needed.

❑ Use the Five Most Difficult approach to assess the child's capabilities (see Chapter 6).

Designing the Sports Environment

❑ In order to challenge these students the coach may need to set goals and standards at a high and demanding level.

❑ These students may require equipment modification; for example, in gymnastics the gifted child may progress to apparatus that challenges his or her skill level.

❑ Instructional challenges come from the coach teaching advanced tactics and strategies, if the child is able to implement them.

Coaching Strategies

❑ It is important to recognize that there is a significant difference between a gifted child and a child who has precocious development. Success at an early age is not necessarily a reflection of athletic giftedness.

❑ Although the coach needs to support and challenge the gifted child, it is critical that age-appropriate activities and emotional support are offered. The giftedness should not be ignored, but it also should not be pandered to. This child is still developing.

Differentiation Strategies

❏ Gifted students may not only have excellent skills, but they may also have a deep understanding of rules, tactics, and strategies. Enrich gifted students' learning by using questioning that challenges the students to analyze the activity and requires them to bring novel solutions to tactical or technical problems.

❏ Design the program around the children's interests, match the content to their skill set, and teach with techniques that challenge their strengths.

❏ Match gifted children with other gifted children in group assignments.

Final Thoughts

Working with students who have either an intellectual disability or have giftedness may appear to be an overwhelming challenge to coach or teacher. Employing the principles of differentiation as outlined in this book allow for students with these needs to be supported or enriched, and this promotes the inclusion and acceptance of each student.

I recommend that parents take a proactive role in advising coaches and teachers of their child's learning strengths and difficulties. With that information, the coach can utilize resources to support (mentors, peer clarifiers) and identify methods to enrich the learning experiences of all students. It is my experience that some parents withhold this information, some in the belief that they are protecting their child, others not wanting to be known as having a child with different needs. Without that information, the effectiveness of coaches and teachers is restricted. Advocating for your child in this context is more fully achieved by disclosure.

CHAPTER 15

Sports for Young Athletes with Specific Learning Disabilities

L ike many of the topics covered in this book, this is an immense subject, and comprehensive coverage is beyond the scope of this text. There are numerous directions this chapter could take, but I focus on just three areas: how difficulties in using memory, attention, and temporal-sequential ordering can impede a child's progress in sports.

Memory

This function of the brain is a critical component of learning—many would argue it is the essence of learning. Children who have difficulties in processing and recalling skills that have been taught are at a disadvantage in a school system that values the excellent retention of information. Memory formation is not a single function but a composite of three areas: short-term memory, active working memory, and long-term memory.

Short-Term Memory

Short-term memory is used for storing information for a brief and limited period. For instance, you may glance at your watch to get a sense of the time, but you will not likely remember the exact minute a few hours or days later. This changes if a very significant event occurs that makes you remember the exact time, in which case this information becomes stored in long-term memory.

Active Working Memory

The area of memory function that I would like to focus on is active working memory. Ashcraft (2002) suggested that there are three components in active working memory:

- The central executive system
- The phonological loop
- The visuospatial workpad

Central Executive System

The central executive system helps to process the information a coach or teacher has given. This system then decides whether the information needs to be transferred to long-term memory; it also plays a key role in focusing the child's attention on relevant information.

Phonological Loop

The phonological loop is the part of this system that processes information (usually words or sounds) and uses them as a store for instant recall. A young athlete who has difficulty in processing and comprehending language may experience challenges in recalling this information in a timely and accurate manner. It is not hard to identify a scenario in which a child who is asked a question has difficulty processing the sounds and recalling the information with accuracy, then feels pressured by peers (or the teacher) for the correct answer, and consequently, may be criticized when he or she makes a mistake.

Visuospatial Workpad

The visuospatial workpad processes the visual imagery in active working memory. A child with difficulty in this area may have problems interpreting tasks that require good spatial awareness. Many sports require the athlete to understand the tactical importance of player positions on the field (both teammates and the opposition), as well as be aware of how these positions quickly change according to the strategy of the game.

How Students with Difficulties in Active Working Memory Are at a Disadvantage

It is clear that children with difficulties in this memory function are at a considerable disadvantage in sports. Active working memory requires that we keep information accessible while we are actually using it. For example, a coach may give the athlete some technical instructions—perhaps it is a certain play in basketball or football. This information is used by the athlete as the play unfolds. Maintaining the idea until it is no longer needed is a key function of active working memory. F. Smith (1975) suggested that an idea in active working memory is only stored for 5–20 seconds.

Children with difficulties in this area may listen intently but cannot execute the task, because the idea has already started to destabilize by the time the coach has finished explaining the concept. Children with ADHD are noted for having impaired functioning of their active working memory system.

Teaching Techniques to Help a Student with Active Working Memory Difficulties

The following list describes some teaching techniques and tips to help a child who has active working memory difficulties:

- Keep the amount of information that you wish to convey concise.
- Understand the child's preferred learning style and present your information in that style. If there is a mismatch between the child's preference and the way that you teach, it only exacerbates the difficulties in active working memory.
- Use visual techniques (e.g., a story board) to allow children to remind themselves of the activity if they are starting to forget.
- Use elaborate rehearsal techniques to reinforce the learning. In this method the coach uses information that the athlete already understands and then tries to "piggyback" new ideas or information.
- Have a peer clarifier to assist this young athlete.
- Encourage the young athlete to observe and follow the lead of his or her peers.

Long-Term Memory

Long-term memories are formed if significance and necessity are attached to the information. On the sports field athletes are taught the rules, the plays, and various techniques that help to bring them success. Our long-term memory functions allow us to store and retrieve this information quickly and efficiently without the need to be taught it all over again. Without practice, sometimes this information in long-term memory deteriorates, and we forget. Repetition or refreshers can keep these skill sets stable in long-term memory.

Attention

A stereotypical view of attention tends to concentrate on the athlete's ability to focus on the coach's words: "Now, pay attention, everyone. This is what I want you to do." There are, however, many facets to this construct. Attention includes how we control mental energy, how we process information, and how we then regulate our behavior.

Mental Energy

There are times when you feel that you just cannot seem to help one of your athletes. The child has low energy, cannot sustain any effort, and seems distant. States of physical arousal (alertness) vary for all of us—we all get tired and lose interest in something, even if it is something that we actually love to do. Coaches who try to coerce extra effort or focus from a tired, low-energy athlete may find that this just undermines the child's interest in this activity. Mental energy can be reinvigorated with rest or the introduction of variety into the sports program.

Processing Information

Young athletes are bombarded with information. Anything from the sights and sounds of the practice or competition, the instructions of the coach, to the cheers or criticisms of peers or parents could be overwhelming for some athletes (and for children with an ASD this can certainly be the case). Athletes with good attention skills figure out what information is relevant, how to concentrate on this information, and then connect it to previous experiences. These are critical skills; if the child makes poor choices, for example, concentrating on the conversation with a peer instead of listening to the coach, he or she can fail to grasp the concepts. The athlete with difficulties in attention processing may focus intensely on something that is not relevant to the successful completion of the task.

Regulating Behavior

Children with difficulties in attention control often have problems with pacing. This may be the case with a child who starts out really well, listens carefully, and does not seem to be distracted but within minutes starts to lose his or her way. This child can then make poor choices because he or she does not take the time to carefully consider options; these decisions then invariably bring the child into conflict with parents, peers, or coaches.

Teaching Techniques to Help a Student with Attention Difficulties

Make Sure that the Student Gets Enough Sleep

Students who are deeply (and genuinely) tired do not bring a high degree of mental energy to a learning situation. So the first thing the parent needs to do (sounds like common sense, I know) is to ensure the child gets consistent sleep.

Use Clear, Jargon-Free Language

Young athletes who have poor ability to determine what information is important and what is irrelevant should not be overwhelmed with choices. Clear, jargon-free language that focuses on specific tasks helps this student.

Monitor Progress

Coaches need to monitor this child's progress with the task. If the young athlete is starting to "drift," change the activity or help the child refocus (perhaps by reinforcing good effort). If the coach does not identify the child's drifting, a disciplinary issue may emerge.

Match the Student with a Peer or Group

Match the child with a peer or group of peers who are very good at sustaining attention, pacing themselves in activities, and so forth. The actions of the other children act as visual cues for this child.

Vary Your Activities

Vary your sports practices so to as attract or keep the attention of your athletes. Activities that are unexpected or perhaps are presented in a novel manner can help focus a student's interest.

Temporal-Sequential Ordering Difficulties

Many sports activities require that we correctly sequence a whole series of movement patterns. We not only have to accurately perceive these patterns (information), we also have to remember the sequences and then apply them in the correct order. For example, a child wishing to make a lay-up in basketball first needs to identify what situation makes the shot selection an appropriate one. This child then needs to coordinate the bouncing (control) of the ball, the correct approach to the basket, the upward swing of the arm, and the release of the ball against the backboard. This can be a challenging sequence of skills for young athletes, and this is especially true for the child who has difficulty following sequenced patterns.

Temporal-sequential difficulties also manifest in time management. Children with poor time-keeping skills or children who cannot understand how to apply time to assigned tasks often have problems in practices. These are the children who never finish the task, not because they lack motivation or effort, but because they distributed the time allocation inappropriately.

Teaching Techniques to Help a Child with Temporal-Sequential Difficulties

Use a Simple, Nonjudgmental Approach to Self-Regulation

It is not helpful to tell a child who has problems with time management, "You just need to organize yourself better," or its companion, "You need to take more responsibility." Neither of these clichés helps the child to improve. Sometimes the simple approach is more effective. I use an egg timer to help the child self-regulate in class. It is a visual and nonjudgmental way of allowing the athlete to keep pace.

Cut Out Some Unnecessary Sequences

Too many sequences overload a child who has a compromised ability to rapidly process them. It's okay to cut out sequences so that the athlete works on skills that can be achieved; for example, I just concentrate on the final steps and ball release in the lay-up analogy. Approaching the basket with speed and bouncing the ball can wait until the child has mastered the shooting technique. Keep the steps simple and allow the child to experience success.

A Checklist to Help Students with Learning Difficulties to Participate in Sports

Assessment

❑ What is the student's preferred learning style?

❑ What are the student's learning strengths?

❑ What are the child's interests in sports?

❑ Are the learning difficulties of this child constant, variable, content/skill–specific, or a general challenge?

❑ Are these learning difficulties a recent phenomenon or life long?

❑ Is there a diagnosis or possible explanation for this challenge?

❑ How does the learning difficulty manifest itself?

❑ How does the child respond when he or she experiences this learning challenge?

❑ What helps the child to cope and learn?

❑ Does the child require a learning assistant?

❑ Does the child use equipment to facilitate learning?

Designing a Successful Learning Environment

❑ Does this child need more time to process instructions?

❑ Are there ways to teach the content that draw on the child's learning strengths and avoids difficulties?

Coaching Techniques that Work Well for This Child

❑ Students with learning difficulties can be self-conscious about the challenges that they face. This is especially true when their difficulties can be observed and possibly ridiculed by teammates. The need for a coach to be compassionate and understanding is especially important.

❑ Use simple but not condescending language to explain the activities.

❑ Avoid the use of jargon, unless it serves the purpose of developing the child's knowledge of the game (language may actually be a strength for some children with a learning difficulty).

❑ Demonstrate the activity with peers.

❑ Once the activity has started and teammates are busy practicing, give a child still having difficulty grasping the concept some one-to-one attention. Rather than explaining with words, guide the student's observations of others and point out how the skill or activity should be conducted.

Differentiation Strategies

❑ Use the assessment information to match the content to the child's needs.

❑ Group your athletes with children who will be supportive and understanding of errors made on the sports field.

❑ Use choice boards to help build the child's confidence.

Final Thoughts

Parents of a student who has either an unusual learning style or difficulty processing and using information in a certain way are encouraged to share this knowledge with the coach or teacher. All students can successfully participate in sports and learn—with support if necessary—the knowledge and skills a teacher or coach is sharing. Modifications may be necessary—and some of these are outlined in this chapter—but the parents and students may have some techniques or learning strategies of their own that are equally (or more) effective. Teachers and coaches are encouraged to welcome any input that helps support the learning and development of the student.

CHAPTER 16

Addressing Anxiety, Stress, and Social Confidence Issues in Young Athletes

The sporting experience, for all the wonderful things that it can offer, can also overwhelm some young children. Such feelings often emerge out of excessive desire or pressure to succeed. This is something that many parents can identify with as they see some children leaving the sports field in floods of tears when the outcome is not what was expected. Setbacks, when framed by parents and coaches as a learning and resilience-building opportunity, can be an integral part of the child's development (Valee, Mayo, & Dellu, 1997). When presented as a statement of the child's lack of skill, effort, or character, however, they can be damaging to the child's emotional well-being.

Although we want success for our children, most responsible parents and coaches would avoid placing athletes in an environment where they feel threatened and overwhelmed. Sports are, after all, meant to be fun and not something that should be feared and avoided. And yet the situations that evoke these kinds of responses in children have become so common that the terms *stress, anxiety, psyched out,* and *choke* are now, regrettably, an accepted part of our sports lexicon.

Children react in many different ways when they experience difficulties in sports. They can feel helpless, have pervasive thoughts of anxiety, and even experience depression. They can respond in physical ways by experiencing the symptoms associated with stress. They can also respond through their behavior, perhaps by being withdrawn or by becoming a bully. Each area is worthy of examination for it underscores the need for coaches and parents to support children with compassion and understanding, plus practical coping strategies.

Coaches from "the school of hard knocks" may dismiss this as "politically correct" nonsense; after all, "Kids need toughening up to get them ready for the world." Although it is true that we want our children to have the emotional competence to face challenges, the adversarial coach's approach is seldom effective at enhancing athletes' resilience; this is especially accurate when they are dealing with children who have challenges.

Anxiety

Anxiety can be considered a feeling, a fear, or a sense of apprehension of something that is either real or is perceived to be real. It is also a natural response of the body for self-preservation, for it helps us to identify possible threats to our well-being. It is something that most, if not all of us have had some experience with, and it can be either long or relatively short lasting.

Anxiety is often the result of our unique interpretation of a particular situation. One person may feel very comfortable taking an exam, an airplane journey, or a free throw in the dying seconds of a basketball game. For other people, these very same situations can make them tense, restless, and exhibit visible signs of distress. These symptoms can disappear quickly when the exam has ended, the plane has landed, or the game is over. A child's sense of anxiety may also emerge out of the interpretation of a situation in which he or she perceives a sense of injustice or victimization—"Nobody likes me and everyone laughs at me when I make a mistake." This perception can be powerfully reinforced if the child perceives the coach to be indifferent, or worse, an amplifier of the injustice.

Parents should not quickly look to the coach or sports environment to assign blame for the anxious reactions of their child, however. It is fair to acknowledge that some children have a general disposition to feel anxiety (also known as trait anxiety), which is exacerbated when they fail to achieve the success that a coach or parent expects to see. Other children may develop anxiety due to the unique circumstances of a sports situation, which has been described as state anxiety, but the anxiety passes once the situation is over.

An Anxious Participant

I can vividly remember the first day that Sara came to our school. I had been forewarned by her parents that she was absolutely terrified about gym. Despite the best efforts of the parents to gently introduce Sara to team sports, her only response was entrenched fear, followed by tears and inactivity. The class was sent into the changing room and Sara was the last to emerge. She timidly poked her head into the gym and looked as if she had seen the school ghost (yes, that's true, but that's another story!). She sat on the bench on the verge of tears. We played a few games of tag, then did a bit of gentle fitness work. Sara participated but with reluctance. It took several months of gentle coaxing and lots of reassurance and praise, but eventually Sara became a fully involved member of the class.

When the anxiety is persistent, it can become a very debilitating condition. It can find expression in anything ranging from simple phobias to obsessive-compulsive disorder. The anxiety response may be something more specific such as a social anxiety disorder; for example, a fear of social situations or, in the context of sports, a fear of performance. The child may also experience panic attacks emerging from feelings of intense anxiety. Rowley (1993) reported that boys (before they reach puberty) are more prone to anxiety arising from competition than girls. The reasoning is that boys seem to attach greater significance to sports outcomes than girls. Anxiety is likely to manifest itself in three ways: in the child's behavior, in his or her thoughts and how they are expressed, and in a physical response (feelings of sickness, and so forth). Each area is worthy of examination to help coaches and teachers recognize signs of anxiety in the child.

Behavioral Responses to Anxiety

Researchers say that all behavior is communication. This is especially true with anxious children who are having difficulty in sports or play. Crying, tantrums, withdrawal from the situation, and seeking constant reassurance from the coach are behavioral indicators of a child feeling anxious. Some children also respond to their anxiety with bullying behavior. There is a risk of overinterpreting a single behavior. The occasional expression of one of these symptoms does not necessarily mean the child is anxious. Knowledge of the child's prior behavior in similar situations can often explain why the behavior is occurring. The child may not have an anxious disposition but may lack the confidence to perform or behave as expected in a unique circumstance; for example, the child happily sings at home and in the school choir, but may become anxious performing a solo in front of a large group of strangers.

Cognitive Responses to Anxiety

It is natural for some children to experience uncertainty when facing (or placed in by their parents) new and challenging situations. This apprehension may be expressed by the child through comments that ask the parent for support to allay fears. A perceptive parent monitors these comments and sees if they become chronic. Ongoing anxious comments require the parents and coaches to examine the sources of the child's anxiety and devise strategies to help the child cope (more on this later). A child's cognitive response to anxiety derived from experiences in sports may also include

- Intrusive thoughts of failure
- Thoughts of hopelessness
- Thoughts that reflect anger, sadness, and many other emotions that articulate feelings of insecurity

Stress: A Physical Response to Anxiety

Williams and Huber (1986, p. 243) defined stress as "a psychological and physical reaction to prolonged internal and/or environmental conditions in which an individual's adaptive capabilities are overextended." When an athlete perceives a threat to his or her well-being, this person's body mobilizes physical resources to help respond to the challenge. For exercise physiologists, stress is a complex series of chemical and neurological reactions to a stimulus—the stressor. With ongoing exposure to these stressors, the athlete's body adapts. All the training that we do, the various ways that we challenge our energy systems and muscles, all are designed to "stress" the body and force it to improve (get fitter). It is in this context that some researchers have applied the term *eustress,* or good stress (French, Kast, & Rosenzweig, 1985, p. 707).

General Adaptation Theory

A classic theory of how the body responds to stress was proposed by Hans Selye (1946). The general adaptation theory (GAS) states that the body responds to stress in three distinct phases. The first response is known as the alarm phase, when the body recognizes that a demand has been placed upon it (e.g., a race is about to start, or you are heading out on a training run). Energy resources are mobilized and various chemicals (e.g., adrenaline) activate the physiological systems to meet the body's needs (e.g., the heart beats faster, breathing rate increases). This has also been called the fight or flight response.

The second stage, the adaptation phase, is when the athlete's body adjusts to the repeated exposure to the stressor (e.g., in the race it might be the need to cope with fatigue, or in training, the way the athlete prepares). If the athlete does not modify the stimulus—how hard he or she runs—the fitness level stays the same (plateau). Changing the intensity, the frequency of training, the duration of effort, and the type of training (e.g., aerobic runs or short anaerobic sprints) forces the body to continue to adapt.

The final stage in Selye's theory is known as the exhaustion phase. If an athlete trains too hard he or she may experience difficulty adapting. The warning signs are initially subtle, then more direct. The athlete may experience low energy, persistent soreness, colds, and so forth. The mental fatigue is characterized by a waning interest in running. Certainly any one of these symptoms in isolation does not necessarily mean the athlete is at the exhaustion stage. A child facing a hostile or unwelcoming sports environment may quickly experience the alarm phase as suggested by Selye. This athlete might feel pressured to achieve a certain standard or behave in a certain way even though his or her skills (emotional and physical) might not be at the required level. This child may respond with any number of standard physical symptoms, which can include the following:

- The classic "butterflies in the stomach"
- Irritability or aggression

- Complaints of physical symptoms that can then be used to excuse participation or "explain away" substandard performances
- Frequent urination—teachers recognize this in the child who always requests a bathroom visit during exam time

He Passed Out!

The Inter Counties Cross Country running championships for 15-year-olds was a huge event. Hundreds of runners jogged on the start line and awaited the starter's gun to release us over the 4-mile muddy course. I was running a really good race and thought I would finish just inside the top 20. With 1 mile left I find myself running stride for stride with a boy who started to make a strange whimpering sound. Soon, the whimpering turned into sobbing, then full-blown crying. Within a few more meters I found out why. His coach and father had been following him all over the course. The father was outraged at his son's lack of effort. "You can at least try!" he shouted viciously. To my surprise the boy yelled back, "I can't!" The coach made his presence known. "Start your sprint now!" I thought that was a bit strange. We still had three quarters of a mile to go and my opponent looked drained of energy. The boy shouted back almost hysterically, "I can't do it!" "Yes, you can!" his father immediately replied. This "to and fro" shouting continued for a few more meters. Suddenly, the boy's legs gave out from under him and he fell face down in the mud. He had passed out! I can still remember the look on the coach's and father's faces: It was a mixture of embarrassment and shock.

According to Selye's theory, a child either adapts to the source of stress (in this example, a culture of hostility) or quickly drops out. Just because the child has adapted does not mean that he or she is suffering any less—thus the "toughen them up" approach is misleading, for this child has only learned to cope. Sometimes the desire to be accepted makes them tolerate disrespect or bullying. The repeated ongoing exposure to stress can sometimes be too much, and despite every effort to develop coping skills, the child becomes actively resistant to the sport. Ultimately, they drop out.

Should All Stressful or Anxiety-Inducing Experiences Be Avoided?

Stress, when it conveys threat, is certainly something to avoid. We do not want to place our children in situations where they feel exposed and humiliated, and a coach who allows that to happen is one to avoid. However, stress, when it challenges the athlete to learn and adapt, is a necessary part of our development. It is easy to be in a comfort zone, but that does not readily lead to improvement. We have to challenge ourselves with realistic and achievable goals.

Perry (1998) has suggested that a child exposed to positive motor, sensory, emotional, cognitive, and social experiences in childhood will develop a capacity to tolerate frustration and be able to control impulsive urges. However, he cautioned that a child exposed to constant stress may be predisposed to behavioral reactivity (acting out, and so forth). Research has shown that when stress is perceived by the athlete as a source of threat it can alter the normal neurodevelopmental processes (Perry & Azad, 1999; Perry, Pollard, & Blakely, 1995). We all respond in different ways when threatened. Some of us become hostile and argumentative, others seek to avoid those situations. A young athlete faced with yet another exposé of his or her poor skills may trigger a learned helplessness response and withdraw from the situation (Caine & Caine, 1997; Le Doux, 1996). Young athletes operating in a state of fear or perceived threat are likely to become "downshifted"; this is a response that moves the individual to do whatever it takes for survival (Hart, 1998)—which likely means dropping out of sports.

Perry (1999) identified two common patterns that children use to cope with stress: hyperarousal and dissociative behavior patterns. The hyperarousal pattern is a classic "fight or flight" stress response. Young athletes (especially teenagers) may become defiant, confrontational, and impulsive in a chronic stress situation. Behavioral consequences are often inconceivable to a child participating in a culture of perceived threat.

The dissociation behavior is characterized by the athlete becoming "distant," introspective, and anxious. The athlete may engage in avoidance behavior. Ironically, after the avoidance phase, the athlete may comply with a coach's request, but only in a passive way. Research suggests that boys are more likely to adopt the hyperarousal response to stress and girls to use the dissociation pattern of coping (Perry et al., 1995).

How Do Stress and Anxiety Influence a Student's Ability to Learn in Sports?
Young athletes participating in a culture of fear or anxiety understandably learn skills and knowledge in a different way than that of a child who is feeling secure. Perry (1997) noted that children in states of stress perceive the concept of time in a different way. When they are stressed, they focus on the immediate time and cannot comprehend the significance of the future. They may arrive late for practices, display no sense of urgency, and appear to "mentally drift" when listening to coaching instructions.

Research has shown that intense emotions influence the child's ability to learn (Ashcraft & Kirk, 2001). When we are stressed we release a hormone called corticosterone, which in turn interferes with the release of a very important chemical known as brain-derived neurotrophic factor (BDNF). BDNF enhances brain neurons' ability to communicate with one another. BDNF appears to be important in learning and in memory-forming processes, thus a reduction in this chemical seems to impair the ability of the brain to learn. Children who are already stressed and are being heavily criticized by peers or coaches do not learn as efficiently as athletes who feel secure in their sporting environment.

Goleman (2006) stated that children's ability to focus, remember, pay attention, and solve problems can be compromised if they feel stressed. Clearly, coaches who repeatedly shout and use intimidation as a teaching tool cannot be effective. Coaches are not immune to the effects of stress. One research study of coaches (Scanlan & Lewthwaite, 1984) revealed that 42.8% quoted disrespect from players as a major source of stress. Other sources of stress were not reaching their athletes (20.7%) and feeling a lack of appreciation from athletes (3%), from the administration (14%), and from the public (6.5%). Almost 85% of the coaches reported being stressed by relationship challenges, not questions about their technical competency.

Students, Sports, and Depression

Childhood should be a time filled with wonderful opportunities that create fond memories. As sports are highly valued by young children, they are a powerful means for providing healthy physical experiences and creating emotion-filled moments. Sadly, some children find that sports are a source of intense unhappiness, and many continue to participate only to meet their parents' expectations or because their peers are playing. Children who are chronically unhappy in sports eventually burn out, drop out, or, if they continue to "suffer through it," become stressed and depressed.

Regrettably, children and youth are increasingly experiencing the symptoms of full-blown depression (Rice, Harold, & Thapar, 2002). The number of children experiencing diagnosable mental disorders is profound: 21% of U.S. children ages 9–17 years have a mental health or addictive disorder that carries at least a minimum impairment; anxiety disorders affect 13% of children, mood disorders 6.2%, disruptive disorders 10.3% (DHHS, 1999). Many teachers and parents recognize that sports participation rates of girls falls away from Grade 7 onward. The reasons for this drop may be a complex blend of social and psychological reasons. A young teenage girl who has poorly developed sports skills, is undergoing significant hormonal and physical changes, and is feeling alienated by a high-pressure, demanding sports culture can be discouraged completely. At worst, such pressures can place these girls at risk of depression (Silberg et al., 1999). In boys, failing to make a sports team was not only a source of stress and disappointment, but potentially a precursor to depression.

It is important to place such studies in context. Episodes of depression that emerge out of unhappiness in sports are not likely to be something that happens just because the athlete was not selected. Consider the whole picture: In a hostile sports culture, repeated exposure to ridicule, chronic low self-image, and constant lack of success can make a young athlete very unhappy. Feelings of hopelessness and failure are often enough to move the child from a state of sadness to depression.

A Love/Hate Relationship

It was obvious that Jill was depressed and that her involvement in sports (running) was the most likely cause. Her parents were very demanding, with expectations of high achievement and intense effort at her practices. She dutifully obliged by winning championship titles (much to the delight of her parents). When she turned 18 she left home and headed to university. This presented her with freedoms and opportunities that she had never experienced before. Jill continued to practice with the intensity that she had been accustomed to, but with no one to prompt her she started to drop out of workouts. She started to cry before, during, and after practices. She became racked with guilt because she could not, and did not want to, run any more. Jill continued to attend practices but was thoroughly miserable. She stopped her healthy eating habits, could not sleep, and fell into a depression. She clearly hated her sport, and what compounded her feelings were fear and guilt because she could not tell her parents how she felt.

With much coaxing from several concerned coaches and teammates, Jill agreed to counseling. She was advised to take a complete break from running—her first in 9 years. To their credit and to the surprise of their daughter, Jill's parents were very supportive of her decision to rest.

A full year later, Jill started to run again. A few months after that, on terms that she dictated, Jill participated in a running race and really enjoyed it. Her joy in sports had returned.

Although sports (and exercise in general) do have a therapeutic effect, the way that some sports are presented to at-risk children actually compounds the problems they are dealing with. Highly anxious girls—who are self-conscious about their body image—are at risk of developing anorexia and depression (Halmi, 1997; Kaye et al., 2004). Students prone to severe disruptive behavior are at risk of being marginalized by coaches and peers and this, in turn, may exacerbate any tendencies for depression.

It is fair to acknowledge that there can be many sources of depression, and the purpose of this section is not to blame coaches and parents. Some children have a predisposition to depression, and such bouts could emerge in whatever social situation they might find themselves. But as the safety and well-being of all children should be the primary concern of sports coaches, they should be mindful of the culture that they are promoting and consider what effects this may have on the emotional state of children who continually face complex challenges.

How Does Exclusion from Sports Damage Self-Confidence?

An athlete with low self-esteem—whether it has been acquired as a result of ridicule and exclusion, or whether it is a natural extension of a shy and nervous personality—requires careful nurturing to ensure a positive experience in sports. Kernis (2003) has suggested that of more concern is not that a child has low (athletic or general) self-esteem, but the degree to which this self-esteem fluctuates. All children need support as they try to develop their self-image; it is often fragile and subject to change. A child with poor athletic skills, but who receives lots of praise and encouragement may develop a stable sense of inner confidence. Conversely, a talented child who is winning races, and so forth, may feel very insecure if there is a high degree of expectation for performance and criticism for setbacks.

Rogers (1959) and Harter (1999) wrote about the debilitating effects of conditional acceptance. This is the notion that learning that acceptance only comes with strings attached (e.g., success on the sports field, or making a meaningful contribution to the game) creates a false state of self. The child then develops an inner dialogue: "I am liked when I do well on the sports field. I am disliked (maybe even loathed) when I make a mistake." Once this dialogue (and its variants) is internalized, the power of self-fulfilling prophecy kicks in.

Stanley Coopersmith (1967) found that self-esteem could be linked to the style of parenting the child receives. Three factors seem to be linked to high self-esteem: the parent's acceptance of their child, the parent clearly defining limits of behavior, and the parent's respect for the child's individuality. There are plenty of examples of parents prowling the sidelines demanding a certain standard of performance from their child, and when the child fails to reach that standard, the child is berated for a lack of effort. A child who receives acknowledgement and praise for his or her effort (despite the outcome) is more likely to develop respect for the coach or parent as a guide in the development of self-esteem.

How to Identify a Young Athlete with Low Self-Esteem

Low self-esteem reveals itself in the thoughts and behaviors of young athletes who may exhibit all or a few of the following characteristics.

Listen for Self-Deprecating Comments

Self-deprecating comments, such as "I am useless at sports—what's the point in playing" or "I can never seem to do anything right" are quite common in children with fragile self-esteem. Reassurance, while important, is not likely to produce a quick fix with a child who has an entrenched view of his or her ability. Indeed, attempts at suggesting otherwise may come across as glib and not effective. Building confidence takes time.

Watch the Girls in Particular

Research has shown that girls are more likely to be excessively critical in evaluating their performances (Pomerantz, Altermatt, & Saxon, 2002). Girls need a lot more emotional encouragement and reassurance on the sports field than boys. A critical coach may only exacerbate feelings of uncertainty and disappointment the young athlete may be experiencing. The research has also suggested that girls tend to look upon their coach or teacher as an ally. This reinforces the potential impact the coach may have on the athlete; thus coaches need to design their methods of instruction and interaction with care. Making consistently positive remarks and providing a strong sense that the children are liked and valued—even if their athletic skills may happen to be poor—provides a framework for children to build their self-image.

Watch for Teasing

Teasing other kids, displaying bullying behavior, reacting in an excessively emotional way to setbacks, refusing to make a serious effort in practices, not following directions, or cheating are behaviors that you may observe in a child with low self-esteem.

Ways of Coping with Stress and Anxiety

Stress reduction and ways to cope with anxiety are multibillion-dollar industries. From counseling to self-help, from pharmaceuticals to naturopathic techniques, there are many ways of dealing with these issues. A comprehensive account of the benefits or weakness of these strategies is beyond the scope of this book, and the information presented throughout this book should not be interpreted as therapy or an endorsement of one treatment over another. Coaches working with anxious children may benefit from an awareness of different strategies that can be used to help reduce stress and promote a child's sense of security and acceptance in sports.

When Is It Appropriate to Use Stress and Anxiety Reduction Techniques?

Before I discuss the range of options that parents and coaches can use to help anxious children, a few cautions are needed. Rather than concentrating on ways to help this child cope, a more important question is, why is this child feeling highly anxious or stressed in the first place? Is the child feeling excessive pressure to perform or behave in a certain way? Does the child believe there are no appropriate outlets for his or her sense of frustration or feelings of insecurity? Commonsense judgment is required from parents, teachers, and coaches. A child experiencing situational anxiety—perhaps it is something that is derived from their desire to do well in a game—probably does not require professional support from trained interventionists. A few well-placed words of compassion and support from parents and coaches can help the child develop competitive resilience and overcome uncertainties.

Behavioral Techniques to Cope with Stress and Anxiety

This book takes the view that a compassionate and supportive-learning sports environment will go a long way to remove the sources of stress and anxiety perceived by young athletes. Coaches should expect that reassuring and supporting children is an important part of their role.

Excessively competitive sports situations actually compound the insecurities and emotional uncertainties of children who are emotionally fragile.

If the young athlete is still very anxious despite receiving compassionate support, removing the child from the source of the anxiety and finding other ways for him or her to be involved in sports may be all that is required. There may be times when a student's stress or anxiety level requires more supportive intervention. A coach may be able to use some of the techniques to be discussed next, but they are also the tools of counseling and should only be used as coaching support, not therapeutic intervention.

Avoidance Reduction

The term *avoidance reduction* is a touch misleading, for the approach encourages the athlete to face discomfort (with support) rather than to avoid it. In this technique the coach and athlete discuss the origins of the anxiety; some of these anxiety/stress precursors may be simple to identify—"I get nervous before the start of the race"—or more complex—"No one on the team likes me." Confidence-building measures that utilize techniques such as visualization and positive self-talk have been shown to help alleviate sources of anxiety (Hatzigeorgiadis, Theodorakis, & Zourbanos, 2004).

Goal Setting and Increasing Athlete Engagement in the Sport

The SMART goal-setting technique was discussed in Chapter 3. It can be used in this context to help an athlete overcome anxiety about participating, for example, in a sport. The goals might include just observing the game, or participating only in elements of the practice that the athlete feels comfortable with, and so forth. The idea is simply to expose the athlete to the source of the stress or anxiety and try to counter it with support from the coach and peer mentors. Once the athlete starts to interact with and engage other participants, and if the sport is presented in a manner that the athlete can relate to, it is hoped that the sources of stress and anxiety will start to dissipate. This process is something that will follow its own timeline. An athlete anxious about joining a new club may quickly become comfortable when the games start. However, a young athlete with a complex anxiety condition may require ongoing support to assist his or her participation.

Cognitive Techniques to Cope with Stress and Anxiety

Cognitive techniques that can be used to cope with stress, anxiety, and depression include stress inoculation training (SIT), mental imagery, visuomotor behavior rehearsal (VMBR), and cognitive restructuring.

Stress Inoculation Training

SIT (Meichenbaum, 1996) is a protocol that trains the student to cope with stress or anxiety-inducing situations. There are three phases in this protocol.

In the conceptualization phase the student learns to recognize what may be causing the stress. The perception of threat or uncertainty is then approached from a problem-solving perspective and a series of goals to deal with these issues are mapped out by the child and the mentor (parent or coach).

The skills acquisition phase trains the student in specific coping skills. These are uniquely tailored to the child's circumstances. Some of these skills can be taught by a coach in the sports context, but most are likely developed in social skills forums (with counselors, support groups, and so forth). Examples of these coping skills include the following:

- Emotional self-regulation—teaching the child to recognize the triggers for stress and anxiety and then employing diversionary or calming strategies to cope
- Self-talk or self-soothing strategies—using positive affirmations to calm oneself or to help direct behavior (e.g., to "psych up" the athlete or energize him or her in preparation for a performance)

The third phase of SIT is the application and follow-through phase. Here the student draws on the skills that have been taught and utilizes them in the situation that threatens emotional security. The student is trained to recognize the warning signs of potential anxiety and employ coping skills accordingly.

Mental Imagery

Mental imagery is a practical skill that all athletes can use to help them overcome some of the challenges that they face. A lack of confidence or self-belief are common symptoms experienced by the children who have difficulties in sports. Imagery skills fall into two basic categories: internal and external imagery. Both techniques help the athlete exercise mastery or coping. Internal imagery has been described as "an approximation of the real life phenomenology such that the person actually feels those sensations which might be expected while participating in the actual situation" (Mahoney & Avener, 1977, p. 136). Children being trained to use mastery internal imagery would think about the sports situation that is challenging, but rather than focusing on how bad they feel, they would focus on positive thoughts and sensations that indicate coping with stress. External imagery is when "a person views him or herself from the perspective of an external observer" (Mahoney & Avener, 1977, p. 137). Athletes using this type of imagery view themselves performing the skill correctly or being calm, confident, and in control of their performance.

Visuomotor Behavior Rehearsal

VMBR is a technique that combines relaxation and mental imagery. The athlete first learns progressive muscular relaxation; this is squeezing the large muscle groups, then relaxing them, so as to identify the difference in tension. With practice, the child learns to recognize the social triggers that increase muscular tension and reduce performance. Once the relaxation component of VMBR has been mastered, the athlete practices imagining performing without anxiety, performing skills with competence, and feeling happy in the sports environment. Lane (1980) noted four main benefits of VMBR:

- The enhancement of relaxation and the reduction of anxiety
- Error correction of sports skills
- An increased ability to concentrate
- Increased skill development

Suinn (1976) noted that VMBR can provide a well-controlled copy of the sporting experience and helps to prepare the mind and body for movement.

Cognitive Restructuring

The Greek Stoic philosopher Epictetus once stated, "Men are not disturbed by things but by the views they take of them" (Arrian, 125 A.D.). Irrational beliefs are significant sources of anxiety and stress, and they can undermine a child's involvement in sports. Ellis (1962) listed five irrational beliefs that generate anxiety:

- *One must be thoroughly competent, adequate, and achieving in every way in order to be worthwhile.* Children with the types of challenges described throughout this book sometimes have to play sports with people who promulgate this belief statement. Such views undermine the child's sense of self-worth and inhibit the enjoyment that the child can receive from sports.

- *It is necessary to be loved or approved of by every other significant person.* When children experience social difficulties with other children you often hear comments like "No one likes me." Although this view is in a general sense irrational, a child not approved of or accepted by an influential peer (or worse, the coach) will have difficulty enjoying the sport.

- *It is catastrophic when things are not the way we would like them to be.* Coaches who exclude or ignore children in need of support can actually reinforce this irrational view. Not being selected for a team, for example, can be a devastating experience to a child. Although selection is a practical neces- sity in many sports, the manner in which it is done can reframe the child's irrational view. Also, providing the children not selected with other op- portunities can lessen that decision's impact.

- *Unhappiness and anxiety are externally caused and we have no control over our feelings.* Taking responsibility for your feelings and deciding on positive ways of reacting to setbacks and adversity are core skills of an emotion- ally resilient child.

- *If something is threatening or dangerous, one must keep thinking that it might happen.* It is understandable that children who have had poor experiences in sports may believe that similar outcomes will occur if they keep partici- pating. The checklists in this chapter emphasize the importance of gath- ering information about the child's experiences, what has worked well, and what should be avoided. Using this information to design the sports environment increases the chances for this child to find success and acceptance; it also helps to change this irrational belief.

It is not realistic to expect children to understand the psychological logic of these irrational beliefs, but affirmation statements can be used to help the child "restructure" these irrational thoughts. Such statements might be simple: "I'm going to have fun today!" They might focus on a certain aspect of thought: "I'm not going to get 'down' when I make a mistake." Or they might emphasize effort: "I am going to really work hard on that particular skill. I know I can achieve it!" In time, the child internalizes positive and self-supporting attributions, thus displacing some (if not all) of these irrational beliefs.

Physical Techniques to Cope with Stress and Anxiety

Physical techniques play an important role in helping to reduce the insidious effects of stress or anxiety. Many of these techniques utilize breathing patterns. It almost goes without saying that breathing is a critical part of a child's sporting performance (and of course, life!). Breathing is part of the body's purification system—it removes poisonous waste products (carbon dioxide) and brings oxygen into the bloodstream, which is then distributed to the tissues and organs; thus, it has both restorative and invigorating properties. It is an autonomic function—it happens without our thinking about it, and yet we can exert some influence over the way it works. Here are some of techniques for controlling breathing.

Tension-Releasing Technique
If you have ever attended an opera, you have probably been amazed at the power and resonance of the singers' voices. These performers will tell you that although their vocal cords shape sound, the volume comes from their use of controlled breaths and the correct use of their diaphragm. Try this to release tension and enhance relaxation: Find a place that is quiet and where there will be no disruptions. Rest your hands over your abdomen (above the belly-button) so that the tips of several fingers touch. Inhale deeply. This should take 3–5 seconds and be slow and controlled. If you are using your diaphragm correctly, your fingertips should gently separate. Let the breath out as slowly as you inhaled. Repeat this process 10 times. Try to empty your mind of any "clutter"—let go of the things that are bothering you.

Quieting Response
This technique uses verbal self-suggestion in combination with relaxation. On inhaling the athlete makes assertive statements like "I am calm." When exhaling the athlete imagines the breath traveling down the inside of the body. This process is repeated three times. This technique is a good one to use in the last few minutes immediately prior to the start of a competition.

Breathing for Relaxation

The three-part breathing program is a technique that can help to induce a state of relaxation. After taking a deep diaphragmatic breath, the athlete visualizes three portions of the lungs, lower, middle, and upper, sequentially filling each with air. This exercise is repeated 3–4 times.

In the "5:1 count" the athlete takes a large breath and then slowly exhales. This breath is termed number 5. After again inhaling and exhaling the athlete states, "I am more relaxed than number 5." The second breath is labeled number 4. The process continues so that by number 1 the athlete is more calm and relaxed.

In the "1:2 ratio" the athlete inhales for the count of four. On exhalation the athlete counts to eight. This technique is repeated until the athlete reaches a deep and relaxed state.

Breathing for Invigoration

There are occasions when young athletes need to switch states from deep relaxation to a more energized approach. Breath in and out rapidly through the nose, but make sure that you keep your mouth tightly shut (thus avoiding hyperventilation). Keep the breaths equal and short. Continue this process for about 30 seconds, then stop. With practice, you should find that this technique fills you with energy and heightens your state of preparation.

Breathing to Enhance Concentration

One technique that, with lots of practice, is particularly effective for pain control is one that combines attention-focusing strategies with controlled breathing. Concentrating on the sensations of breath moving in and out of the nose and mouth can help to shift the focus away from exercise discomfort (or pain). Having an external focal point (for example, a landmark in a running race) and alternating that with a focus on relaxed abdominal breaths can also reduce the perception of discomfort. Athletes may prefer to combine their breathing skills with an internal focal point, for example, thinking of a time and a place (or race) when their breathing and performance seemed to be perfectly in synch. The breathing patterns in a race situation should include controlled, deep, invigorating inhalations and exhalations.

Whatever your intended use for these breathing techniques, remember to keep them natural and unstrained. Breathing patterns that are not comfortable for a child are not particularly effective.

A Checklist to Help Students with Stress and Anxiety to Participate in Sports

Assessment

❑ Asking what are this student's strengths, interests, and areas of support helps a coach to plan for an anxious student's inclusion in sports. Anxiety often emerges when an athlete faces an uncertain and potentially threatening (by the student's interpretation) situation. Identifying what those situations are and helping the athlete either to cope or to avoid those situations reduces the anxiety.

❏ There are a number of sports questionnaires available for coaches and teachers to use to assess the type and degree of anxiety their athletes may be experiencing. One of the most practical instruments is the Sports Competitive Anxiety Test (SCAT) developed by Rainer Martens (1977). The SCAT asks athletes 15 questions relating to their feelings prior to sports competitions. Their responses are given a numerical value, which, in turn, indicates their level of anxiety. The SCAT can be particularly useful for identifying specific areas that cause an athlete anxiety. For example, some athletes may experience intense anxiety just before the competition and yet be completely relaxed once the event starts. Other athletes may experience anxiety and uncertainty for the duration of the event.

Designing a Successful Learning Environment

❏ A lack of confidence in their sports abilities and/or social competence can be precursors to the athletes who experience anxiety. Coaches who design practices that highlight an anxious child's lack of competence—for example, they make fun of mistakes the athlete makes or ridicule the way the athlete looks, speaks, behaves, and so forth—will be a catalyst for increased anxiety for this young athlete.

❏ A successful learning environment is built on principles of inclusion, acceptance, compassion, and understanding.

❏ Coaches and teachers should discuss with the parents the origins of this athlete's anxiety and determine what practical measures can be used to support this athlete.

Coaching Techniques that Work Well for This Child

❏ Coaches should understand that their manner of interaction will be influential in this athlete's perception of anxiety. Coaches who shout, threaten, or cajole their athletes to achieve better performances may possibly have the desired effect with highly resilient children (until they get fed up with being shouted at!), but are almost ineffective with an athlete who is sensitive and overwhelmed with anxiety by such approaches.

Differentiation Strategies

❏ Group your anxious athletes with children who will be supportive and understanding of errors made on the sports field.

❏ Use choice boards to help build the child's confidence.

❏ Use variable pacing learning techniques. These techniques allow the athletes to slow down their pace of learning if they feel the rate of introduction of new skills and concepts is too fast and is causing them uncertainty (and thus, anxiety).

Final Thoughts

This book has cautioned coaches not to use some of the information presented as therapy; that is particularly the case for young athletes who may be exhibiting symptoms of stress or anxiety. With anxiety and stress, some of the characteristics may be sports specific; for example, the athlete may want to do really well but faces competition from a gifted rival. Once the race or game is over, the stress and anxiety disappear. Such experiences can be supported by the coach employing some of the strategies discussed. But when the athlete reports not eating or sleeping, self-harm behavior, and so forth, this is clearly beyond the domain of coaching. The child should be referred to the parents with the recommendation that they pursue an appropriate medical consultation.

CHAPTER 17

Putting It All Together:
Creating a Sporting Environment
Where All Children Can Thrive

Helping all children find success in sports requires the coordination of the themes covered throughout this book: creating the right environment, understanding what motivates your athletes, deciding which teaching and coaching strategies would best meet the child's needs, and so forth. This chapter brings these themes together and offers a practical plan to help achieve full inclusion in sports.

Creating opportunities for all children to play sports—either in school or on community teams—requires systems-level support (Villa & Thousand, 2003). Inclusive sports environments emerge from school and community organizations where there is strong and visionary leadership that has created a framework for these children to find a place in sports. These leaders provide administrative support (providing the resources), redefine the roles of the coaching staff, obtain adult support (from parents, mentors, and aides), and secure collaboration from other groups. Visionary leaders recognize that sports organizations—while desiring success in their various leagues—should also be recognized for the opportunities that they offer to less able members of society.

These leaders understand the benefits that sports can provide and wish to reach out to all children. Visionary leaders are bold and understand that some people suggest that providing inclusive sports is not within the mandate of their organization. But these leaders are driven by a noble purpose; they recognize the joy that a child with poor physical skills feels when he or she completes a game as part of a team. These leaders understand the pride of parents when they see their child playing as an accepted member of a team. These leaders set out a plan and then market it to the organization and community. A sound plan responds to the needs of the people in the community. It does not just cater to the fit and capable, but recognizes the benefits of "Sport For All."

Designing the Plan for Inclusive Sports

This plan invariably draws on principles enveloped in an athlete's Code of Rights and Responsibilities (see Chapter 5) and the themes articulated throughout this book. Here are the important elements that should be included:

- Promote active living. Sports organizations can play an influential role in promoting values and attitudes to sports. Success in a competition is admirable (if not strongly desirable), but this should be balanced with seeking to instill an appreciation for healthy living and provide opportunities for participants, not just for the season, but hopefully for life.
- Train coaches to employ differentiation and other pedagogical practices that recognize the varying needs of athletes.
- Ensure the physical safety and emotional security of all participants in the sports environment.
- Provide opportunities for volunteerism and mentoring. Encouraging parent and athlete advocacy helps organizations understand the needs of the community.
- Work with other community programs and sports organizations to see if there is a way to augment or complement their programs. Working in partnership may create new ways of making sports attractive to children of different backgrounds, learning styles, and special needs.

Developing a Communications Plan
to Help Vulnerable Children Participate in Sports

When developing a communications plan to help students participate in sports, it is important to consider the following:

- Decide how you are going to pitch the idea of participating to the child. How might the child respond to your approach?
- Just like any advertising campaign, you must present a product that is (or could be) appealing.
- Demonstrate a need to the child; perhaps you emphasize that new friendships and exciting social opportunities are to be found in this sport.
- Have a plan to cope with dissonance (disagreement or refusal).
- Have fun and provide rewards—recognize the child's efforts with lots of genuine praise and a reward.

Community Involvement and Sports

It is easy to say that there is no demand for programs of adapted sports. After consultation and some parent advocacy our local recreation center decided to offer an adapted swimming program. We were initially told there was no need, nor had there been any requests for such programs. When the program was announced, the recreation center was inundated with requests from parents of children with disabilities and special learning needs. They sold out within the first day and had to hire more staff to meet the demand. Credit is due to the community sports programmer for recognizing that these children (unable to participate in regular swim programs) craved the same opportunities as their more able peers.

Poor community sports facilities, the absence of parental involvement (thus a lack of positive role modeling), and the costs associated with sports programs all inhibit the participation of children from these communities. Statistics can, of course, be misleading, and invariably the reality is more complex than a number would indicate. Some communities, even though they may have a high number of low-income inhabitants, have thriving sports organizations and strong rates of participation.

Community sports programs that are successful likely have high levels of parent involvement and offer a collaborative partnership that is designed to put the child's best interests first. These programs promote social relationships, offer support for staff (professional development), and provide not only activities that are inclusive but also differentiated coaching to meet the varied learning styles of the athletes.

Advocating for Your Child

Creating a sporting environment where children of all abilities are included may require the advocacy of parents to initiate changes. Children with challenging needs are often misunderstood, and it is fair to assume that some coaches and organizations may believe that they cannot cope with these children. Knowledge and understanding of the child's needs not only serves to inform and clear up misconceptions, but also allays fears. The person who takes the most influential role in this process is the parent. Parents advocate for their child, that is, they act and speak on behalf of another person. Following are a few practical suggestions to consider when advocating for your child.

Have a Clear Goal

Having a clear goal is important. What exactly do you want, and is this in the child's best interests? Is it practical for the sports organization to accommodate this goal? Don't forget that these organizations (schools) are charged with the mandate of providing the best service they can for many children, not just yours. Be realistic. Are your requests reasonable?

Research Whether There Have Been Similar Requests

Find out about previous requests to this organization. Have there been other individuals who have made similar requests? How were these requests handled?

Respect the Organization and the Coaches

Respect the organization and the coaches involved. Anger and hostility are not part of the profile of parents who are effective advocates for their child. Calm, thoughtful, reasoned appeals to the representatives of the organization will have a greater chance of success than threats of lawsuits.

Understand that Partnership Requires at Least Two Willing Members

The sports organization may be willing to accommodate your requests, but the organization may lack knowledge of the matter. This lack of information may make the organization uncertain. It is your job as the advocate for your child to relay relevant information, such as providing explanations of your child's challenges or preferred learning styles. It is not fair to let others discover your child has difficulties and not provide them with a plan or guidance to help your child.

Join a Support Group

When you join a support group, you may find that other parents have been through similar experiences and may be able to offer advice. This advice can be helpful when advocating for your child.

Work with Coaches

Try to work closely with the coaches who work with your child. Offer them your support and recognize that many of these individuals are volunteers who devote much of their spare time for the love of the sport.

Talk to Other Parents

Talking to and engaging with other parents may provide information that may help your child's path to inclusion. You will find that most (reasonable) parents empathize with your desire to see your child happy and accepted by peers; these parents may discuss your child's needs and secure the understanding of their children. This proactive step can be a very effective tool in preparing children and other parents for your child's introduction into the sport.

Involve Your Child in the Advocacy Process

Help your child to understand that success and frustration is part of sports. Encourage him or her to share these feelings with you, the coach, and teammates. Eventually you will want your child to be able to advocate for him- or herself (or others in a similar situation); this empowers the child on a path to personal responsibility. Encourage your child to stand up for him- or herself.

> Consider the rights of others before your own feelings, and the feelings of others before your own rights.
> —John Wooden (as cited in Williams, Walton, and Wimbish, 2006, p. 95)

Final Thoughts

This book has offered a lot of advice to help children with different challenges find acceptance from their peers and personal success in sports. The degree of compassion and understanding from those who interact with these children determines the effectiveness of these techniques. Coaches may be willing to accommodate or modify their programs, but just as important is positive role modeling of the virtues that promote healthy respect for all athletes. Coaches who are recognized as excellent motivators are also likely to be skilled analysts of athlete behavior. They understand the varying needs of their athletes and can draw on a vast range of strategies to help support them. The needs of children with challenges may be different, their motives for participation in sports perhaps not typical, but the coach who takes the time to understand these athletes can exert a significant influence on their development.

To all children questioning if they should even participate in sports, I offer these final words of advice:

- Find a coach who believes in you and wants to help you fulfill your athletic potential.

- Don't be deterred by your challenges—may they spur you to achieve great things.

- Never let anyone or anything stop you from enjoying all the wonderful things that playing sports has to offer.

References

Aicinena, S. (1991). The teacher and student attitudes toward physical education. *The Physical Educator, 48*(1), 28–32.

Altarac, M., & Saroha, E. (2007, February). Lifetime prevalence of learning disability among US children. *Pediatrics, 119*, S77–S83.

American Academy of Pediatrics. (2000). Intensive training and sports specialization in young athletes. *Pediatrics, 106*(1), 154–157.

American Academy of Pediatrics. (2001). AAP policy statement: Children, adolescents, and television, *Pediatrics, 107*(2), 423–426.

American Obesity Association. (2002). *AOA Survey on Parents' Perceptions of their Children's Weight.* (Online) http://www.obesity1.tempdomai

American Psychiatric Association. (2000). *Diagnostic and statistical manual of mental disorders* (4th ed.). Washington, DC: Author.

Andersen, R.E., Crespo, C.J., Bartlett, S.J., Cheskin, L.J., & Pratt, M. (1998). Relationship of physical activity and television watching with body weight and level of fatness among children: Results from the Third National Health and Nutrition Examination Survey. *JAMA, 279*, 938–942.

Anderson, C.B., Hughes, S.O., & Fuemmeler, B.F. (2009). Parent-child attitude congruence on type and intensity of physical activity: Testing multiple mediators of sedentary behavior in older children. *Health Psychology, 28*, 4.

Armstrong, T. (1998). *Awakening genius in the classroom.* Alexandria, VA: Association for Supervision and Curriculum Development.

Armstrong, T. (2001, November). IKSWAL—Interesting kids saddled with alienating labels. *Educational Leadership, 59*, 38–40.

Arrian. (125 A.D.). *Enchiridion—Handbook of Epictetus.*

Ashcraft, M.-H. (2002). *Cognition* (3rd ed.). Upper Saddle River, NJ: Prentice Hall.

Ashcraft, M., & Kirk, E. (2001). The relationship among working memory, math anxiety and performance. *Journal of Experimental Psychology, 130*, 224–227.

Austin, I. (2007, September 24). Girl denied chance to play soccer. *The Vancouver Province.*

Auxter, D., Pyfer, J., & Huettig, C. (1997). *Principles and methods of adapted physical education and recreation* (8th ed.). St. Louis: Mosby.

Balyi, I., & Hamilton, A. (2004). *Long-term athlete development: Trainability in childhood and adolescence. Windows of opportunity. Optimal trainability.* Victoria, British Columbia, Canada: National Coaching Institute British Columbia & Advanced Training and Performance.

Barber, M.A., Milich, R., & Welch, R. (1996). Effects of reinforcement schedule and task difficulty on the performance of attention deficit hyperactivity disordered and control boys. *Journal of Clinical Child Psychology, 25*, 66–76.

Barkley, R.A. (1997). ADHD and the nature of self-control. New York: Guilford Press.

Barkley, R.A. (1998). Attention-deficit hyperactivity disorder. *Scientific American, 279*(3), 66–71.

Barnett, N.P., Smoll, F.L., & Smith, R.E. (1992). Effects of enhancing coach-athlete relationships on youth sport attrition. *The Sport Psychologist, 6*, 111–127.

Baron, R.A., & Byrne, D. (1984). *Social psychology: Understanding human interaction* (4th ed.). Newton, MA: Allyn & Bacon.

Barynina, I.I., & Vaitsekhovskii, S.M. (1992, August). The aftermath of early sports specialization for highly qualified swimmers. *Fitness Sports Review International*, 132–133.

Baumeister, R.F., & Leary, M. (1995). The need to belong: Desire for interpersonal attachments as a fundamental human motivation. *Psychological Bulletin, 117*(3), 497–529.

Bauminger, N., & Kasari, C. (2000). Loneliness and friendship in children with high functioning autism. *Child Development, 71*(2), 447–456.

Bedini, L., & Henderson, K. (1994). Women with disabilities and the challenge to leisure service providers. *Journal of Park and Recreation Administration, 12*(1), 17–34.

Beilock, S., & Carr, T. (2005). When high powered people fail: Working memory and "choking under pressure" in math. *Psychological Science, 16*, 101–105.

Biddle, S., & Goudas, M. (1996). Analysis of children's physical activity and its association with adult encouragement and social cognitive variables. *Journal of School Health, 66*(2), 75–78.

Blair, T. (2008, July 21). An uplifting power. *Time, 171*, 26–27.

Block, M.E. (1999). Did we jump on the wrong bandwagon? Problems with inclusion in physical education. *Palaestra, 15*(3), 30–36.

Bloom, B.S. (Ed.). (1956). *Taxonomy of educational objectives: Book 1, Cognitive domain.* New York: Longman.

Bloom, G.A., Durand-Bush, N., Schinke, R.J., & Salmela, J.H. (1998). The importance of mentoring in the development of coaches and athletes. *International Journal of Sport Psychology, 29*, 267–281.

Boiduck, B. (2004, May). Inclusion: We all belong. *Early Intervention Nova Scotia Newsletter, 7.*

Brady, F. (2004, February). Children's organized sports: A developmental perspective. *Journal of Health, Physical Education, Recreation, and Dance 75*(2), 35–41.

British Department of Health. (2006). *Measuring childhood obesity: Guidance to primary care trusts.* Retrieved from http://www.dh.gov.uk/assetroot/04/12/64/04126406

Brockner, J. (1983). Low self-esteem and behavioral plasticity. In L. Wheeler & P.R. Shaver (Eds.), *Review of personality and social psychology* (Vol. 4, pp. 237–271). Beverly Hills: Sage Publications.

Brown, T.E. (2000). Emerging understandings of attention deficit disorders and comorbidities. In T.E. Brown (Ed.), *Attention-deficit disorders and comorbidities in children, adolescents and adults* (pp. 3–55). Washington, DC: American Psychiatric Press.

Brustad, R.J. (1988). Affective outcomes in competitive youth sport: The influence of intrapersonal and socialization factors. *Journal of Sport and Exercise Psychology, 10*, 307–321.

Brustad, R.J. (1996). Parental and peer influence on children's psychological development through sport. In F.L. Smoll & R.E. Smith (Eds.), *Children and youth in sport: A biopsychosocial perspective* (pp. 112–124). Madison, WI: Brown & Benchmark.

Bryan, T. (1974). Peer popularity of learning disabled children. *Journal of Learning Disabilities, 7*, 31–35.

Burckes-Miller, M.E., & Black, D.R. (1988). Male and female college athletes: Prevalence of anorexia nervosa and bulimia nervosa. *Athletic Training, 23*(2), 137–141.

Burdette, H.L., & Whittaker, R.C. (2005). Resurrecting free play in young children: Looking beyond fitness and fatness to attention, affiliation and affect. *Archives of Pediatric Adolescent Medicine, 159*, 46–50.

Burgeson, C.R., Wechsler, H., Brener, N.D., Young, J.C., & Spain, C.G. (2001). Physical education and activity: Results from the School Health Policies and Programs Study 2000. *Journal of School Health, 71*, 279–293.

Butcher, J. (2002). Fit for life. *Future Reflections, 22*(1), 38–42.

Butler, L.F. (2000). Fair play: Respect for all. *Journal of Physical Education, Recreation and Dance, 71*(2), 32–35.

Caine, R., & Caine, G. (1997). *Unleashing the power of perceptual change: The potential of brain-based teaching.* Alexandria, VA: Association for Supervision and Curriculum Development.

Calfas, K. & Taylor, W. (1994). Effects of physical activity on psychological variables in adolescents. *Pediatric Exercise Science, 6,* 406–423.

Canadian Fitness and Lifestyle Research Institute. (2002). Increasing physical activity: Assessing trends from 1998–2003. *Physical Activity Monitor.*

Cassidy, J., & Ditty, K. (2001). Gender differences among newborns on a transient otoacoustic emissions test for hearing. *Journal of Music Therapy, 38,* 28–35.

Castelli, D.M., Hillman, C.H., Buck, S.M., & Erwin, H.E. (2007). Physical fitness and academic achievement in third and fifth grade students. *Journal of Sport and Exercise Physiology, 29,* 239–252.

Center on Education Policy. (2007, December). *Choices, changes, and challenges: Curriculum and instruction in the NCLB era.* Washington, DC: Author.

Center on Education Policy. (2008, February). *Instructional time in elementary schools: A closer look at changes for specific subjects.* Washington, DC: Author.

Center on Education Policy. (2008, August). *Time out: Is recess in danger?* Washington, DC: Author.

Centers for Disease Control and Prevention. (1997). Guidelines for school and community programs to promote lifelong physical activity among young people. *Morbidity and Mortality Weekly Report, 46*(RR-6), 1–36.

Centers for Disease Control and Prevention. (1999). Youth risk behavior surveillance United States. *Morbidity and Mortality Weekly Report, 49*(SS-5), 1–94.

Centers for Disease Control and Prevention. (2007, February 9). Autism and developmental disabilities monitoring. *Morbidity and Mortality Weekly Report, 56*(SS-01), 12–28.

Centers for Disease Control and Prevention. (2007, August 29). Prevalence of children with a learning disability. *Morbidity and Mortality Weekly Report, 57*(34), 947.

Centers for Disease Control and Prevention. (2008, June 6). Youth risk behavior surveillance 2007: Prevalence of childhood obesity. *Morbidity and Mortality Weekly Report, 57*(SS-04), 1–131.

Centers for Disease Control and Prevention (2009, August). *Autism spectrum disorders (ASDs).* Retrieved 12/21/2009 from http://www.cdc.gov/ncbddd/autism/index.html

Centers for Disease Control and Prevention. (2009, December 18). Prevalence of autism spectrum disorders—Autism and developmental disabilities monitoring network, United States, 2006. *Morbidity and Mortality Weekly Report, 58*(SS10), 1–20.

Children's participation in sports. (2000, Autumn). *Canadian Social Trends,* 20–24.

Chomitz, V., Slining, M., McGowan, R., Mitchell, S., Dawson, G., & Hacker, H. (2009). Is there a relationship between physical fitness and academic achievement? Positive results from public school children in the northeastern United States. *Journal of School Health, 79*(1), 30–37.

Clark, B. (2002). *Growing up gifted* (5th ed.). Columbus, OH: Merrill.

Clarke, A., & Hubball, H. (2001). Physical education methods course as an immersion experience in an elementary school setting. *Avante, 7*(2), 11–27.

Coaching Association of Canada. (1996). *Straight talk about children and sport: Advice for parents, coaches and teachers.* Ontario: Mosaic Press.

Coakley, J. (1992). Burnout among adolescent athletes: A personal failure or a social problem? *Sociology of Sports Journal, 9,* 271–285.

Cochlear Corporation. (1996). *Static electricity and cochlear implants.* Englewood, CO: Author.

Coie, J.D., & Kuiper-Schmidt, A. (1983). A behavioral analysis of emerging social status in boys' groups. *Child Development, 54,* 1400–1416.

Coil, C. (2004). Standards-based activities and assessments for the differentiated classroom. Marion, IL: Pieces of Learning.

Comings, D.E., Himes, J., & Comings, B.G. (1989). An epidemiological study of Tourette syndrome in a single school district. *Journal of Clinical Psychology, 51,* 463–469.

Cone-Wesson, B., & Ramirez, G. (1997). Hearing sensitivity in newborns estimated from ABRs to bone-conducted sounds. *Journal of the American Academy of Audiology, 8,* 299–307.

Coopersmith, S. (1967). *The antecedents of self-esteem.* New York: W.H. Freeman.

Corsaro, W. (2003). *We're friends, right? Inside kids' culture.* Washington, DC: Joseph Henry Press.

Corso, J. (1959). Age and sex differences in thresholds. *Journal of the Acoustical Society of America, 31,* 489–507.

Cote, J. (2005, August). *Building pathways towards youth sports performance and continued participation.* Symposium conducted at the 11th World Congress of Sports Psychology of the International Society of Sports Psychology, Sydney, Australia.

Cothran, D.J., & Ennis, C.D. (1998). Curricula of mutual worth: Comparisons of students' and teachers' curricular goals. *Journal of Teaching in Physical Education, 17,* 307–327.

Crocker, J., & Wolfe, C.T. (2001). Contingencies of self-worth. *Psychological Review, 108,* 593–623.

Csikszentmihalyi, M., Rathunde, K., Whalen, S., & Wong, M. (1993). *Talented teenagers: The roots of success and failure.* New York: Cambridge University Press.

Curtner-Smith, M.D. (1996). The impact of an early field experience on preservice physical education teachers' conceptions of teaching. *Journal of Teaching in Physical Education, 15*(2), 224–250.

Daley, A.J. (2009). Can exergaming contribute to improving physical activity levels and health outcomes in children? *Pediatrics, 124*(2), 763–771.

Damiano, D.L., & Abel, M.F. (1998). Functional outcomes of strength training in spastic cerebral palsy. *Archives Physical Medical Rehabilation, 79,* 119.

Darrah, J., Wessel, J., Nearingburg, P., & O'Connor, M. (1999). Evaluation of a community fitness program for adolescents with cerebral palsy. *Pediatric Physical Therapy, 11,* 18–23.

Davidson, K., & Decker, T. (2006). Bloom's and beyond: Higher level questions and activities for the creative classroom. Marion, IL: Pieces of Learning.

Deci, E.L. (1975). *Intrinsic motivation.* New York: Plenum.

Deci, E.L., & Ryan, R.M. (1985). *Intrinsic motivation and self-determination in human behavior.* New York: Plenum.

Deshaies, P., Vallerand, R., & Guerrier, J.P. (1984). *La connaissance et l'attitude des jeunes sportifs Québécois face à l'esprit sportif.* Québec, Canada: À la Régie de la sécurité dans les sports du Québec.

Devine, M., & Broach, E. (1998). Inclusion in the aquatic environment. *Park and Recreation,* 60–67.

Dietz, W.H. (1983). Childhood obesity: Susceptibility, cause, and management. *Journal of Pediatrics, 103*(5), 676–686.

Dillingham, T.R. (2002). Limb amputation and limb deficiency: Epidemiology and recent trends in the United States. *Southern Medical Journal, 95,* 875–883.

Dodd, M. (1990, September 10). Children say having fun is no. 1. *USA Today.*

Doolittle, S.A., Dodds, P., & Placek, J.H. (1993). Persistence of beliefs about teaching during formal training of preservice teachers. *Journal of Teaching in Physical Education, 12*(4), 355–365.

Douglas, V.I. (1983). Attention and cognitive problems. In M. Rutter (Ed.), *Developmental neuropsychiatry* (pp. 280–329). New York: Guilford Press.

Duncan, B., Boyce, W.T., Itami, R., & Puffenbarger, N. (1983). A controlled trial of a physical fitness program for fifth grade students. *Journal of School Health, 53*(8), 467–471.

Dunn, J.M., Morehouse, J.W., & Fredericks, H.D. (1986). *Physical education for the severely handicapped: A systemic approach to data based gymnasium.* Austin, TX: PRO-ED.

Durstine, J.L., & Moore, G.E. (Eds.). (2003). *Exercise management for persons with chronic diseases and disabilities: Epilepsy.* Champaign, IL: Human Kinetics.

Dykens, E.M., Rosner, B.A., & Butterbaugh, G. (1998). Exercise and sports in children and adolescents with developmental disabilities: Positive physical and psychosocial effects. *Child and Adolescent Psychiatric Clinics of North America, 7*(4), 757–771.

Dyson, B. (2001). Cooperative learning in an elementary school physical education program. *Journal of Teaching in Physical Education, 20,* 264–281.

Dyson, B., & Grineski, S. (2001). Using cooperative learning structures to achieve quality physical education. *Journal of Physical Education, Recreation & Dance, 72*(2), 28–31.

Elliott, R.O., Dobbin, A.R., Rose, G.D., & Soper, H.V. (1994). Vigorous, aerobic exercise versus general motor training activities: Effects on maladaptive and stereotypic behaviors of adults with both autism and mental retardation. *Journal of Autism and Developmental Disorders, 24*(5), 565–576.

Ellis, A. (1962). *Reason and emotion in psychotherapy.* New York: Lyle Stuart.

Ennis, C.D., Solmon, M.A., Satina, B., Loftus, S.J., Mensch, J., & McCauley, M.T. (1999). Creating a sense of family in urban schools using the sport for peace curriculum. *Research Quarterly for Exercise and Sport, 70,* 273–285.

Epstein, J. (1988). Effective schools or effective students? Dealing with diversity. In R. Haskins & B. MacRae (Eds.), *Policies for America's public schools* (pp. 89–126). Norwood, NJ: Ablex.

Epstein, L.H., Wing, R.R., Koeske, R., & Valoski, A. (1987). Long-term effects of family-based treatment of childhood obesity. *Journal of Consulting and Clinical Psychology, 55*(1), 91–95.

Erikson, E.H. (1950). *Childhood and society.* New York: Norton.

European Union. (2001). *A charter for sport. Improving physical education and sport for children and young people in all European countries.* Bureau of the Committee for the Development of Sport, R (92) 13 rev., pp. 3–5.

Ewen, R. (2003). *An introduction to theories of personality* (6th ed.). Mahwah, NJ: Lawrence Erlbaum Associates.

Ewing, M.F., & Seefeldt, V. (1992). Patterns of participation and attrition in American agency-sponsored youth sports. In F.L. Smoll & R.E. Smith (Eds.), *Children and youth in sport: A biophysical perspective* (pp. 31–41). Dubuque, IA: Brown & Benchmark.

Falk, B., Bar-Or, O., Calvert, R., & MacDougall, J.D. (1992). Sweat gland response to exercise in the heat among pre-mid and late-pubertal boys. *Medicine Science and Sports Exercise, 24,* 313–319.

Falvey, M., Forest, M., Pearpoint, J., & Rosenberg, R. (1997). *All my life's a circle. Using the tools: Circles, MAPS and PATH* (2nd ed.). Toronto: Inclusion Press.

Falvey, M.A., Givner, C.C., & Kimm, C. (1995). What is an inclusive school? In R.A. Villa and J.S. Thousand (Eds.), *Creating an inclusive school* (pp. 34–58). Alexandria, VA: Association for Supervision and Curriculum Development.

Faucette, N., & Patterson, P. (1989). Classroom teachers and physical education: What they are doing and how they feel about it. *Education, 110*(1), 108–114.

Ferguson, R. (2002, November). *What doesn't meet the eye: Understanding and addressing racial disparities in high-achieving suburban schools* (pp. 20–21). Naperville, IL: Learning Point Associates.

Fernie, D.E., Kantor, R., & Whaley, K.L. (1995). Learning from classroom ethnographies: Same places, different times. In J.A. Hatch (Ed.), *Qualitative research in early childhood settings* (pp. 156–172). Westport, CT: Praeger.

Filipek, P.A., Accardo, P.J., Ashwal, S., Baranek, G.T., Cook, E.H., Jr., Dawson, G., et al. (2000). Practice parameter: Screening and diagnosis of autism: Report of the quality standards subcommittee of the American Academy of Neurology and the Child Neurology Society. *Neurology, 55*(4), 468–479.

Fland, G.F, Blair, S.N, & Blumenthal, J. (1992). Statement on exercise. Benefits and recommendations for physical activity programs for all Americans. *Circulation, 86*(1), 340–344.

Forest, M., O'Brien, J., & Pearpoint, J. (1993). *PATH: A workbook for planning positive, possible futures.* Toronto: Inclusion Press.

Frankl, D. (1998, March 5–8). *Children's and parents' attitudes toward competitive youth sports programs.* Paper presented at the 65th Annual CAHPERD State Conference, San Diego.

Freedman, D.S., Zuguo, M., Srinivasan, S.R., Berenson, G.S., & Dietz, W.H. (2007). Cardiovascular risk factors and excess adiposity among overweight children and adolescents: The Bogalusa Heart Study. *Journal of Pediatrics, 150*(1), 12–17.

French, W.L., Kast, F.E., & Rosenzweig, J.E. (1985). *Understanding human behavior in organizations.* New York: Harper & Row.

Gagné, F. (1985). Giftedness and talent: Reexamining a reexamination of the definitions. *Gifted Child Quarterly, 29,* 103–112.

Gaily, R.S., Gailey, A.M., & Sendelbach, S.J. (1995). *Home exercise guide for lower extremity amputees.* Miami, FL: Advanced Rehabilitation Therapy.

Gandini, L. (1993, November). Fundamentals of the Reggio Emilia approach to early childhood education. *Young Children, 49*(1), 4–8.

Gardner, H. (1983). *Frames of mind: The theory of multiple intelligences.* New York: Basic Books.

Gardner, H. (November, 1995). Reflections on multiple intelligences: Myths and messages. *Phi Delta Kappan, 200*–209.

Gardner, H. (1998). Reflections on multiple intelligences: Myths and messages. In A. Woolfolk (Ed.), *Readings in educational psychology* (2nd ed., pp. 64–66). Boston: Allyn & Bacon.

Gardner, H. (1999). *Intelligence reframed.* New York: Basic Books.

Gardner, H. (2007). *Five minds for the future.* Boston: Harvard Business School Press.

Geralis, E. (Ed.). (1991). *Children with cerebral palsy: A parents' guide.* Rockville, MD: Woodbine House.

Gershon, J. (2002). A meta-analytic review of gender differences in ADHD. *Journal of Attention Disorders, 5*(3), 143–154.

Gibbins, S.L., Ebbeck, V., & Weiss, M.R. (1995). Fair play for kids: Effects on the moral development of children in physical education. *Research Quarterly for Exercise & Sport, 66,* 247–255.

Gillberg, C. (1990). Autism and pervasive developmental disorders. *Journal of Child Psychology and Psychiatry, 31*(1), 99–119.

Ginsburg, K.R. (Ed.). (2007). The importance of play in promoting healthy child development and maintaining strong parent-child bonds. *Pediatrics, 119,* 1.

Glasser, W. (1986). *Control theory in the classroom.* New York: Harper & Row.

Goethals, G.R., & Nelson, R.E. (1977). Social comparison theory: An attributional approach. In J.M. Suls & R.L. Miller (Eds.), *Social comparison processes: Theoretical and empirical perspectives.* Washington, DC: Hemisphere.

Goleman, D. (2006). Social intelligence: *The new science of human relationships.* New York: Bantam Books.

Gould, D., Chung, Y., Smith, P., & White, J. (2002). *Coaching life skills: High school coaches' views.* Unpublished manuscript.

Gould, D., Feltz, D., Horn, T., & Weiss, M. (1982). Reasons for attrition in competitive youth swimming. *Journal of Sport Behavior, 5,* 155–165.

Gould, D., Lauer, L., Rolo, S., Jannes, C., & Sie-Pennisi, N. (2004). *The role of parents in junior tennis success and failure. Final report.* U.S. Tennis High Performance Sport Science Grant.

Graham, G. (1992). *Teaching children physical education: Becoming a master teacher.* Champaign, IL: Human Kinetics.

Greendorfer, S.L., Lewko, J.H., & Rosengren, K.S. (1996). Family influence in sport socialization: Sociocultural perspectives. In F. Smoll & R. Smith (Eds.), *Children and youth in sport* (pp. 89–111). Dubuque, IA: Brown & Benchmark.

Greenfield, D., Quinlan, D.M., Harding, P., Glass, E., & Bliss, A. (1987). Eating behavior in adolescent population. *International Journal of Eating Disorders, 6,* 99–111.

Grineski, S. (1996). *Cooperative learning in physical education.* Champaign, IL: Human Kinetics.

Guevremont, D. (1990). Social skills and peer relationship training. In R. Barkley (Ed.), *Attention-deficit hyperactivity disorder* (pp. 540–572). New York: Guilford Press.

Guozhen, C., Jinghai, L., Yimin, S., & Shaoqiu, X. (1992). On the conformity of moral judgement among children aged from 8–12. *Acta Psychologica Sinica, 24*(3), 267–275.

Halle, J.W., Gabler-Halle, D., & Bembren, D.A. (1989). Effects of a peer mediated aerobic conditioning program on fitness measures with children who have moderate and severe disabilities. *The Journal of the Association for Persons with Severe Handicaps, 14,* 33–47.

Halmi, K.A. (1997). Models to conceptualize risk factors for bulimia nervosa. *Archives of General Psychiatry, 54,* 507–508.

Hamilton, L.H., Brooks-Gunn, J., Warren, M.P., & Hamilton, W.G. (1986, July/August). The impact of thinness and diet on the professional ballet dancer. *CAHPER Journal, 52*(4), 30–35.

Hamilton, L.S., & Klein, S.P. (1998). *Achievement test score gains among participants in the Foundations school-age enrichment program.* Santa Monica, CA: Rand.

Hanson, S., & Krause, R. (1998). Women, sports and science: Do female athletes have an advantage? *Sociology of Education, 71,* 93–110.

Hart, L.A. (1998). *Human brain and human learning* (Rev. ed.). Kent, WA: Books for Educators.

Harter, S. (1999). *The construction of the self: A developmental perspective.* New York: Guilford Press.

Hastie, P.A. (1998). The participation and perceptions of girls within a unit of sport education. *Journal of Teaching in Physical Education, 17,* 157–171.

Hatzigeorgiadis, A., Theodorakis, Y., & Zourbanos, N. (2004). Self-talk in the swimming pool: The effects of self-talk on thought content and performance on water polo tasks. *Journal of Applied Sport Psychology, 16,* 138–150.

Heacox, D. (2002). *Differentiating instruction in the regular classroom.* Minneapolis, MN: Free Spirit Publishing.

Heider, F. (1958). *The psychology of interpersonal relations.* New York: John Wiley & Sons.

Hellison, D.R., & Templin, T.J. (1991). *A reflective approach to teaching physical education.* Champaign, IL: Human Kinetics.

Henry, W.A., III (1995). *In defense of elitism.* New York: Anchor.

Himle, M.B., Woods, D.W., Piacentini, J.C., & Walkup, J.T. (2006). Brief review of habit reversal training for Tourette syndrome. *Journal of Child Neurology, 8,* 719–725.

Hodge, K.P. (1989). Character-building in sport: Fact or fiction? *New Zealand Journal of Sports Medicine, 17*(2), 23–25.

Hoover-Dempsey, K.V., & Sandler, H.M. (1997). Why do parents become involved in their children's education? *Review of Educational Research, 67,* 3–42.

Horn, T., & Lox, C. (1993). When coaches' expectations become reality. In J.M. Williams (Ed.), *Applied sports psychology* (pp. 68–81). Mountain View, CA: Mayfield.

Hume, S. (2008, April 26). Gender parity in sports thwarted on the island. *Vancouver Sun.*

Hutchinson, N.L. (2002). *Inclusion of exceptional learners in Canadian schools.* Toronto: Prentice Hall.

Ifedi, F. (2008). *Sports participation in Canada in 2005.* Ottawa, Canada: Statistics Canada.

International Federation of Sports Medicine. (1991). Excessive physical training in children and adolescents: A position statement. *Sports Health, 9(1)*, 23–24.

Jacques, N., Wilton, K., & Townsend, M. (1998). Cooperative learning and social acceptance of children with mild intellectual disability. *Journal of Intellectual Research, 42*(1), 29–36.

Jarrett, O.S. (2002, July). *Recess in elementary school: What does the research say?* ERIC Clearinghouse on Elementary and Early Childhood Education.

Jordan, W., & Nettles, S. (1999). *How students invest their time out of school: Effects on school engagement, perceptions of life chances and achievement* (Report No. 29). Baltimore: Center for Research on the Education of Students Placed at Risk.

Kagan, S. (2001, October). Teaching for character and community. *Educational Leadership, 50*–55.

Kaiser Family Foundation. (1999). *Kids & media @ the new millenium* [Monograph]. Menlo Park, CA: Author. Kaiser Family Foundation.

Kalish, N. (2008, January 14). The early bird gets the bad grade. *New York Times.*

Katz, J.L. (1986). Long distance running, anorexia nervosa and bulimia: Report of the two uses. *Comprehensive Psychiatry, 27*(1), 74–78.

Kaye, W.H., Bulik, C.M., Thornton, L., Barbarich, L., Masters, K., & the Price Foundation. (2004, December). Collaborative group comorbidity of anxiety disorders with anorexia and bulimia nervosa. *American Journal of Psychiatry, 161*, 2215–2221.

Keays, J. (1993). *The effects of regular (moderate to vigorous) physical activity in the school setting on students' health, fitness, cognition, psychological development, academic performance and classroom behavior.* North York, Ontario, Canada: North York Community Health Promotion Research Unit.

Kernis, M.H. (2003). Toward a conceptualization of optimal self-esteem. *Psychological Inquiry, 14*, 1–26.

Kitahara, K. (1984). *Daily life therapy* (Vol. 3). Tokyo: Musashino Higashi Gakuen School.

Kogan, M., et al. (2009, October 5). Parent reported diagnosis of autism spectrum disorder among children in the United States, 2007. *Pediatrics* (online), http://www.pediatrics.aapublications.org

Kohn, A. (2005, September). Unconditional teaching. *Educational Leadership*, 20–24.

Kun, I. (2002). Psychomotor state of 10-year-old soccer players. *Proceedings of the European Congress of Sports Science.*

Kunesh, M., Hasbrook, C.A., & Lewthwaite, R. (1992). Physical activity socialization: Peer interactions and affective responses among a sample of sixth grade girls. *Sociology of Sport Journal, 9*, 385–396.

Ladd, G.W., Kochenderfer, B.J., & Coleman, C.C. (1997). Classroom peer acceptance, friendship and victimization: Distinct relational systems that contribute uniquely to children's school adjustment. *Child Development, 68*, 1181–1197.

Lane, J.F. (1980). Improving athletic performance through VMBR. In R.M. Suinn (Ed.), *Psychology in sports.* Minneapolis, MN: Burgess.

Latner, J.D., & Stunkard, A.J. (2003). Getting worse: The stigmatization of obese children. *Obesity Research, 11*(3), 452–456.

Lavay, B.W., French, R., & Henderson, H.L. (1997). *Positive behavior management strategies for physical educators.* Champaign, IL: Human Kinetics.

Le Doux, J. (1996). *The emotional brain.* New York: Simon & Schuster.

Leckman, J.F., Zhang, H., & Vitale, A. (1998). The course of tic severity in Tourette syndrome: The first two decades. *Pediatrics, 102*,14–19.

Lee, M.J., Whitehead, J., & Balchin, N. (2000). The measurement of values in youth sport: Development of the youth sport values questionnaire. *Journal of Sport and Exercise Psychology, 22*, 307–326.

Lieberman, L.J., James, A.R., & Ludwa, N. (2004, May/June). The impact of inclusion in general physical education for all students. *Journal of Health, Physical Education, Recreation, and Dance, 75*(5), 37–42.

Longmuir, P.E., & Bar-Or, O. (2000). Factors influencing the physical activity levels of youth with physical and sensory disabilities. *Adapted Physical Activity Quarterly, 17,* 40–53.

Lopez-Williams, A., et al. (2005, September). Athletic performance and social behavior as predictors of peer acceptance in children diagnosed with attention-deficit/hyperactivity disorder. *Journal of Emotional and Behavioral Disorders,* 173–180.

Lindner, R.M. (1944). *Rebel without a cause.* New York: Grune and Stratton.

Lord, J. (1991). *Lives in transition: The process of personal empowerment.* Kitchener, Ontario, Canada: Centre of Research and Education in Human Services.

Ludwig, D.S. (2007). Childhood obesity: The shape of things to come. *New England Journal of Medicine, 357,* 2325–2327.

Mackay, W. (1986). The Charter's equality provisions and education: A structural analysis. *Canadian Journal of Education, 11,* 293–312.

Magill, R.A. (2001). *Motor learning: Concepts and applications.* New York: McGraw-Hill.

Mahoney, J. (2000). School extracurricular activity participation as a moderator in the development of antisocial patterns. *Child Development, 71*(2), 502–516.

Mahoney, M.J., & Avener, M. (1977). Psychology of the elite athlete: An exploratory study. *Cognitive Therapy and Research, 1,* 135–141.

Maker, C.J., & Nielson, A.B. (1995). *Teaching models in education of the gifted* (2nd ed.). Austin, TX: PRO-ED.

Malaguzzi, L. (1993, November). For an education based on relationships. *Young Children, 49*(1), 9–12.

Malina, R.M. (1984). Human growth, maturation and regular physical activity. In R.A. Boileau (Ed.), *Advances in pediatric sports sciences* (pp. 2–26). Champaign, IL: Human Kinetics.

Mandigo, J.L., & Couture, R.T. (1996). An overview of the components of fun in physical education, organized sport, and physical activity programs. *Avante, 2,* 56–72.

Manning, M.L. (2000). Understanding diversity, accepting others: Realities and directions. *Educational Horizons, 78*(2), 77–79.

Marsh, H.W., & Peart, N.D. (1998). Competitive and cooperative physical fitness training programs. Effects on physical fitness and multidimensional self-concepts. *Journal of Sport and Exercise Psychology, 10,* 390–407.

Martens, R. (1993). Psychological perspectives. In B.R. Cahill & A.J. Pearl (Eds.), *Intensive participation in children's sports* (pp. 9–17). Champaign, IL: Human Kinetics.

Martens, R. (1996). Turning kids onto physical activity for a lifetime. *Quest, 48,* 303–310.

Martin, J., & Smith, K. (2002). Friendship quality in youth disability sport: Perceptions of best friend. *Adapted Physical Activity Quarterly, 19,* 472–482.

Martinez-Gomez, D., Tucker, J., Heelan, K., Welk, G., & Eisenmann, J. (2009). Associations between sedentary behavior and blood pressure in young children. *Archives of Pediatrics & Adolescent Medicine, 163*(8), 724–730.

McClelland, D.C., Atkinson, J.W., Clark, R.A., & Lowell, E.L. (1953). *The achievement motive.* New York: Appleton Century Crofts.

McGinnis, J.M., Kanner, L., & DeGraw, C. (1991). Physical education's role in achieving national health objectives. *Research Quarterly of Exercise and Sport, 62*(2), 138–42.

McKay, L.O., & Keyes, D.W. (2001). Developing social competence in the inclusive primary classroom. *Childhood Education, 78,* 70–78.

McNeal, R. (1995). Extracurricular activities and high school dropouts. *Sociology of Education, 68,* 62–81.

Mehrabian, A. (1968). Communication without words. *Psychology Today, 2*(9), 52–55.

Meichenbaum, D. (1996). Stress inoculation training for coping with stressors. *The Clinical Psychologist, 49,* 4–7.

Missiuna, C. (1995). *Management of children with developmental coordination disorder: At home and in the classroom* (2nd ed.) [Booklet]. Ontario, Canada: McMaster University.

Morrell, D.S., Pearson, J.M., & Sauser, D.D. (2002). Progressive bone and joint abnormalities of the spine and lower extremities in cerebral palsy. *Radiographics, 22,* 257–268.

Murphy, C.C., Yeargin-Allsopp, M., Decoufle, P., & Drews, C.D. (1993). Prevalence of cerebral palsy among ten-year-old children in metropolitan Atlanta, 1985 through 1987. *Journal of Pediatrics, 123,* S13–S20.

Murphy, N.A., & Carbone, P.S. (2008, May). Promoting the participation of children with disabilities in sports, recreation, and physical activities. *Pediatrics, 121*(5), 1058.

Murray, H.A. (1938). *Explorations in personality.* New York: Oxford University Press.

National Center for Education Statistics. (2006, May). *Calories in, calories out: Food and exercise in public elementary schools, 2005.* Fast Response Survey System (FRSS 2005). Publication No. 2006057.

National Coaching Certification Program. (1989). *Level 1 Theory.* Ottawa, Canada: Coaching Association of Canada.

National Collegiate Athletic Association (NCAA). (1991). *Nutrition and eating disorders in college athletics.* Overland Park, KS: NCAA.

National Health and Nutrition Survey. (2002). *Prevalence of overweight among children and adolescents.* Hyattsville, MD: U.S. Department of Health and Human Services, Centers for Disease Control and Prevention, National Center for Health Statistics.

National Institute of Mental Health. (1993). *Eating disorders* (NIH Publication No. 93-3477). Washington, DC: U.S. Government Printing Office.

National Institutes of Health. (2008). *Dwarfism* (online), http://www.nlm.nih.gov/medlineplus/dwarfism.html

National Institute on Deafness and Other Communication Disorders. (2009, August). *Cochlear implants* (NIH Publication No. 09-4798). Washington, DC: U.S. Government Printing Office.

Newell, K. (1984). Physical constraints to the development of motor skills. In J. Thomas (Ed.), *Motor development during childhood and adolescence* (pp. 105–120). Minneapolis, MN: Burgess.

Noreau, L., & Shepard, R.J. (1995). Spinal cord injury, exercise, and quality of life. *Sports Medicine, 20*(4), 226–250.

Norman, J.F., Bossman, S., Gardner, P., & Moen, C. (2004). Comparison of the energy expenditure index and oxygen consumption index during self-paced walking in children with spastic diplegia cerebral palsy and children without physical disabilities. *Pediatric Physical Therapy, 16,* 206–211.

Norwich, B. (2005, December). Inclusion and educational policy in English schools. *Curriculum Management Update,* 32–35.

Nylund, D. (2000). *Treating Huckleberry Finn: A new narrative approach to working with kids diagnosed ADD/ADHD.* San Francisco: Jossey-Bass.

Odom, S., & Diamond, K. (1998). Inclusion of young children with special needs in early childhood education: The research base. *Early Childhood Research Quarterly, 13*(1), 3–26.

Office of Special Education and Rehabilitation Services, OSE/RS, 34, CFR 300 (2002).

Office of the United Nations High Commission for Human Rights. (1989). *Convention on the rights of the child.*

Olashansky, S.J., Passaro, D.J., Hershow, R.C., Layden, J., Carnes, B.A., Brody, J., et al. (2005). A potential decline in life expectancy in the United States in the 21st century. *New England Journal of Medicine, 352,* 1138–1145.

Orlick, T. (1982). *Cooperative games and sport.* New York: Pantheon Books.

Padden, C., & Humphries, T. (1988). *Deaf in America: Voices from a culture.* Cambridge, MA: Harvard University Press.

Page, R.M., Frey, J., Talbert, R., & Falk, C. (1992). Children's feelings of loneliness and social dissatisfaction: Relationship to measures of physical fitness and activity. *Journal of Teaching in Physical Education, 11,* 211–219.

Pangrazi, R.P. (2001). *Dynamic physical education for elementary school children* (13th ed.). Boston, MA: Allyn & Bacon.

Pangrazi, R.P., & Dauer, V.P. (1992). *Dynamic physical education for elementary school children* (10th ed.). New York: Macmillan.

Panskepp, J. (1998). *Affective neuroscience: The foundation of human and animal emotions.* New York: Oxford University Press.

Pastor, P.N., & Reuben, C.A. (2008). Diagnosed attention deficit hyperactivity disorder and learning disability: United States, 2004–2006. *Vital Health Statistics, 10*(237). Hyattsville, MD: U.S. Department of Health and Human Services.

Pate, R.R, & Hohn, R.C. (1994). Health-related physical education—A direction for the 21st century. In R.R. Pate & R.C. Hohn (Eds.), *Health and fitness through physical education* (pp. 215–217). Champaign, IL: Human Kinetics.

Pate, R.R., Small, M.L., Ross, J.G., Young, J.C., Flint, K.H., & Warren, C.W. (1995). School physical education. *Journal of School Health, 65*(8), 312–318.

Pellis, S.M. (1992). The role of the cortex in play fighting by rats: Developmental and evolutionary implications. *Brain, Behavior & Evolution, 39,* 5.

Pellis, S., & Pellis, V. (2007). Rough and tumble play and the development of the social brain. *Current Directions in Psychological Research, 16*(2), 95–98.

Perrenoud, P. (1991). Towards a pragmatic approach to formative evaluation. In P. Weston (Ed.), *Assessment of pupils' achievement: Motivation and school success* (pp. 77–101). Amsterdam: Swets & Zeitlinger.

Perry, B.D. (1997). Incubated in terror: Neuro-developmental factors in the cycle of violence. In J. Osofsky (Ed.), *Children, youth and violence: The search for solutions* (pp. 124–148). New York: Guilford Press.

Perry, B.D. (1998). Memories of fear: How the brain stores and retrieves physiologic states, feelings, behaviors and thoughts from traumatic events. In J.M. Goodwin & R. Attias (Eds.), *Splintered reflections: Images of the body in trauma* (pp. 26–47). New York: Basic Books.

Perry, B.D. (1999). *The trauma academy. Memories of fear. How the brain stores and retrieves physiologic states, feelings, behaviors, and thoughts from traumatic events.* [Online serial] Available FTP: http://www.bcm.tmc.edu/civitas/Memories.htm

Perry, B.D. (2001). The neurodevelopmental impact of violence in childhood. In D. Schetky & E. Benedek (Eds.), *Textbook of child and adolescent forensic psychiatry* (pp. 221–238). Washington, DC: American Psychiatric Press.

Perry, B.D., & Azad, I. (1999). Post-traumatic stress disorders in children and adolescents. *Current Opinion in Pediatrics, 11,* 121–132.

Perry, B.D, Pollard, R., & Blakely, T. (1995). Childhood trauma, the neurobiology of adaptation and "use-dependent" development of the brain: How "states" become "traits." *Infant Mental Health Journal, 16*(4), 271–291.

Petlichkoff, L.M. (1996). The drop-out dilemma in youth sports. In O. Bar-Or (Ed.), *The child and adolescent athlete* (pp. 418–430). Oxford, United Kingdom: Blackwell Science.

Pierce, W.J. (1981). *Psychological perspectives of youth sport participants and nonparticipants.* Unpublished doctoral dissertation, Virginia Polytechnic Institute and State University.

Piéron, M., Telama, R., Almond, L., & Carreiro da Costa, F. (1997). Lifestyle of young Europeans: Comparative study. In J.J. Walkuski, S.C. Wright, & S.K.S. Tan (Eds.), *Proceedings of the world conference on teaching, coaching and fitness needs in physical education and the sport sciences* (pp. 403–415). Singapore: Association Internationale des Ecoles Supérieures d'Education Physique (AIESEP).

Polloway, E.A., Patton, J.R., & Serna, S. (2001). *Strategies for teaching learners with special needs* (7th ed.). Upper Saddle River, NJ: Prentice Hall.

Pomerantz, E., Altermatt, E., & Saxon, J. (2002). Making the grade but feeling distressed: Gender differences in academic performance and internal distress. *Journal of Educational Psychology, 94*(2), 396–404.

Pooley, J. (1981). *Dropouts from sports: A case study of boys' age-group soccer.* Paper presented at American Alliance for Health, Physical Education, Recreation and Dance (AAHPERD) Convention, Boston, Massachusetts.

President's Council on Physical Fitness and Sport. (2009). *Physical activity facts.* Washington, DC: U.S. Department of Health and Human Services.

Prevalence of diagnosed Tourette syndrome in persons aged 6–17—United States, 2007. (2009, June 5). *Morbidity and Mortality Weekly Report, 58*(21), 581–585.

Putallaz, S. (1987). Maternal behavior and children's sociometric status. *Child Development, 58,* 324–340.

Quill, K., Gurry, S., & Larkin, A. (1989). Daily life therapy: A Japanese model for educating children with autism. *Journal of Autism and Developmental Disorders, 19*(4), 625–635.

Quinn, P., & Wigal, S. (2004). Perceptions of girls and ADHD. *Medscape General Medicine, 6*(2), 2.

Rajecki, D.W. (1982). *Attitudes, themes and advances.* Sunderland, MA: Sinhauer Associates.

Rehabilitation Act of 1973, PL 93–112, 29 U.S.C. § 701 *et seq.*

Rice, F., Harold, G., & Thapar, A. (January 2002). The genetic aetiology of childhood depression: A review. *Journal of Child Psychology and Psychiatry and Allied Disciplines, 43*(1), 65–79.

Rich, S.M. (2000). Instructional strategies for adapted physical education. In J.P. Winnick (Ed.), *Adapted physical education and sport* (pp. 75–91). Champaign, IL: Human Kinetics.

Rief, S. (1993). *How to reach and teach ADD/ADHD children: Practical techniques, strategies, and interventions for helping children with attention problems and hyperactivity.* San Francisco: Jossey-Bass.

Rimmer, J. (2005). The conspicuous absence of people with disabilities in public fitness and recreation facilities: Lack of interest or lack of access? *American Journal of Health Promotion, 19*(5), 327–329.

Rink, J.E. (2001). Investigating the assumptions of pedagogy. *Journal of Teaching in Physical Education, 20*(2), 112–128.

Robert Wood Johnson Foundation. (2007, Fall). *Active education: Physical education, physical activity and academic performance.* Research brief.

Roberts, J.L., & Roberts, R.A. (2001). Writing units that remove the learning ceiling. In F.A. Karnes & S.M. Bean (Eds.), *Methods and materials for teaching the gifted* (pp. 213–252). Waco, TX: Prufrock Press.

Robinson, T.N. (1999). Reducing children's television viewing to prevent obesity: A randomized controlled trial. *Journal of the American Medical Association, 282,* 1561–1567.

Rogers, C. (1959). A theory of therapy, personality and interpersonal relationships as developed in the client-centered framework. In S. Koch (Ed.), *Psychology: A study of science: Vol. 3. Formulations of the person and the social context.* New York: McGraw-Hill.

Rogers, M.T. (1986). *A comparative study of developmental traits of gifted and average children.* Unpublished doctoral dissertation, University of Denver, Denver, CO.

Rosen, L., McKeag, D.B., Hough, D.O., & Curley, V. (1986). Pathogenic weight control behavior in female athletes. *The Physician and Sports Medicine, 14,* 79–84.

Rosenbloom, A.L. (2002). Increasing incidence of type 2 diabetes in children and adolescents: Treatment considerations. *Paediatric Drugs, 4,* 209–221.

Rosenshine, B. (1986). Synthesis of research on explicit teaching. *Educational Leadership, 43*(7), 60–69.

Rosenthal, R., & Jacobson, L. (1968). Pygmalion in the classroom: Teacher expectation and pupils' intellectual development. *The Urban Review, 3,* 1.

Rosenthal-Malek, A., & Mitchell, S. (1997). Brief report: The effects of exercise on the self-stimulating behaviors and positive responding of adolescents with autism. *Journal of Autism and Developmental Disorders, 27*(2), 193–202.

Rowland, T.W. (1990). *Exercise and children's health.* Champaign, IL: Human Kinetics.

Rowland, T. (1998). Predicting athletic brilliancy, or the futility of training till the sal-chows come home. *Pediatric Exercise Science, 10,* 197–201.

Rowley, S. (1993). Causes of children's anxiety in sport. *Coaching children in sport.* London: E & FN Spon.

Rubin, K.H. (1985). Socially withdrawn kids: An at-risk population? In B.H. Schneider, K.H. Rubin, & J.E. Ledingham (Eds.), *Children's peer relations: Issues in assessment and intervention.* New York; Springer-Verlag.

Sage, G. (1998). Does sport affect character development in athletes? *The Journal of Physical Education, Recreation, and Dance, 69,* 15–18.

Sage, G.H. (1984). *Motor learning and control: A neuropsychological approach.* Dubuque, IA: William C. Brown.

Salinger, J.D. (1945). *The catcher in the rye.* Boston: Back Bay Books.

Sallis, J.F., McKenzie, T.L., Kolody, B., Lewis, M., Marshall, S., & Rosengard, P. (1999). Effects of health-related physical education on academic achievement: Project SPARK. *Research Quarterly for Exercise and Sport, 70*(2), 127–134.

Sallis, J.F., Prochaska, J.J., Taylor, W.C., Hill, J.O., & Geraci, J.C. (1999). Correlates of physical activity in a national sample of girls and boys in grades 4 through 12. *Health Psychology, 18,* 410–415.

Sallis, J.F., Simons-Morton, B.G., Stone, E.J., Corbin, C.B., Epstein, L.H., Faucette, N., et al. (1992). Determinants of physical activity and interventions in youth. *Medicine and Science in Sports and Exercise, 24*(Suppl. 6), S248–S257.

Salmela, J. (2005, August). Uncoached excellence in Brazilian football. Symposium conducted at the 11th World Congress of Sports Psychology of the International Society of Sports Psychology, Sydney, Australia.

Sapon-Shevin, M. (2003, October). Inclusion: A matter of social justice. *Educational Leadership, 61*(2), 25–28.

Saracho, O.N. (2002). Developmental play theories and children's social pretend play. In O.N. Saracho & B. Spodek (Eds), *Contemporary perspectives on early childhood curriculum* (pp. 41–62). Greenwich, CT: Hampton Press.

Scahill, L., Bitsko, R.H., Visser, S.N., & Blumberg, S.J. (2009). Prevalence of diagnosed Tourette syndrome in persons aged 6–17 years—United States, 2007. *Morbidity and Mortality Weekly Report, 58*(21), 581–585.

Scanlan, T. (1986). Competitive stress in children. In M.R. Weiss & D. Gould (Eds.), *Sport for children and youths* (pp. 113–118). Champaign, IL: Human Kinetics.

Scanlan, T., & Lewthwaite, R. (1984). Social psychological aspects of competition for male youth sport participants: I. Predictors of competitive stress. *Journal of Sport Psychology, 6,* 208–226.

Schleien, S. (1993). Access and inclusion in community leisure services. *Parks and Recreation, 28*(4), 66–72.

Schwimmer, J.B., Burwinkle, T.M., & Varni, J.W. (2003). Health-related quality of life of severely obese children and adolescents. *Journal of the American Medical Association, 289,* 1813–1819.

Seefeldt, V., Ewing, M.E., & Walk, S. (1992). *Overview of youth sport programs in the United States.* Washington, DC: Carnegie Council on Adolescent Development.

Selman, R.L. (1981). The child as friendship philosopher. In S.R. Asher & J.M. Gottman (Eds.), *The development of children's friendships.* Cambridge, UK: Cambridge University Press.

Selman, R.L., & Schultz, L.H. (1981). *Making a friend in youth.* Chicago: University of Chicago Press.

Selye, H. (1946). The general adaptation syndrome and the diseases of adaptation. *Journal of Clinical Endocrinology, 6,* 117–230.

Shank, J., Coyle, C., Boyd, R., & Kinney, W. (1996). A classification scheme for therapeutic recreation grounded research in the rehabilitative sciences. *Therapeutic Recreation Journal, 30,* 179–196.

Sharma, A.J., Grummer-Strawn, L.M., Dalenius, L., Galuska, D., et al. (2009, July 24). Obesity prevalence among low-income, preschool-aged children—United States, 1998–2008. *Morbidity and Mortality Weekly Report, 58*(28), 769–773.

Shephard, R. (1982). *Physical activity and growth.* Chicago: Year Book Medical Publishers.

Sherrill, C. (1998). In *Adapted physical activity, recreation, and sport: Cross-disciplinary and lifespan* (pp. 184–209). Boston: McGraw-Hill.

Shields, D.L., & Bredemeier, B.L. (1995). Moral growth through physical activity. In *Character development and physical activity* (pp. 173–195). Champaign, IL: Human Kinetics.

Siedentop, D. (1998). *Introduction to physical education, fitness, and sport* (3rd ed.). Mountain View, CA: Mayfield.

Sieg, K., Gaffney, G., Preston, D., & Hellings, J. (1995). SPECT brain imaging abnormalities in attention deficit hyperactivity disorder. *Clinical Nuclear Medicine, 20,* 55.

Silberg, J., Pickles, A., Rutter, M., Hewitt, J., Simonoff, E., & Maes, H. (1999). The influence of genetic factors and life stress on depression among adolescent girls. *Archives of General Psychiatry, 56,* 225–232.

Silverman, L.K., & Ellsworth, B. (1980). The theory of positive disintegration and its implications for giftedness. In N. Duda (Ed.), *Theory of positive disintegration: Proceedings of the third international conference* (pp. 179–194). Miami, FL: University of Miami School of Medicine.

Singer, H.S. (2005). Tourette's syndrome: From behaviour to biology. *Lancet Neurology, 4*(3), 149–159.

Skinner, R.A., & Piek, J.P. (2001). Psycho-social implications for poor motor coordination in children and adolescents. *Human Movement Science, 20,* 73–94.

Smith, A.L. (1999). Perceptions of peer relationships and physical activity participation in early adolescence. *Journal of Sport & Exercise Psychology, 21,* 329–350.

Smith, F. (1975). *Comprehension and learning: A conceptual framework for teachers.* New York: Holt, Rinehart & Winston.

Smith, M. (1975). Adult domination in kids' sports. *Recreation Canada, 33,* 51.

Smith, R.E., Smoll, F.L., & Barnett, N.P. (1995). Reduction of children's sport performance anxiety through social support and stress-reduction training for coaches. *Journal of Applied Developmental Psychology, 16,* 125–142.

Smith, R.E., Smoll, F.L., & Curtis, B. (1979). Coach effectiveness training: A cognitive behavioral approach to enhancing relationship skills in youth sport coaches. *Journal of Sport Psychology, 1,* 59–75.

Smith, R.E., Smoll, F.L., & Hunt, E.B. (1977). A system for the behavioral assessment of athletic coaches. *Research Quarterly, 48,* 401–407.

Smith, S. (1993). Investigating the physical education curriculum in the primary school. In *Proceedings of the AIESEP International Meeting of Experts* (pp. 219–232). Singapore: Association Internationale des Ecoles Supérieures d'Education Physique (AIESEP).

Smoll, F.L. (2001). Coach-parent relationships in youth sports: Increasing harmony and minimizing hassle. In J.M. Williams (Ed.), *Applied sports psychology: Personal growth to peak performance* (pp. 150–161). Mountain View, CA: Mayfield.

Smyth, M.M., Anderson, H.I., & Church, A. (2001). Visual information and the control of reaching in children: A comparison between children with and without developmental coordination disorder. *Journal of Motor Behavior, 33,* 306.

Spaggiari, S. (1993). The community-teacher partnership and the governance of the schools. In C. Edwards, L. Gandini, & G. Forman (Eds.), *The hundred languages of children: The Reggio Emilia approach to early childhood education* (pp. 91–99). Norwood, NJ: Ablex.

Sport Canada. (2006). *Policy on sports for persons with a disability.* Ottawa, Canada: Canadian Heritage.

Statistics Canada. (2006). *Leisure-time physical activity, by age group and sex, household population aged 12 and over, Canada, provinces, territories, health regions (June 2005 boundaries) and peer groups, every 2 years* (CANSIM Table 105-0433). Ottawa: Statistics Canada, 2006.

Statistics Canada. (2006). *Self-reported youth body mass index (BMI), by age group and sex, household population aged 12 to 17 excluding pregnant females, Canada, provinces, territories, health regions (June 2005 boundaries) and peer groups, every 2 years* (CANSIM Table 105-0408). Ottawa: Statistics Canada.

Stice, E. (2001). Risk factors for eating pathology: Recent advances and future directions. In R. Striegel-Moore & L. Smolak (Eds.), *Eating disorders: Innovative directions in research and practice* (pp. 51–73). Washington, DC: American Psychological Association.

Stone, W., & LaGreca, A.M. (1994). Social deficits in children with learning disabilities. In A. Capute, P. Accardo, & B. Shapiro, *Learning disabilities spectrum*. Timonium, MD: York Press.

Stormont, M. (2001). Social outcomes of children with ADHD: Contributing factors and implications for practice. *Psychology in Schools, 38,* 521–531.

Strean, W.B. (1995). Youth sport contexts: Coaches' perceptions and implications for intervention. *Journal of Applied Sport Psychology, 7,* 23–37.

Suinn, R.M. (1976). Body thinking: Psychology for Olympic champions. *Psychology Today, 10,* 38–43.

Sung, E., & Kirchner, D. (2000). Depression in children and adolescents. *American Family Physician, 62,* 2297–2308, 2311–2312.

Swain, A.B., & Harwood, C.G. (1996). Antecedents of state goals in age-group swimmers: An interactionist perspective. *Journal of Sports Sciences, 14,* 111–124.

Synder, E.E., & Spreitzer, E. (1979). Orientations toward sport: Intrinsic, normative and extrinsic motivation. *Journal of Sports Psychology, 1,* 170–175.

Szatmari, P., Offord, D.R., & Boyle, M.H. (1989). Ontario Child Health Study: Prevalence of attention deficit disorder with hyperactivity. *Journal of Child Psychology and Psychiatry, 30,* 219–230.

Tajfel, H., & Turner, J.C. (1979). An integrative theory of intergroup conflict. In W.G. Austin & S. Worchel (Eds.), *The social psychology of intergroup relations.* Monterey, CA: Brooks-Cole.

Tannock, R. (2000). Attention deficit disorders with anxiety disorders. In T.E. Brown (Ed.), *Attention-deficit disorders and comorbidities in children, adolescents and adults* (pp. 231–295). Washington, DC: American Psychiatric Press.

Tannock, R., & Brown, T.E. (2000). Attention-deficit disorders with learning disorders in children, adolescents. In T.E. Brown (Ed.), *Attention-deficit disorders and comorbidities in children, adolescents and adults* (pp. 231–295). Washington, DC: American Psychiatric Press.

Tomlinson, C. (1999). *The differentiated classroom: Responding to the needs of all learners* (p. 10). Alexandria, VA: Association for Supervision and Curriculum Development.

Tomlinson, C. (2002). Invitations to learn. *Educational Leadership, 60*(1), 6–10.

Tomlinson, C. (2003). Fulfilling the promise of the differentiated classroom. Alexandria, VA: Association for Supervision and Curriculum Development.

Tomlinson, C.A., & Allan, S.D. (2000). Reasons for optimism about differentiation: Its basis in theory and research. In C.A. Tomlinson & S.D. Allan, *Leadership for differentiating schools and classrooms.* Alexandria, VA: Association for Supervision and Curriculum Development.

Tomlinson, C.A., Callahan, C.M., & Lelli, K. (1997). Challenging expectations: Case studies of high potential, culturally diverse, young children. *Gifted Child Quarterly, 41,* 5–17.

Tsai, L.T. (1998). Briefing paper: Pervasive developmental disorders. *National Information Center for Children and Youth with Disabilities, 20,* 1–16.

United States Military Academy. *Physical program.* (Online), http://www.usma.edu/wpe/physicalprogram.htm

U.S. Census Bureau. (2000, October). *Who's minding the kids? Child care arrangements.* (Online), www.census.gov/prod/2005pubs/p70-101.pdf

U.S. Department of Education Fast Response Survey System. (2005). *Foods and physical activity in public elementary schools* (FRSS, 87). Washington, DC: National Center for Education Statistics.

U.S. Department of Health and Human Services. (1996). *Physical activity and health: A report of the Surgeon General.* Atlanta, GA: U.S. Department of Health and Human Services, Centers for Disease Control and Prevention, National Center for Chronic Disease Prevention and Health Promotion.

U.S. Department of Health and Human Services. (1999). *Mental health: A report of the surgeon general.* Atlanta, GA: U.S. Department of Health and Human Services, Centers for Disease Control and Prevention, National Center for Chronic Disease Prevention and Health Promotion.

U.S. Department of Health and Human Services. (2000, November). *Healthy people 2010: Understanding and improving health* (2nd ed.). Washington, DC: U.S. Government Printing Office.

U.S. Department of Health and Human Services, Centers for Disease Control and Prevention. (2009, December 18). Prevalence of autism spectrum disorders—Autism and developmental disabilities monitoring network, United States, 2006. *Morbidity and Mortality Weekly Report, 58*(SS-10), 1–20.

U.S. Military Academy, West Point Admissions. (n.d.). *The West Point experience—Cadet development: Physical.* Retrieved 3/29/2008 from http://admissions.usma.edu/prospectus/wpe_physical.cfm

Vallee, M., Mayo, W., & Dellu, F. (1997). Prenatal stress induces high anxiety and postnatal handling induces low anxiety in adult offspring: Correlation with stress-inducing corticosterone secretion. *The Journal of Neuroscience, 17,* 2626–2636.

Vallerand, R.J., & Reid, G. (1984). On the causal effects of perceived competence on intrinsic motivation: A test of cognitive evaluation theory. *Journal of Sports Psychology, 6,* 94–102.

Villa, R.A., & Thousand, J.S. (2003, October). Making inclusive education work. *Education Leadership, 61*(2), 19–23.

Vogler, E.W., Koranda, P., & Romance, T. (2000). Including a child with severe cerebral palsy into physical education: A case study. *Adapted Physical Activity Quarterly, 9,* 316–329.

Vygotsky, L.S. (1978). *Mind in society: The development of higher psychological processes* (M. Cole, J. Scribner, V. John Steiner, & E. Souberman, Eds.). Cambridge, MA: Harvard University Press.

Walkup, J.T., Mink, J.W., & Hollenback, P.J. (Eds.). (2006). *Advances in neurology: Vol. 99. Tourette syndrome.* Philadelphia: Lippincott, Williams & Wilkins.

Watters, R.G., & Watters, W.E. (1980). Decreasing self-stimulatory behavior with physical exercise in a group of autistic boys. *Journal of Autism and Developmental Disorders, 10,* 379–387.

Watts, S., & Markham, R. (2005, September). Etiology of depression in children. *Journal of Instructional Psychology.*

Weber, R.C., & Thorpe, J. (1992). Teaching children with autism through task variation in physical education. *Exceptional Children, 59*(1), 77–86.

Weiner, B. (1992). *Human motivation: Metaphors, theories and research.* Newbury Park, CA: Sage Publications.

Weinstein, C.E. (1994). Learning strategies and learning to learn. In K.W. Prichard & R. Mclaran Sawyer (Eds.), *Handbook of college teaching: Theory and applications* (pp. 375–386). Westport, CT: Greenwood Press.

Weiss, J., Diamond, T., Demark, J., & Loval, B. (2003). Involvement in Special Olympics and its relations to self-concept and actual competency in participants with developmental disabilities. *Research in Developmental Disabilities, 24*(4), 281–305.

Weiss, M.R. (1993). Psychological effects of intensive sport participation on children and youth: Self-esteem and motivation. In B.R. Cahill & A.J. Pearl (Eds.), *Intensive participation in children's sports* (pp. 39–69). Champaign, IL: Human Kinetics.

Weiss, M.R., & Duncan, S.C. (1992). The relation between physical competence and peer acceptance in the context of children's sport participation. *Journal of Sport and Exercise Psychology, 14,* 177–191.

Wiersma, L.D. (2000). Risks and benefits of youth sport specialization: Perspectives and recommendations. *Pediatric Exercise Science, 12,* 13–22.

Wilder, D.A. (1977). Perception of groups, size of opposition, and social influence. *Journal of Experimental Social Psychology, 13,* 253–268.

Williams, J.C., & Huber, G.P. (1986). *Human behavior in organizations.* Cincinnati, OH: South-Western.

Williams, J.M. (Ed.). (1998). *Applied sport psychology: Personal growth to peak performance* (3rd ed.). Mountain View, CA: Mayfield.

Williams, P., Walton, B., Wimbish, D. (2006). *How to be like coach Wooden: Life lessons from basketball's greatest leader.* Deerfield Beach, FL: HCI Books.

Winnick, J.P. (2005). *Adapted physical education and sport.* (4th ed.). Champaign, IL: Human Kinetics.

Wohlwend, K.E. (2005, Winter). Chasing friendship: Acceptance, rejection, and recess play. *Childhood Education,* 77-82.

Wolf, A.M., & Colditz, G.A. (1998). Current estimates of the economic cost of obesity in the United States. *Obesity Research, 6*(2), 97–106.

Wolf, M.C., Cohen, K.R., & Rosenfeld, J.G. (1985). School-based interventions for obesity: Current approaches and future prospects. *Psychology in the Schools, 22,* 187–200.

Wood, B. (2003). Risk management is responsible practice. *RespectEd for Sport, Culture, and Recreation Project.* Canadian RedCross (online): http://www.RedCross.Ca/ article

Wood, K.C., Becker, J.A., & Thompson, J.K. (1996). Body image dissatisfaction in preadolescent children. *Journal of Applied Developmental Psychology, 17,* 85–100.

Wright, D. (2008). *Healthy people 2010. Nutrition and overweight progress review.* Washington, DC: U.S. Department of Health and Human Services.

Wyatt, N. (2007, February 27). Rules forbid hijab, says Quebec Soccer Federation. *The Star.*

Xiang, P., Lowy, S., & McBride, R. (2002). The impact of a field-based elementary physical education methods course on preservice classroom teachers' beliefs. *Journal of Teaching in Physical Education, 21*(2), 145–161.

Yair-Bar, D., Urkin, J., & Kozminsky, E. (2005). The effects of voluntary dehydration on the cognitive functions of elementary school children. *Acta Paediatrica, 94*(11), 1667–1673.

Yates, A., Leehey, K., & Shisslak, C.M. (1983). Running: An analogue of anorexia? *New England Journal of Medicine, 308,* 251–255.

Yilmaz, I., Yanarda, M., Birkan, B., & Bumin, G. (2004). Effects of swimming training on physical fitness and water orientation in autism. *Pediatrics International, 46,* 624–626.

- National Association of the Deaf (NAD)   http://www.nad.org
- National Association for Girls and Women in Sport
  http://www.aahperd.org/nagws
- National Association for Health & Fitness   http://www.physicalfitness.org
- National Association for Sport and Physical Education
  http://www.aahperd.org/naspe
- National Center for Learning Disabilities   http://www.ncld.org
- National Center on Physical Activity and Disability
  http://www.ncpad.org
- National Coalition for Promoting Physical Activity
  http://www.ncppa.org
- National Consortium for Physical Education and Recreation for Individuals
  with Disabilities   http://www.ncperid.org
- National Crime Prevention Council   http://www.ncpc.org
- National Dissemination Center for Children with Disabilities
  http://www.nichcy.org
- National Institute of Neurological Disorders and Stroke
  http://www.ninds.nih.gov/disorders/tourette
- National Softball Association of the Deaf   http://www.nsad.org
- National Sports Center for the Disabled   http://www.nscd.org
- National Tourette Syndrome Association   http://www.tsa-usa.org
- National Wheelchair Basketball Association   http://www.nwba.org
- National Youth Violence Prevention Resource Center
  http://www.safeyouth.org
- Obesity Society   http://www.obesity.org
- Ontario Cerebral Palsy Sports Association   http://www.ocpsa.com
- PACER   http://www.pacer.org
- *Palaestra*   http://www.palaestra.com
- PE Central   http://www.pecentral.org
- Penn Resiliency Program   http://www.ppc.sas.upenn.edu/prpsum.htm
- President's Council on Physical Fitness and Sports   http://www.fitness.gov
- RespectEd   http://www.redcross.ca/article.asp?id=000294
- Special Olympics   http://www.specialolympics.org
- Spokes 'n Motion   http://www.spokesnmotion. com
- Sports, Play, and Active Recreation for Kids (SPARK)
  http://www.sparkpe.org
- Tourette Syndrome Association of Ontario
  http://www.tourettesyndromeontario.ca
- Tourette Syndrome Foundation of Canada   http://tourette.ca

- United Cerebral Palsy   http://www.ucp.org
- United States Association of Blind Athletes   http://www.usaba.org
- United States Power Soccer Association   http://www.powersoccerusa.net
- United States Quad Rugby Association   http://www.quadrugby.com
- U.S. Adaptive Recreation Center   http://www.usarc.org
- U.S. Electric Wheelchair Hockey Association   http://www.powerhockey.com
- U.S. Handcycling   http://www.ushandcycling.org
- U.S. Paralympics   http://www.usparalympics.com
- USA Deaf Sports Federation   http://www.usdeafsports.org
- Wheelchair and Ambulatory Sports USA   http://www.wsusa.org
- Women's Sports Foundation   http://www.womenssportsfoundation.org

Index